de Gaulle

SAM WHITE

de Gaulle

SAM WHITE

HARRAP · LONDON

First published in Great Britain 1984
by HARRAP LIMITED
19–23 Ludgate Hill, London EC4M 7PD

ISBN 0 245–54213–2

Designed by Roger King Graphic Studios
Typeset by Acorn Origination Bournemouth
Printed and bound in Great Britain
by Billings, Worcester

Contents

Illustrations

Georges Pompidou with the General in 1968 *(Popperfoto)*
De Gaulle visits Brittany in 1968 *(Popperfoto)*
The General's funeral, November 1970 *(Rex Features)*
The memorial mass at Notre Dame *(Rex Features)*
De Gaulle and 'La Gloire' *(Camera Press)*

Acknowledgments

Grateful acknowledgment
is made to Mr Louis Kirby of the *Standard*
for his kind permission to reproduce the articles
in this collection.

1
Return to Power 1958

THE TOP THREE IN A LAND OF TERROR

Three remarkable men dominate the Algerian scene. They are the Resident Minister for Algeria, M. Robert Lacoste, the Jesuit-educated 47-year-old Mayor of Algiers, M. Jacques Chevalier, and the paratroop general who commands the Algerian Region, 49-year-old General Jacques Massu.

Take Lacoste first.

A former trade union leader, he greatly resembles in his stubbornness and earthy patriotism the late Ernest Bevin. And like Bevin he enjoys the confidence of his Socialist Party leader, M. Mollet. This is important because in the state of the present French Parliament no government can be formed without the Socialists.

Furthermore, to the 1,200,000 Europeans here, Lacoste has become such a symbol of resistance to the rebels that any move to depose him would very likely reproduce the very riots which led to his appointment two years ago.

What happened to this veteran member of a traditionally anti-Colonialist party which makes such a resolute foe of the Nationalists?

Lacoste told me: 'Algeria is not a colonial problem like the others. The bulk of the Europeans here are humble folk who have been here for generations and have a right to remain.

'I felt we could not abandon them to a Cairo-inspired rebellion. Take it from me that a Right-wing government in Paris would long ago have ratted on these people.'

He is convinced that the overwhelming majority of Muslims do not want independence but only complete equality as French citizens.

Chevalier, a Catholic intellectual, is by temperament and background the complete opposite of Lacoste.

A one-time Minister in the Mendès-France Government, he has been the brilliantly successful Mayor of Algiers since 1953.

His great achievement has been a series of superb building projects which have provided cheap flats for nearly eight thousand families numbering some thirty-seven thousand people.

These flats are divided on a fifty-fifty basis between European and Muslim families.

He enjoys tremendous prestige among the Muslims. Relations between him and Lacoste are often difficult.

Chevalier was an outspoken critic of the repressive measures used in Algiers to purge the city of terrorists.

General Jacques Massu is a tall, hawk-nosed man who served under Leclerc during the War. He and his paratroops smashed the terrorists in Algiers.

He was given this job when the police were overwhelmed by it, and he did it with ruthlessness and efficiency.

Surprisingly enough he is politically well on the Left. He believes that reforms should have followed swiftly on the heels of repression and he bitterly regrets that the French Parliament wasted precious months before finally passing the framework laws.

The basic tragedy of Algeria is that the rebellion is taking place at a time of a great French Renaissance, and nowhere is this Renaissance more evident than in Algeria itself.

In the past two years there has been unleashed here a burst of reforming zeal of such energy and imagination that it is transforming the country.

The main engine for what is virtually a social revolution is the Army, and what a magnificent army it is.

It is an army which does more than fight. It clears slums, builds houses, re-settles entire villages, teaches in schools, administers health services, short-circuits bureaucracy on behalf of nomadic Muslims and generally does everything but baby-sit.

Take hideous 'Bidonville' (so-called because the shacks are made of tins) on the outskirts of Algiers.

There until recently 15,000 Arabs who flocked into Algiers for seasonal work as dockers lived in appalling squalor on a 24-acre allotment. On an absurdly small budget, fifteen paratroop officers detached from normal army service have worked a miracle here. They are in the process of demolishing the shacks and putting in their place wooden homes. Even these are temporary, for already plans are being made to replace these with fourteen-storey apartment houses.

Even as the demolition work goes forward, schools and medical centres function in the area, and a local council made up from the Muslims helps in the administration.

Is it too late to win back the Muslims on the basis of the promise of full equality? There are ominous signs that it may be so.

Evening Standard
Friday, March 7, 1958

THE BIG CHANGE IN DE GAULLE

A friend of mine who sees de Gaulle once a year, and saw him this week, gives me the following interesting impressions of the General.

He found de Gaulle looking greatly aged and grey with fatigue. A deep pessimism reflected his marked physical decline. He did not look at all like a man eager to take up the burdens of office.

On the contrary he gave the unmistakable impression that he will accept power reluctantly and only as a matter of the most compelling duty. His ideas on public issues were vague, often outdated, and reluctantly given.

His principal interest seems to be the completion of his memoirs. Apart from that, he seemed to be half-hearted about everything, even about his classic fates.

He was deeply conscious of his age – he is 68 – and referred to it again and again.

My friend found that his principal task at the interview was to try to cheer the General up a bit.

In fact the only subject raised during the talk which brought a glint of enthusiasm to the General's eyes was a reference to Britain. He was full of generous praise of Britain, and warm nostalgic affection for the country where he had some of his most bitter setbacks and greatest triumphs.

It provided the only cheering moments in an interview as drab as the drab, faded office in which it took place.

Evening Standard
Friday, March 28, 1958

FRENCH ULTIMATUM TO ALGIERS C-IN-C
De Gaulle's ex-aide misses last plane out

The French Cabinet met today and decided to confront General Salan, C-in-C in Algeria, with a clear choice of either siding with the rebels or accepting orders from the government.

The general's exact relationship with the rebel Committee of Public Safety in Algiers is not yet clear in Paris.

A statement made on General Salan's behalf, in a communiqué broadcast from Algiers, said he accepted civil and military powers to assure the protection of person and property and the continuation of military operations.

The communiqué added that the Committee of Public Safety would work in co-operation with General Salan. Now the French Cabinet has charged him with the maintenance of order and the continuation of military operations on its behalf.

It remains to be seen whether General Salan will become a prisoner of the rebel generals or if he will throw his lot in with them.

General de Gaulle arrived in Paris today on his normal weekly visit to the capital. His first act was to cancel all his Paris appointments for the next two days.

Jacques Soustelle, the burly former right-hand man of General de Gaulle, who is generally believed to have been the chief inspirer of the generals' revolt, is virtually under house arrest at his Paris home in the fashionable Avenue Henri Martin today.

It was officially stated, however, by Paris police that M. Soustelle is under police protection in case of Algerian terrorist attacks against him.

Clearly the Committee of Public Safety set up by Parachute General Massu in Algiers yesterday expected M. Soustelle to join them there during the night.

Algiers radio announced today that M. Soustelle was in Algiers. M. Soustelle and several other politicians had made reservations on the last aeroplane to leave Paris for Algiers last night. They were all prevented from leaving.

A Ministry of Interior order, it was revealed today, prevented British and American newspapermen from leaving on the same aeroplane. French reporters were allowed to proceed.

M. Soustelle is one of four French politicians who today called for a 'government of national salvation'.

A statement, signed by M. Soustelle, M. Georges Bidault, leader of the

Right Wing of the Popular Republican (Catholic) Party, Senator Roger Duchet, a Conservative leader, and M. André Morice, Right Wing Radical, described the actions taken by French officers and civilians in Algeria as 'the expression of a patriotic awakening, a further proof of their will to remain French. The tragic misunderstanding (in Algeria) of which M. Pierre Pflimlin, the Premier, has spoken must be dispelled at the earliest, the unity of the nation restored, and the authority of the Republic re-established. These objectives of salvation demand most urgently the setting up of a government of union and of national salvation'.

The French Cabinet sat until five-thirty this morning to consider urgent measures to cope with the situation in Algiers.

It was understood that the Prefects of two important departments — Oran and Constantine — have remained loyal to the Republic and refuse to join the revolt.

President of the Republic, M. Coty, made a solemn and unprecedented broadcast appeal to the 400,000 troops in Algeria to remain loyal to the Republic and to obey only orders from Paris.

In it, he said: 'Guardians of national unity, I make this appeal to your patriotism and to your good sense not to add to the motherland's trials that of a division of Frenchmen before the enemy. Lack of discipline can only profit those whom we fight. In my capacity as Chief of the Army according to Article 33 of the Constitution, I give you the order to fulfil your duties under the authority of the Government of the French Republic'.

M. Coty made his plea as constitutional Chief of the Army. He was preceded on the radio by the new Premier, M. Pflimlin, who told the nation that his Government 'would see to it that the laws of the republic are respected'.

He asked French people in Algeria to 'do their duty' and added: 'The Government will not fail in its task'.

He declared that the 'responsibilities will be established' for the events in Algeria.

The intentions of his new Government had been systematically distorted and it had been falsely accused of wanting to carry out a policy of abandonment in Algeria.

'In reality its action programme, approved by the National Assembly, envisages new sacrifices by the nation so that a victorious peace shall crown as soon as possible the effort of our army. The Government will never allow the bonds linking Algeria to France to be broken. But Algeria can be saved only by a national effort carried out in unity and discipline under the lawful authority'.

One hundred and forty arrests of Right-wing extremists were made by the Paris police during the night. Police claim that they discovered

17

documents showing that Commando groups of the Right-wingers had received instructions to attack public buildings, among them the Elysée Palace, the residence of President Coty.

Senior police officers were summoned to a special meeting at the Ministry of the Interior early today. Afterwards guards were placed outside all public buildings, ministries and civil service officers. The homes of several Right-wing politicians were watched by police.

The British Embassy in Paris has been unable to make contact with the British consul in Algiers. The US Embassy, however, has communicated by teletype with its consul there.

Paris today was calm after the widespread police raids on suspected Right-wing extremists.

Three Right-wing members of the new Pflimlin Government are considering resigning. They have asked for twenty-four hours to consider their positions.

The influential morning paper, *Le Figaro,* has this editorial comment on the army coup: 'Thirty days of quietness of which those responsible can now measure the lunacy have presented France with a tragic spectacle. The duty today, the only duty, is to re-establish legal authority of which all will be lost for France and everything will be gained by Communism. The only danger is death for the nation'.

Evening Standard
Wednesday, May 14, 1958

DE GAULLE DRAMA
He prepares a communiqué as Algiers C-in-C acclaims him

General de Gaulle will make a statement on the Algerian revolt this evening. The statement, on which the General has been working today at his country retreat, will be in the form of a communiqué. It will be issued by his headquarters in Paris. General de Gaulle will make it clear that he has always been ready to serve the Republic.

According to official circles in Paris, the main danger in Algeria now is to avoid the possibility of the Army being used to suppress rioting by armed French settlers.

It is now revealed that a senior officer was secretly flown from Paris to

Algiers to see General Salan, C-in-C Algeria, on behalf of the French Chief of Staff, General Ely, on Tuesday afternoon.

This followed an anguished warning by General Salan on Monday to General Ely that the situation in Algiers was getting out of hand and there was great danger of a secession movement.

General Ely's chief concern was to avert a split in the Army which might eventually produce a clash between those who remained loyal to the Republic and those who work in revolt against it.

The avoidance of a split in the Army has now become the main preoccupation of senior officers here, no matter what their opinions are as to General Massu's action.

There is an increasing belief here that the Army's principal purpose is to control the growing rebellious character of the agitation among the settlers with a view to averting a total break between Algiers and Paris.

In this task there are increasing signs of conflict between the military authorities and the leaders of the settlers' Home Guard. The local militia, as far as the leadership is concerned, seems determined to carry the fight still further.

It is these para-military organisations among the civilians which are creating the greatest disquiet here and not the loyalty of the military High Command.

In Algiers earlier today General Salan addressed a crowd of 2,000 outside Government headquarters. He appeared on the balcony with Generals Massu, Allard and Jouhaud and some civilian members of the Committee of Public Safety.

General Salan was cheered frantically and there were cries of 'Power to the Army' and 'Vive Salan'.

He said: 'We shall continue the war against the Fellaghas (Algerian Muslim Nationalists) and we shall win it. In showing the world your determination to remain French you will be helping Algeria to save France. Seven thousand Moslems deposited wreaths yesterday in honour of the three French soldiers executed by the Fellaghas. That is victory. With this Army which you love led by the generals around me who have protected you against the Fellaghas we will win because we will have deserved victory'.

General Salan concluded: 'Long live France, long live French Algeria, long live de Gaulle'. [The French radio in Paris broadcast parts of the speech but cut out the cry 'Long live de Gaulle'.]

Earlier General Salan told his listeners: 'My friends, you must know that I am one of yourselves since my son is buried here in the Clos Salembier cemetery. I shall never forget that'.

The crowd was asked to leave quietly. It did. Then the area quickly refilled with other demonstrators.

France is to have the toughest Minister of the Interior in its post-war history as a result of the entry of the Socialists into the Pflimlin Government today. He is M. Jules Moch, who was Minister of the Interior in the immediate post-war years and showed great severity in smashing Communist and Right-wing sedition.

Leader of the Socialists, M. Guy Mollet, has also joined the Government as Deputy Premier.

The new Minster for Defence, M. de Chevigne, has issued fresh orders for the strict enforcement of discipline among troops stationed in metropolitan France.

In Saint-Etienne, Central France, unidentified motor-cyclists hurled a grenade at a Communist Party bookshop. No one was hurt.

Evening Standard
Thursday, May 15, 1958

FRENCH GENERALS ARRESTED

Several senior Army officers, including some generals, have been arrested in France during the last twenty-four hours, it is reliably reported in Paris today. No official confirmation of the arrests has yet been given.

This report came out as one of the most fateful Parliamentary sittings since 1940 opened. A tense, crowded French Parliament listened to Premier Pflimlin while he appealed for emergency powers for three months to cope with the Algerian rebellion and gave an account of events in Algiers.

The House was ringed with steel-helmeted, rifle-carrying Republican Guards as the Premier spoke. He looked pale and there were heavy shadows under his eyes, indicating lack of sleep.

The course of the debate showed overwhelming support for the Government. The absence of two controversial figures from Parliament this morning was widely commented upon – M. Lacoste, the outgoing Resident Minister for Algeria, and M. Soustelle, who is widely credited with complicity in the generals' revolt in Algiers.

It was notable that several members of the Catholic Party walked out when their most eminent member, M. Bidault, a former Premier and Foreign Minister who is now a staunch supporter of the Extremist Right, started to speak.

'Two things are clear at the moment.

'1 – There will be no spontaneous appeal by Parliament to General de Gaulle's offer to take power.

'2 – The only danger of civil war in France is from a landing of troops from Algiers.

'The Communists will add their 159 votes to give the Government a crushing majority. This will be the first time the Communists have voted for a Government since 1948.'

When the debate began the semi-circular green plush benches of the Assembly were packed. The public galleries were crowded, but not unusually so. The Soviet Ambassador, Mr Vinagadov, was among the diplomats who listened to the Premier's speech.

M. Pflimlin said: 'There has been a plot against the Republic and established order.' Certain civilian leaders (whom he did not name) had 'tried to create an insurrectional situation in the metropolis and in Africa at one and the same time'.

The Government would act with the utmost vigour against the authors of this plot, dissolving certain organisations and prosecuting some of their members. 'All the leaders responsible will be brought into court,' he said. The Paris police prefect, Maurice Papon, was under stringent orders to smash any anti-Republican demonstration.

M. Pflimlin said the situation was 'too serious' to permit the Government to save the Republic without special powers. The Assembly and the Senate must bolster the régime by passing the State of Emergency Bill without fail today.

M. Pflimlin added: 'This is not a time for words, but for deeds.'

M. Pflimlin began by giving an outline of events in Algeria during the past three days. He said: 'The Committee of Public Safety set up in Algiers is made up of people who appear to have a responsibility in the riots there. General Massu [the paratroop leader who heads the Committee] might be supposed to have acted with a desire to avert further excesses. As to his true intentions the information I have available does not yet allow a proper verdict. Today General Salan has replaced civil servants without consulting the Government. I am obliged to pose the problem gravely in the place of the Army in relation to the nation.

'It seems that certain officers have taken a path dangerous to the unity of the country. The Army chiefs should understand that the unity of the nation can only be maintained under the Republic. It is only the Republic which can maintain national integrity.'

M. Pflimlin said the Government had the duty to face up to the situation. He said it understood the emotional state of the French in Algeria who had been told that the Government was preparing to abandon them.

Then with great vehemence M. Pflimlin added: 'That is a calumny against which I make a solemn protest. This calumny has been spread deliberately by men who have placed themselves in a state of insurrection against the State. Their intention is to create a revolutionary situation in Algeria and in France.'

M. Pflimlin said forty-eight people have been arrested for plotting against the State and said the Government discovered a 'veritable plot against the Republic'. He said that all measures have been taken to maintain public order.

M. Bidault, a former Premier who was General de Gaulle's Foreign Minister just after the war, said it was intolerable that the man who had restored the Republic should now be accused of being its enemy. 'It is better to obey God than men and one's conscience rather than political prudence', he said. 'I cannot vote for the Bill.'

Despite the huge concentration of police and troops in Paris, the city, and indeed the whole country, remains calm except for isolated bomb incidents.

A plastic bomb exploded during the night in front of the Premier's villa at Hendaye near the Spanish frontier. It caused some damage.

Two more bombs were found at the Ministry of the Interior and at the Ministry of Economic Affairs in Paris. They were made harmless.

Two bombs were thrown at the local Communist Party headquarters in Marseilles. No one was injured.

General de Gaulle, who is in his country villa with his wife and two servants, is refusing to receive any visitors today.

There is good reason for believing that General de Gaulle did not connive with the generals in Algeria. It was learned in Paris that two senior French officers visited him recently before the insurrection to ask him for his support but he refused to make any statement. The general feeling in France is that de Gaulle has damaged his reputation by his statement.

Had he condemned the generals' revolt for its unconstitutional character – he has always claimed that he would act only constitutionally – while at the same time condemning the system for its weaknesses, General de Gaulle would have been today the most popular man in France.

Communist, Socialist and Independent trade unions are proceeding today to prepare for a general strike should the situation deteriorate. Leaflets are circulating in all big factories in Paris warning the workers to remain ready to strike at any moment.

De Gaulle's open following in the French Parliament numbers no more than fifty. Nevertheless, should the situation worsen many MPs of all parties, with the exception of the Communists, might be prepared to recommend that power should be handed over to de Gaulle.

The significant pointer to Conservative opinion in France is in an editorial in the highly-respected *Le Figaro* which, in carefully chosen terms, rebukes de Gaulle and calls for support of the Government. Censorship in Algiers is now extremely strict and often exercised at the point of a paratrooper's tommy-gun.

From a brief telephone conversation I had with a reporter in Algiers this morning I gathered that he was being extremely cautious as to what he said and would not welcome any embarrassing questions.

The special powers which M. Pflimlin is asking for and which he will be granted, it seems, by an overwhelming majority empower the Government to establish a Press censorship, to confine people in house arrest and to close cafés, cinemas and theatres.

It was raining heavily in Paris today, which in itself would be sufficient to discourage demonstrations.

Evening Standard
Friday, May 16, 1958

DE GAULLE'S AIDE FLIES TO ALGIERS
Pflimlin sends an envoy to the General

Jacques Soustelle, the Gaullist MP who inspired the generals' revolt in Algiers, reached Algiers by air today. He left France secretly. He could only have gone there with the direct approval of General de Gaulle.

At the same time talks are going on at General de Gaulle's village of Colombey between a representative of the General and of Premier M. Pflimlin. The talks are being held in the tiny police station of the village. M. Pflimlin's representative is a member of his staff, M. Diebold, who is Prefect for the Marne, and General de Gaulle's principal secretary Captain Sabot.

Througout the day M. Soustelle's Paris telephone number was given as temporarily out of order.

News from Algiers, which is heavily censored, says that thousands of Muslims are joining the French settlers in demonstrations for the return of General de Gaulle.

[Algiers radio, after announcing M. Soustelle's arrival, asked the population to assemble immediately in front of Government House to hear 'an important announcement'.]

23

General de Gaulle will break this silence on the French crisis for the second time on Monday afternoon at three o'clock. He has called a Press conference at the Hotel Palais d'Orsay.

This follows a challenge issued by the Prime Minister, M. Pflimlin, in a speech to the Senate early this morning. His speech carried a clear indication to the General to make clear his position.

Said M. Pflimlin: 'I do not believe that General de Gaulle would ever act against the Republic, but we would like him to clarify his position toward the events in Algeria'.

M. Pflimlin also invited the General to explain how he intended to serve the Republic.

The mystery of the two generals whose arrests had been reported and denied was cleared up this afternoon.

It was learned that General André Challe (Air Deputy of the Chief of the General Staff, General Ely) was 'virtually under house arrest' at the home of the Commander-in-Chief of the naval forces at Brest, and that General Challe's deputy, General Jacques Martin, was under the 'same kind of surveillance at Metz'.

The Ministry of National Defence refused to confirm that the generals have been arrested. But there is a possibility that a statement will be issued after a full Cabinet meeting this evening.

The Ministry of Defence did say that General Henri Lorillot, Commander of France's ground army, who was reported to have been dismissed this morning, was in fact at his office today. The general was Commander-in-Chief in Algeria before General Salan took over.

As for General Ely, the French Army Chief of Staff, it is not yet known whether President Coty has accepted his resignation offered last night as a protest, it was said, against suspicion cast on members of his staff.

Evening Standard
Saturday, May 17, 1958

DE GAULLE SPEAKS — 'I AM NO DICTATOR'
Underground stops as he says 'Now I shall return to my village and wait'

At two minutes past three this afternoon General Charles de Gaulle told France and the rest of the world: 'If the people want it, I am ready to take over the leadership of the Government of the French Republic.'

The General spoke for twenty-eight minutes and immediately afterwards was quizzed by Press men. The key question was: 'What do you mean by "assuming the powers of the Republic"?' The General replied: 'The powers of the Republic can only be those which the Republic delegates. I shall make no attempt to violate the Republic, but to obtain by legal means the changes in the political system that seem necessary.'

After this reply the general feeling in Paris was that it is not a question of de Gaulle returning to power or not, but of when and how.

The central problem is to reunite the legal power of the Government in Paris with a usurped power in Algiers. The only man capable of doing this, it is almost unanimously felt among French MPs, is de Gaulle. The problem is not so much to fight de Gaulle as to 'legalise' him.

General de Gaulle's last words at his conference, held in the Palais d'Orsay Hotel, were: 'I am now going back to my village and there I shall remain at the disposition of the country.'

As General de Gaulle spoke all traffic on the Paris Underground came to a halt as strikers cut off the current. At the same time some of the city buses left their routes and headed for garages in response to the strike call by the Communist-led General Confederation of Labour. Communists had called on workers to down tools at three o'clock 'to break the Fascist plot against the Republic'.

General de Gaulle entered the conference room at three o'clock and, after allowing two minutes for pictures, he began speaking. He said: 'It is three years since I had the pleasure of seeing you. My last meeting with you showed my anxiety and I was determined to maintain silence until it was possible for me to come to the country's aid. Since then, events have become more and more serious. What has been happending in North Africa for the past four years has been a very heavy burden for the country and perhaps will lead to an extremely grave national crisis. But it also may be the beginning of a kind of resurrection. That is why I think it might be useful for me to address myself once more to France.'

The General said he was ready to head a French government again if the people wished it.

'If the people want it, I am ready, as in the preceding national crisis, to take the leadership of the Government of the French Republic,' he declared. [The 'preceding' crisis was apparently a reference to the time he took over leadership of the Free French movement on July 18, 1940.]

'The fact that the exclusive régime of political parties has not settled, is not settling, and will not settle our enormous political problems such as the association of the peoples of our overseas territories and life in Algeria is a well-established fact. Everyone must take note of the fighting in Algeria and the fever that reigns there. If things continue in this way, we know that the present régime, such as it is, will find no result. It will work out a multitude of solutions without achieving any result. In such a case we might be facing the risk of a solution by force, which would be the worst solution for France. I do not confuse myself with any party or any organisation. I belong to no one and I belong to everyone.'

*   *   *

This ended the General's prepared statement. Then he threw the conference open to questions.

The first was: 'What do you mean by being ready to assume the powers of the Republic?'

The General replied: 'The powers of the Republic – I could only assume them if they had been delegated to me by the Republic. There was a time when the Republic was rejected by the parties themselves. I fought in the war and I saw to a victory for all without distinction and that it should be equally a victory for the Republic. I re-established it. In my name its Government accomplished an immense task of national renovation.'

Asked about a question put to de Gaulle last week in Parliament by the Socialist leader, M. Guy Mollet, as to whether the General would be prepared to accept power only in a strictly constitutional manner, General de Gaulle said: 'I have always had a great respect for M. Mollet. I followed his political career from afar and my sentiments have not changed. The questions he put to me are not, however, the most important ones. It would be absolutely lamentable if the connection between France and Algeria were broken. 'The only thing to do is to prevent Algeria from breaking with France. As for the Army, it is an instrument of State. But of course there must be a State.'

Then came a dramatic passage.

'I re-established political liberty in France', he said. 'Why should I at sixty-seven years of age start a new career as a dictator?'

Evening Standard
Monday, May 19, 1958

PFLIMLIN ENVOY GOES TO SEE GENERAL DE GAULLE

The French political drama today presents a strange spectacle of an unofficial emissary of the Government travelling to the village of

Colombey-les-deux-Eglises to make the first informal approach on behalf of the Government to General de Gaulle.

The emissary is M. Antoine Pinay, the highly-respected leader of the Conservative-Independents, a former Prime Minister and Foreign Minister and a man of honour who would certainly not go to see de Gaulle without first obtaining the permission of Premier Pflimlin.

For the past two days M. Pinay has been urging M. Pflimlin to open talks with de Gaulle. Finally he offered to go himself. This morning his offer was accepted on the condition that the visit committed no one but M. Pinay.

The political centre of France has for the time being moved to de Gaulle's country residence.

Before leaving by road for Colombey M. Pinay was assured that General de Gaulle would receive him.

The stated reason for this visit to de Gaulle is that M. Pinay intends to plead with the General to ask him to use his influence with the generals in Algiers so that relations between Paris and Algiers could be normalised.

He will point out to the General that to await a call from President Coty is one thing but that the situation in Algeria borders on the edge of disaster.

General Salan, he will point out, is walking a tightrope and may be overthrown at any moment if the other rebel generals feel he is seeking a settlement with the Pflimlin Government.

In that case, M. Pinay will tell de Gaulle, the situation will become uncontrollable and tragedy looms before Algeria. He will appeal to de Gaulle to try and avert the tragedy by direct appeal to the army in Algeria.

Meanwhile the link between the constitutional reforms the Government intends pushing through Parliament in the next five days and the minimum conditions which General de Gaulle would accept as a basis for a return to power become more and more clear.

A declaration by General Massu made last night that was held up by censorship either in Algiers or Paris was released by the French news agency AFP this morning.

In the declaration, General Massu says he has been told of certain rumours being spread in Algiers, 'rumours which serve the interests of those in France who are trying to asphyxiate us'.

General Massu then said the army has the power here (in Algeria). 'General Salan is still civil and military head. He will remain that until our aims are achieved; that is to say, the constitution of the Government of Public Safety in Paris. Meanwhile, Soustelle is our friend and counsellor. He helps us with all his knowledge, his influence and his ability. There is no misunderstanding on this point. If you hear calumnies do not listen to them. These are simply the continuation of a psychological and subversive war. You, the people, must help us. Unmask those who spread false news. They are traitors. Give me their names. I shall take care of the rest.'

It is not known to what rumours General Massu is referring but it is thought in Paris that he could only have been referring to reports that General Salan was doing 'a deal' with the Pflimlin Government.

But in spite of the lifting of the censorship on Massu's overnight declaration there is still no lifting of the black-out in Paris on Randolph Churchill's sensational interview with General Massu published in yesterday's *Evening Standard*.

There is no direct censorship in Paris, but editors have been asked to exercise a voluntary censorship.

The silence of the Paris Press on General Massu's statements adds point to the General's remark to Churchill that he wished his views to be made known 'in London and through London to Paris'.

A curious feature of the crisis remains the undisturbed calm of Parisians. This coming Whitsun week-end, for example, a record number of Parisians are expected to leave for holiday resorts.

With the appearance today of the literary and political weeklies a curious split on the subject of de Gaulle becomes apparent. Many noted left-wing intellectuals have come out in favour of him.

Evening Standard
Thursday, May 22, 1958

PFLIMIN GOES ONE STEP NEARER DE GAULLE
Discussions begin about sending a Minister to the General

The French Government today opened discussions with General de Gaulle's headquarters in Paris regarding a suitable member of the Cabinet to go and see the General. At the same time the Government decided to postpone until next Tuesday a preliminary debate on its proposals for constitutional reform. M. Pinay, the Conservative leader who saw de Gaulle yesterday, advised the Premier, M. Pflimlin, on his return to open direct discussions with de Gaulle.

Some major political transformation in Paris is now becoming a matter of the greatest urgency. The fear in Government circles is that the army in Algeria is prepared to go to any extent to secure the recall of

General de Gaulle, even to the point of invading Tunisia. Such an action, it is thought here, would be based on the principle that the bigger the mess the more imperative it will be to secure de Gaulle's return.

The influential newspaper, Le Monde, has summed up the situation by saying that there are, in fact, three distinct powers governing the situation: 'The Government in Paris, General de Gaulle at Colombey, and the army in Algeria.'

Le Monde goes on to speculate gloomily regarding the future, saying that unless the situation is quickly resolved there is a risk of creating a 'state within a state' and a complete separation between France and the Army administration in Algeria.

Any meeting between General de Gaulle and M. Pflimlin would have to be arranged on 'neutral' ground and cannot be held, in M. Pflimlin's view, either at de Gaulle's country residence or at M. Pflimlin's official residence, the Matignon Palace.

M. Pinay told M. Pflimlin that General de Gaulle has assured him that he had no intention of taking power by any other but constitutional means on the direct request of the leaders of all parties in Parliament with the exception of the Communists.

On M. Pinay's major request, that de Gaulle should issue a public statement asking the Army in Algiers to remain loyal to the Government, de Gaulle replied that he would consider the matter but at the moment he did not see how he, a private citizen, could intervene in the situation.

The drastic reforms strengthening the power of the Executive, which M. Pflimlin plans to rush through Parliament next week, will provide him with his decisive test. If M. Pflimlin feels that the parties will delay these projected reforms he will resign immediately.

The issue is rendered all the more doubtful by the fact that these reforms can only be passed under the Constitution by a two-thirds majority of the House. Such a majority is doubtful. The projected reforms have already created considerable alarm among anti-de Gaulle MPs.

Thus M. Mendès-France, who has now established himself as the spokesman for a kind of popular front against de Gaulle, describes them as 'tailor-made' for the General. The projected reforms are, in fact, of a nature which could make it possible for de Gaulle to assume power under a new Constitution largely of the kind he has been demanding. The constitutional reforms whch M. Pflimlin is planning would give the Government executive power on specific issues without any reference to Parliament.

It would also strengthen the Government's position in relation to Parliament by insisting that a government can only be overthrown if an alternative policy is outlined and an alternative premier is designated.

A significant pointer to the future has been the steady rise in prices on the Paris Stock Exchange. This is taken as a sign of confidence in de Gaulle's return to power. The rise has been particularly striking in Sahara oil shares. There has been heavy foreign buying, especially from Switzerland, in Sahara shares.

Evening Standard
Friday, May 23, 1958

DE GAULLE IS IN – PFLIMLIN OUT
The General 'taking steps to form government'

The French Government of M. Pflimlin abdicated this afternoon. General Charles de Gaulle left his country residence of Colombey to receive a call from President Coty to form a new government. In a message released today General de Gaulle asked for an end to disorders and called for the loyalty of the army, navy and air forces in Algeria to its chiefs.

The Communist-called general strike against General de Gaulle has been a flop.

These are the main highlights of a day which will change the whole course of French history.

And here is the full text of the momentous message which General de Gaulle issued from his Paris office:

*   *   *

I began yesterday the regular procedure necessary for the establishment of a Republican Government capable of ensuring the unity and independence of the country.

I expect that this procedure will continue and that the country will show by its calm and its dignity that it hopes to see it succeed.

In these circumstances every action, from whatever quarter it may come, against public order, runs the risk of having grave consequences.

Even taking circumstances into account, I could not approve of them.

I await from the land, sea and air forces in Algeria that they remain exemplary in their behaviour under the orders of their chiefs – General Salan, Admiral Auboyneau and General Jouhaud.

To these leaders I express my confidence and my intention of taking up contact with them immediately.

*   *   *

M. Pflimlin, who spent 50 minutes with President Coty after the General's communiqué was made public, will tender his resignation in Parliament. Then President Coty will call on the General to form the next government. Afterwards, the President will see M. Pflimlin for the second time. The Cabinet will meet this evening.

When Parliament reassembled the Speaker apologised for the absence of M. Pflimlin and asked the House to be patient. He said the Premier was in conference with the Foreign Minister, M. Pleven.

There are violent scenes when the Speaker announced that the session, owing to the absence of the Premier, would be adjourned to nine o'clock tonight. Led by the Communist leader M. Duclos, the Communists raised violent protests. They banged their desks and shouted 'Fascism shall not pass'. The vote for the adjournment was carried by a heavy majority. All but the Communists and a few Left-wingers voted against.

Radio Algiers interrupted its programme to announce de Gaulle's communiqué. A spokesman for General Salan said: 'We are delighted at the news but we never doubted for a moment General de Gaulle's return.'

There is, however, a considerable feeling of disappointment and frustration in Right-wing circles in Algiers at the news. They hoped that the movement started in Algiers would gather momentum so quickly that a democratic solution to the crisis would become impossible.

Ironically enough, the chief concern for public order now is in Algiers where the revolt started. Right-wing settlers were convinced that there would be a military coup d'état. This was the reason why they allied themselves with the Army. Now disillusion has set in and fear of de Gaulle is uppermost in the minds of many settlers with a strong Vichy past.

General de Gaulle's statement came about eight hours after a car dash to Paris during the night from Colombey. He returned to Colombey at five o'clock this morning. It is now known that M. Guy Mollet, Socialist leader and Vice-Premier, talked to de Gaulle during his visit. It is not known whether M. Pflimlin was present. It was also reported that while in the capital, the General met M. Maurice Schumann, who was acting as in intermediary between the Government and the General. M. Schumann, wartime Free French spokesman in London, is a member of M. Pflimlin's Catholic Party.

No one at the General's Paris headquarters had advance notice that he intended issuing a statment. The General personally telephoned his declaration from Colombey to his orderly officer, Lieutenant-Colonel Bonneval, in Paris. Colonel Bonneval had the statement duplicated and news agencies and newspapers were advised by telephone.

Earlier today, Parliament met to consider the first stages of M. Pflimlin's constitutional reform Bill strengthening the executive powers of the Government and curbing Parliament's power to overthrow governments. After fifteen minutes it decided to postpone debate on the Bill until tomorrow. The proposed reforms are in line with General de Gaulle's thinking on the subject.

M. Robert Lacoste, a close friend of de Gaulle and a Socialist former Minister for Algeria, today made public the text of a moving telegram he sent to de Gaulle.

The telegram said: 'I wish to inform you that General Salan and the non-politician patriots of Algeria are losing control of events and adventurers and hot-headed officers are taking control of them. The Corsican affair is a deplorable consequence of this fact. I beg you to contribute by your high authority to the maintenance of public peace by giving your opinion of the conduct of irresponsible elements.'

Evening Standard
Tuesday, May 27, 1958

COTY SPEEDS MOVE TO CALL DE GAULLE

In an effort to secure a quick agreement, the President of the Republic, M. Coty, today insisted on seeing the leaders of the three principal non-Communist parties — M. Mollet, Socialist; M. Teitgen, Catholic; and M. Pinay, Conservative, to decide the next step after the fall of the Pflimlin Government.

I understand that President Coty wishes all three to consult with him and de Gaulle in Paris. If they agree, a Presidential call for General de Gaulle to come to Paris from his villa in Colombey will be sent out later today.

Much now depends on whether M. Mollet can persuade his party to change its attitude and rally to a Government headed by General de Gaulle.

President Coty, at five o'clock this morning, accepted in principle M. Pflimlin's resignation but has asked him to remain in office until a successor is found. M. Pflimlin quit after his failure to secure the necessary absolute majority for his constitutional reform proposals in Parliament last night.

Yesterday the 115-strong Socialist Parliamentary group voted almost unanimously to oppose General de Gaulle. It was notable, however, that M. Mollet did not attend the meeting, nor the Minister of the Interior, M.

Moch, nor the former Minister for Algeria, M. Lacoste.

This hardening of the Socialists' attitude, combined with an anti-de Gaulle demonstration called by them for this evening, will make it more difficult for them to switch sides in the next few days. But observers here believe that the switch will come, and if so General de Gaulle will be assured of the support of all the non-Communist parties. The man who could work this seeming miracle: M. Mollet himself. Privately he favours a de Gaulle solution. He has been in constant contact with the General throughout the crisis. My own prophecy is that within three days France will have a de Gaulle Government, in which M. Mollet will be Vice-Premier.

Meanwhile, de Gaulle's statement yesterday appealing to the Army to remain loyal to its chiefs should be sufficient to avert any military moves in Metropolitan France at least for the next three days.

M. Paul Reynaud, the veteran French politician and former Premier, summed up the situation this morning in these words: 'If General de Gaulle proposed to come to power unconstitutionally I would be the first to oppose him. On the contrary, however, he gives us every assurance that he will respect the constitution.

'I appeal to the Socialists to change their attitude. De Gaulle is the only man who can cope with our immediate problems.

'To turn one's back on de Gaulle is to turn one's face to disaster.'

This morning two cars arrived at Colombey, and eighty minutes later left for Paris. The occupants included one of the General's aides.

The General was ready to travel to Paris last night in response to a call from President Coty. He was apparently confident that M. Pflimlin would resign yesterday afternoon. His return to power is now considered inevitable on all sides. He is expected to undertake office for a limited period – one year or six months – and for specific purposes: the reform of the constitution and a solution to the Algerian war.

The only constitutional alternative to de Gaulle is a popular front government. Not only do the Socialists refuse to join with the Communists in such a project but also if it were attempted it would inevitably be the signal for a military coup in France.

M. Pflimlin obtained 408 votes against 165 in the Assembly last night. The 147 Communists voted solidly for him but M. Pflimlin refused to take their votes into consideration in judging his majority. His resignation in these circumstances indicates clearly that he wished to make way for de Gaulle.

There is considerable nervousness in Paris regarding the demonstration this evening called by the Socialists. Demonstrators are to assemble at the Place de la Nation and march to the Place de la République. This will be the first public demonstration since the crisis commenced fifteen days ago. The Communist Party has appealed to its followers to join the demonstration. There is still a possibility that M. Moch will ban it at the last moment. If it takes place the large Communist element among the demonstrators may provoke incidents.

Sporadic one-hour strikes called for by the Socialists are taking place today all over France. There is continuing apprehension here regarding the possibility of a Corsica-style uprising in either Marseilles or Toulouse.

Evening Standard
Wednesday, May 28, 1958

COTY ULTIMATUM
Pick de Gaulle — or I go

President Coty gave France an ultimatum this afternoon. He told Parliament: 'Accept General de Gaulle or I resign.' The President's statement was read by M. Le Troquer, the Speaker, to a crowded Assembly which remained standing. M. Coty warned that France was on the brink of civil war. As he spoke General de Gaulle was on his way back from Colombey to Paris — for the third time in three days.

In the four-page statement President Coty said he saw no alternative to de Gaulle. He intended to designate de Gaulle as Chief of Government and if the Assembly did not accept him he would resign and turn the Presidency of the Republic over to M. Le Troquer, the man constitutionally in line to take M. Coty's office.

While the message was being read someone from a seat in the public gallery showered pamphlets on the deputies. When the message had been read Communists, Socialists and Mendesist (Left-wing) Radicals sang the 'Marseillaise'. The Poujadists started singing it, too, but were constantly interrupted by Communist shouts of 'Fascism shall not pass'. The Communists and some of the Socialists then sang a revolutionary song containing the words 'Tyrants, descent into your coffins'.

Amid cries of 'To Moscow' from the Right and 'To Corsica' from the Left, the Speaker announced that the session was adjourned until later.

When the Communists and about two-thirds of the Socialist deputies (total 100) rose to sing the 'Marseillaise' and a revolutionary song, the Left-wing radical leader, M. Pierre Mendès-France, stood with them looking pale as death.

Police inspectors and Parliamentary ushers rushed into the public gallery to apprehend the persons who had showered pamphlets on the deputies.

In his message, M. Coty mourned that France, one of the oldest of democracies, was also one of the weakest.

'Thus, if I have passed the traditional limits which were imposed upon my predecessors, I believe myself authorised to do so', he said in this, his first official statement to the Assembly since he thanked them on taking office in 1954.

'The State does not cease to be divided. Now we find ourselves on the brink of civil war'.

After more than forty years of wars against outside enemies, M. Coty asked: 'Are the French now going to fight against the French?'

When M. Le Troquer reached the point of calling for General de Gaulle to come to power 'because both sides seem to be preparing for a fratricidal struggle' the Communists sat down glumly. At the end of M. Le Troquer's speech tumult broke out in the Chamber with the Communists roaring disapproval and the Right cheering General de Gaulle.

The Premier, M. Pierre Pflimlin, the Vice Premier, M. Guy Mollet, and the Interior Minister, M. Jules Moch – the real powers in the outgoing Cabinet – stood expressionless.

Before the House assembled the Speaker, a Socialist, had reported unfavourably to the Socialist Party on his conversations last night with General de Gaulle.

He told them that, in conversations at President Coty's request that he and M. Monnerville, Speaker of the Upper House, had had with de Gaulle, the General demanded that Parliament be suspended for a minimum period of a year.

A possible majority for General de Gaulle emerged following the meeting this morning of the French Socialist Party. It is now estimated that, apart from the Communists, the Socialist Party is split on the issue and more than sixty MPs out of 115 are prepared to go over to de Gaulle.

Thus on present Parliamentary calculations only Communists and about fifty Socialists and some Radicals numbering no more than twenty in opposition would ensure de Gaulle a clear majority.

This morning President Coty made a special announcement from the Elysée Palace. It said:

*   *   *

'The President of the Republic received last night the President of the National Assembly (André Le Troquer) and the President of the Senate (Gaston Monnerville), who reported to him on their talk with General de Gaulle.

'In the gravity of the approaching hours, the Chief of State counts on the patriotism of those who live under the protection of the French national flag *(le Tricolore)* to await with cool-headedness and with a respect for order the decisions which will be taken very shortly'.

*　　　*　　　*

The President's message to Parliament was unprecedented in the history of the Fourth Republic. The Constitution permits it but it is a privilege only very rarely exercised in the entire history of France.

President Coty called on his predecessor, the former President Auriol, a Socialist, to ask him to act as intermediary between the Socialist Party and de Gaulle. M. Auriol has refused this task.

The style of the General's statement of two days ago in which he said that he was in process of forming a government infuriated the Socialists because of its imperial flavour. Not knowing anything of the background of the negotiations between their own leader, M. Mollet, and General de Gaulle, they were enraged that de Gaulle should make such a statement while a legally elected government was still in power. General de Gaulle, on his side, has been saddened and baffled by the blank Socialist refusal to support him after having received M. Mollet's assurances that he could win the Party over to him.

A curfew has been imposed in the south-western town of Tarbes as from today. The use of all private airfields in France has been forbidden by the Government and a special security watch is being kept on the principal civil airfields.

It is as well to be clear as to what is at stake. The threat is that if General de Gaulle's return to power is delayed for another forty-eight hours there will be an invasion of France by the Army from Algeria. The situation in Algeria is out of the control of General Salan. The young officers, and especially the paratroop officers, have made their own plans and are ready to execute them. The revolt in Corsica was a sop to them by General Salan to avert an invasion of southern cities in France. Now that Corsica is in their hands it could be used by them exactly as it was in 1943 as a base for landings on France's Mediterranean coast.

Once the military acted in this way there is no force in Metropolitan France, apart from a general strike, to stop them. The army here would side with the Allgerian rebels. So would all the security forces. Not a gendarme's baton would be raised against them. This is the stark reality of the situation. That is why everyone here who knows the facts – facts hidden by the censorship – is watching with anguish as the hours slip by.

The anti-de Gaulle demonstrators yesterday evening who chanted the slogan 'To factories with the paratroopers' little thought in what an ironic manner their slogan could be realised.

After the tremendously impressive and moving demonstration

against de Gaulle it becomes even more difficult than ever for the
Socialists to go back on the resolution they passed hastily on Tuesday
afternoon, pledging their opposition to de Gaulle.

Evening Standard
Thursday, May 29, 1958

DE GAULLE PLANS TRIP TO ALGIERS
Left Wing parties move to him

The last misunderstandings between General de Gaulle and the French
non-Communist Left are being cleared up today in conferences the
President, M. Coty, is having with Socialist and Radical leaders on
General de Gaulle's behalf at the Elysée Palace.

Ironically enough, as the confidence of the Left grows in General de
Gaulle's intentions, so disquiet is beginning to show itself among the
diehards in Algiers. Certain members of the Committee of Public Safety
in Algiers have stated that they will view with 'vigilance' the composition
of a de Gaulle government. De Gaulle's first act on becoming Premier will
be to go to Algiers as a gesture symbolising 'national reunion'.

In Paris, meanwhile, it is learned that General de Gaulle has given an
assurance that he will not seek a renewal of his mandate after a period of
a year.

At the same time General de Gaulle, in private letters to such personal
friends and political enemies as Mendès-France, has given the most
categoric assurances about his intentions.

He has also assured those who are worried by the fate of such
European integration schemes as the Common Market and the Coal and
Steel Pool that 'he is not in the habit of renouncing France's signed
obligations'.

Similarly he has made it clear that he will remain a supporter of the
Atlantic Alliance.

The situation inside the Socialist Party, whose leader, M. Mollet, saw
President Coty today, is that the party is divided into three groups, some
for de Gaulle, some hesitant and some obstinately against. Nevertheless
a clear majority of the Socialist Party is now emerging in favour of de
Gaulle.

A great deal hinges on the statement de Gaulle will make to
Parliament when he seeks a vote of confidence either tomorrow or

Sunday morning. If he gets the vote – which seems certain – then there is little doubt that he will form a Left-of-the-Centre government, and thus M. Mollet is certain to be his Vice-Premier.

The Ministry of Finance may go to M. Mendès-France. The Ministry of Defence will probably be placed under Marshal Juin. All the other major posts will go to Centre party and Left-of-Centre politicians.

Feeling on the subject of de Gaulle's relations with Britain and Amerian is summed up by *Le Monde:* 'Our Anglo-Saxon allies may find it more satisfactory to deal with a man no matter how difficult who is at least there and will stay there for a definite period rather than with phantom Foreign Ministers who come and go every other week.'

The delay in calling in de Gaulle is now more than ever seen as a tragic misunderstanding between the Left and the General, with his fabulous inability to gauge political sensibilities. On Algeria itself it is notable that the General, in an outline of the main points of his policy, does not mouth the classic Right-wing slogan of 'Algeria is French' but talks instead of a relationship between France and the associated states.

General de Gaulle's principal proposals are:

*　　　*　　　*

1–Full executive powers for a limited period.
2–Reform of the constitution and proposal form will then be submitted to a national referendum.
3–Equal rights for European and Muslims in Algiers, with Algeria becoming part of a North African Federation with Tunisia and Morocco – the Federation itself to be closely linked with France.
4–A reduction in the number of Parliamentary sessions.
5–Electoral reform.

*　　　*　　　*

Meanwhile the French Communist Party is completing detailed plans to go underground while the Communist-dominated Confederation of Labour called today for a general strike. No strike call, however, has come from the Socialist or Christian trade unions.

The General, during his period of office, will have to grapple with a severe financial crisis and a threat of an economic crisis for the autumn. This time it is unlikely that Washington will come to France's aid with a dollar loan, and a loan from the Federal German Republic will depend on de Gaulle's views on European unity and such matters as the Common Market and the Coal and Steel Pool. De Gaulle was an 'anti-Europeaner' in the days when the European Army plan was being discussed.

A proposal which one cannot help viewing with some relish is that some of the people who have been shouting loudest for de Gaulle will be most dismayed by his policies. Thus the Poujadists and Conservatives are likely to receive rude shocks on such matters as higher taxation and rationing, both of which seem inevitable.

The General is now at his country home at Colombey where he will probably remain for the weekend, returning to Paris on Monday.

Last night's rejoicing in the West End of Paris over President Coty's call to de Gaulle continued until dawn, at which time cars were still driving along the Champs Elysées klaxoning their horns to the slogan 'de Gaulle to power'.

Despite these pro-de Gaulle demonstrations the general mood is one of resigned relief, especially relief at having averted an imminent army *putsch* in Metropolitan France. There is genuine regret among many of de Gaulle's admirers that he should have come to power seemingly as the result of an Army ultimatum.

Evening Standard
Friday, May 30, 1958

DE GAULLE PLANS TO BREAK UP THE ALGERIAN CONSPIRATORS
Will General Massu be brought back to France?

Conforming to the best traditions of some 'banana republic', the Algerian revolt was largely the work of colonels. They are four in number and are about as frightening a collection of political delinquents as this decade has produced.

All four are in their early fifties, all fought in Indo-China, all but one are paratroopers and all are addicted to a strange political philosophy deriving from the days when they fought Communists in Indo-China. It consists of taking the doctrines of the Chinese Communist leader Mao Tse-tung and standing them on their head.

The most important is Colonel Trinquier, fifty-two, a veteran of counter-terrorism, who gained his experience in this type of work when he was Chief of Staff to General Massu at a time when the paratroopers were chiefly engaged in extricating information from terrorists in Algiers. He commands the most famous of the parachute regiments – the 3rd – having taken over from the almost legendary Colonel Bigeard just before the revolt. It was Trinquier who organised and trained the settlers' Home Guard and it was also he who organised support for the rebellion among some politicians and military leaders in Paris before the actual revolt took place. Muscular and brimming with energy, he is the personification of the popular idea of a dashing, swashbuckling paratroop officer.

Next comes Colonel Godart, aged fifty-three. He like Trinquier is a superbly handsome man and also a specialist in counter-terrorism. He now runs internal security throughout Algeria where he commands an unrivalled network of spies.

Then there is Colonel Thomaso, fifty-four, a bull-terrier of a man who wears a leather patch over his shattered nose. He came into sudden prominence when he was appointed Military Governor of Corsica after the revolt there. Both his sons were killed fighting, one in Indo-China and the other in Algeria. Their loss understandably has made him an extremely embittered man.

Finally there is Colonel Lacheroy, fifty, the only non-paratrooper among the four. He is General Salan's spokesman and the intellectual of the group. He has written a number of works on political warfare.

Apart from the works of Mao Tse-tung there is another strange volume which is required reading among senior officers in Algeria. It is a work entitled *The Theory of Counter-Revolution,* written by an anonymous author and published in Belgium. It is a muddled and pretentious work, but General Massu thinks so highly of it that he always has a copy of the book beside him on his desk.

All four of these officers have a considerable influence on Massu who is intellectually their inferior: there is little doubt that de Gaulle will disperse all four of them in the near future and that Massu, who is only a one-star general, will soon receive a promotion and a posting to a garrison town in France.

The most interesting appointment to de Gaulle's cabinet is undoubtedly that of the novelist André Malraux, one of the most luminous and exciting minds of this century. Malraux, in addition to being France's foremost novelist, is a living legend as a man of action. A former Communist, whose early novels were concerned with the Chinese Revolutionary movement of the 'Twenties, Malraux was for a time a Comintern agent when the Communist International was in existence. He commanded an air force squadron on the Republican side during the Spanish Civil War and ended the last war as a brigade commander under de Gaulle. A man of striking, malevolent handsomeness, and an intense preoccupied manner, he is a dazzling conversationalist with an astonishing erudition.

Three times married, he lives with his third wife – the widow of a half-brother killed by the Nazis – and with three children in a large house outside Paris. Something of a recluse, his only relaxation is talking.

He has an intense hero-worship for de Gaulle. Shortly before the new government was formed he denounced, in a letter to the President of the Republic, the use of torture in Algeria.

*　　　*　　　*

Historical Note: The strong French sense of history has resulted in General de Gaulle being compared to almost every famous and infamous figure in French history. When, however, a speaker in Parliament compared him to Robespierre, de Gaulle murmured: 'Curious, I always thought I was Joan of Arc. How little one knows oneself.'

*　　　*　　　*

Quotes

Writer *Claude Bowdet:* 'The trouble with Soustelle dates back to the time de Gaulle made him head of his Secret Service in London. Secret Service work has a fatal effect on the mentality of an intellectual. Consider what would happen in England if Graham Greene were head of MI5 and Cyril Connolly the boss of the Special Branch.'

André Malraux: 'France is a country suffering from political paralysis. Let us not worry so much whether it can rival the twentieth-century world powers, let us merely ask why France is incapable of building as many workers' flats as Holland.'

General Massu: 'All these complaints about torture are the fault of Pétain. It was Pétain who made France into a masochistic country.'

Evening Standard
Friday, June 13, 1958

DE GAULLE YES OR NO SPLITS THE STARS

Here is the line-up, on what might be described as the 'celebrity front', two days before France's nation-wide and Empire-wide referendum on General de Gaulle's new constitution. Of course, it is not so much a referendum as a plebiscite for or against de Gaulle.

The issue has inevitably produced some interesting family divisions. For example, film actress Michèle Morgan will be voting YES, but her husband, film actor Henri Vidal, will be voting NO.

That brilliant couple, the former French Premier, Edgar Fauré, and his fashionable and talented wife, Lucie, are also split on the issue: he is a YES, she a NO. The stage and screen are riddled with dissension on the issue. Gérard Philippe is a fervent de Gaullist. Jean Marais is equally enthusiastic. Danièle Delorme is voting NO. Micheline Presle YES. Yves

41

Montand and his actress wife, Simone Signoret, will drive their luxurious English car to the polling station to vote NO. Maurice Chevalier will vote YES, Edith Piaf will be a NO, Line Renaud a YES. The older generation of writers seems to have gone overboard for de Gaulle. Among those who will be voting YES are François Mauriac, André Maurois and Jules Romains. The opposition among the writers is led by Jean-Paul Sartre ('God is more modest than de Gaulle') and includes Simone de Beauvoir and two post-war Goncourt prize-winners: Robert Merle and Pierre Gascar.

France's two leading scientists are opposed: de Broglie, the leading mathematician, is a YES; Perrin, Director of France's Atomic Energy Establishment, is a NO.

An overwhelming majority of French film directors are voting NO.

The Pretender to the French Throne, the Count of Paris, has come out strongly for de Gaulle. But he is not being followed by other royalists. Among them is the composer Henri Sauguet, who writes: 'I have cried too long "Long live the King!" to be trapped into voting for an illegitimate one.'

It is clear that the stridency of the Government's propaganda, combined with a general tactlessness, has made many reluctant YES voters into reluctant NO voters. Whatever the size of de Gaulle's majority, it will be largely an unenthusiastic and somewhat resentful one. It is, for example, deeply resented by many that the voting should take place under a threat of a military coup if the General does not receive a majority. The latest public opinion poll is that de Gaulle has seventy-two per cent of the votes. It would not surprise me, however, if his vote fell below sixty-five per cent.

Evening Standard
Friday, September 26, 1958

DE GAULLE ROUTS THE COMMUNISTS
A million sliced off their vote

General de Gaulle will be undisputed master of France for the next four months after his landslide victory in yesterday's referendum on his proposed new constitution.

His government will have almost dictatorial powers until the transition from the Fourth to the Fifth Republic is completed with the election of a new President next January.

De Gaulle is expected to take advantage of his emergency powers to deal with some of France's key problems. Foremost among these is the four-year-old Algerian war, and the General goes to Algeria next Thursday. He is expected to clarify his policy on Algeria in a speech there.

Another urgent problem is Algerian terrorism in France, and the Government is expected to take stringent measures, including the setting up of concentration camps for suspects, to cope with this problem.

It is also possible that some action will be taken against the French Communist Party.

Latest figures of yesterday's vote show that de Gaulle polled 79·25 per cent of the votes. The figures in Metropolitan France were 17,666,828 for, and 4,624,478 against. The vote against de Gaulle was well below the normal Communist vote in France.

As many others apart from Communists voted against the proposed new Constitution, it is estimated in Paris that the Communists lost between 1,000,000 and 1,500,000 votes.

The highest vote in favour of the Constitution was in Algeria, where 96 per cent of the 83 per cent who voted declared in favour of de Gaulle. Paris recorded a 77·6 per cent vote in favour and only 22·3 against. In the famous Red belt around Paris the Communist vote in many cases dropped 40 to 50 per cent below the Communist vote in the 1956 General Election.

The principal Communist leaders, Maurice Thorez and Jacques Duclos, were unable to carry their own constituencies against the Constitution.

Only French Guinea among France's colonies voted against the new Constitution and, therefore, automatically opted for withdrawal from the French Union.

In accordance with de Gaulle's warning that France will not tolerate 'subsidised independence' all French technicians will be withdrawn from the colony within the next two months and the massive financial assistance that France has poured into the colony since the War will be stopped immediately.

De Gaulle's success can be explained by a longing on the part of a nation for Government stability and for an end to nightmare threats of military coup d'états and civil war. It is above all an overwhelming expression of faith in one man.

General de Gaulle slipped back quietly into Paris today to avoid any sort of triumphal welcome. He arrived at his office after driving from his home at Colombey-les-Deux-Eglises.

Evening Standard
Monday, September 29, 1958

DE GAULLE INVITES ALGERIAN REBEL LEADERS TO PARIS

General de Gaulle today offered to open direct negotiations with the leaders of the Algerian revolt to end the four-year-old war.

This is the most daring proposal made by a French Prime Minister since the rebellion began.

Had it been made by any other Premier it would have meant his instant overthrow by Parliament with riots in Algeria and Paris.

General de Gaulle made his offer at a Press conference. Speaking of the so-called Algerian Government, he invited its members to see him in Paris and offered them safe conduct. They only had to ask at the French Embassy in Morocco or Tunisia.

'I gave them my word of honour that they will be free to leave after our talks to return to Cairo.'

This was far from the snub General de Gaulle was expected to deliver to the Cairo-based Algerian Government.

The statement was full of tributes to the Algerian rebels' courage and promised there could be no settlement without taking into account the 'courageous Algerian personality'. He promised rebel field commanders they could 'cease fire' without humiliation.

'They will be treated honourably', he added.

'The future of Algeria is in Algeria', he went on. 'And the road is now open in Algeria to an immense transformation which will link the country closely with France and with Tunisia and Morocco in a fraternal civilisation.'

The General spoke with great self-assurance. There was none of the wounding irony which often creeps into his statements. The Churchillian brilliance of his language held his audience captivated.

Evening Standard
Thursday, October 23, 1958

CAN DE GAULLE KEEP UP HIS BALANCING ACT?

Tomorrow General de Gaulle takes over the Presidency of the Republic from President Coty, and his faithful follower M. Michel Debré becomes

France's first Prime Minister under the new Fifth Republic.

Thus ends the first stage of the revolution begun in Algiers last May and the second and more decisive stage opens.

Superficially General de Gaulle enters upon his seven-year Presidency in a France almost as thoroughly renovated as the salons of the Elysée Palace, which is now being spring-cleaned to receive the General, his wife and a huge secretariat.

It is as though all the windows have suddenly been opened in a house long shuttered against fresh air.

In the past two weeks while General de Gaulle's emergency powers have still been in force a cascade of some 200 fundamental reforms touching every phase of national life – the judiciary, education, national defence and even marketing – has descended upon a country dazed by the speed of it all.

Everyone in the past has agreed on the need of every one of these reforms; no government in France has ever dared tackle them for fear of offending some powerful lobby or losing a fraction of the support on which its life depended.

Symbolic of this sweeping away of much that is old and musty in France has been de Gaulle's last-minute attack on that almost feudal stronghold of entrenched privilege – Paris's central market Les Halles, the so-called 'Belly of Paris'.

For half a century the criminal absurdity of Les Halles's location has been denounced – and denounced in vain. Not only is it not near a railhead, not only does it cause fantastic traffic jams, but it is the headquarters of hereditary middlemen whose activities are largely responsible for the low prices paid to the farmer and the high prices charged in the shops.

Now Les Halles is to be moved to a more suitable location and central markets near railway stations will be set up in all provincial capitals.

It is now almost thirteen years to the very day that de Gaulle resigned office and went into voluntary retirement. On that bleak January day in 1946 in a Paris largely unheated and hungry, de Gaulle first stunned and then delighted his Cabinet of bickering Socialists, Communists and Catholics by announcing: 'I have decided to resign; my decision is irrevocable.'

He then left the Cabinet Room while his ministers' faces gradually broke into broad smiles of relief like schoolboys witnessing the departure of a harsh headmaster.

They were relieved to see him go, not only because they were supremely confident of being able to rule France without benefit of de Gaulle, but also because they were impatient to revert to the profitable political intrigues and pastimes of pre-war France.

They never realised that twelve years later they would be pleading with de Gaulle to save them from the consequences of their own follies. A few days later de Gaulle made his first (and for several years only) public reference to this resignation. He said: 'The regime of the parties, unchecked by a strong executive responsible to Parliament but separated from it, will lead France into chaos and democracy to the abyss.'

De Gaulle now takes over a France far different from the one inherited after the War. It is now a country in plain renaissance in every field of activity and indeed it was the existence of this renaissance which made the revolutionary change in the outworn political system inevitable.

It has a bounding birthrate which has already changed and will continue to change even more drastically the old political allegiance.

The three dominating figures of the new Republic will be de Gaulle himself, his Prime Minister, M. Debré, and, in the wings for the time being, M. Jacques Soustelle.

Forty-seven-year-old M. Debré is a man of strong opinions but whatever his views he will carry out the General's wishes in all fields of policy.

He dislikes the new Budget, but he will apply it; he loathes the Common Market, but he will swallow it; he detests the Germans, but he will be nice to them. An extreme Nationalist, his nationalism takes the form of complete identification with de Gaulle.

Debré's intense nationalism probably springs from the fact that he is Alsatian. His grandparents left Alsace in 1870 because they did not want to become Germans. His grandfather was a rabbi. He is an intellectual and the author of the New Constitution. Unlike other de Gaullists, he consistently refused to hold office under the old Republic. He was a thorn in the side of successive governments and averaged at least ten extremely embarrassing parliamentary questions a week.

Soustelle's future is a mystery – a mystery bound up with a so far indiscernible outcome of the de Gaulle experiment itself. So far de Gaulle is refusing him any of the key posts in the Government – Interior, Foreign Affairs or Defence – and it may well be that Soustelle will stay out of the Government altogether and devote himself entirely to the leadership of his new party, the UNR, the largest in the present Parliament.

Two aspects of de Gaulle's policy as they may affect Soustelle to say nothing of France itself have now become clear.

1–France will stay in Algeria hoping that military pressure and economic betterment will produce the conditions for a settlement on terms far short of the present rebel demand. Soustelle will oppose negotiations with them on any terms.

2–De Gaulle has chosen a financial policy so classically Conservative that one has to go back to the Twenties in Britain to find a parallel.

This is completely opposed to the policy advocated by Soustelle and his party, which is one of continuing with the present inflationary boom. Soustelle at the moment intends to lie low, consolidate his party, and emerge as an effective Left-wing Opposition leader should de Gaulle's policy fail. This is completely in character with the man who started as a revolutionary and remains one.

Not only is he himself essentially a man of the Left, but his electoral support is very largely Left of centre. It is no accident that his party picked up over a million former Communist votes in the last election.

He has heavy support, too, among the junior ranks in the Army, and the French Army of today is not the traditionally Conservative force it used to be. It is heavily impregnated with the mystique of a kind of French National Socialism.

I doubt if Soustelle's success in the elections was due to his party's seeming identification with de Gaulle. If de Gaulle had given his public blessing, say, to the Socialists, I doubt very much if that would have gained them one extra seat or cost Soustelle's party any important loss of votes.

The fact is the old parties, with the possible exception of the Communists, are finished – their numbers are not only insignificant in the present Parliament but their doctrines and slogans are meaningless in the ears of the new generation.

M. Mollet has, of course, resigned from de Gaulle's government and refuses to serve in the new one. Instead, he has told the General that he and the Socialists will go into 'constructive opposition'.

The Socialists could not really swallow the new budget, and fear that they would be outflanked by the Communists if industrial opposition to the budget was sufficient to ensure a Socialist withdrawal from the Government.

But who in ten years' time will vote for M. Mollet's Dickensian Socialists, or the Radicals? In the new Parliament the great debate will be between the two bulk parties – M. Pinay's Conservatives on the Right and M. Soustelle's revolutionary Nationalists on the Left.

Between them, if the new economic programme falters in the next six months, de Gaulle will hold an uneasy balance.

Evening Standard
Wednesday, January 7, 1959

2
Algeria
1959 - 1962

WILL THE ARMY STAND BY DE GAULLE?

It is easy now to reflect that General de Gaulle, in facing a new uprising in Algeria, is reaping the whirlwind he himself has sown.

He accepted power as a result of a revolt against the legally-established French Government and now the people who brought him into power are demanding the price of their support.

It is easy, as I said, to put this interpretation on the present Algerian uprising – easy, but only partly true. Nevertheless it is in the simplified version of the events of May 13, 1958, in which the 1,200,000 French settlers and large sections of the Army believe. They have had the exhilarating experience of overthrowing a French government and an entire political system without a shot being fired, and simply as a result of some demonstrations and bellicose speeches. How that Government succumbed in terror and humiliation is engraved on their minds.

Today the situation in one important respect is different. De Gaulle can draw on reserves of authority which were not available to the discredited politicians of the Fourth Republic. For him there can be no retreat in facing the challenge.

It is easy now in the light of events to see some of the errors de Gaulle has made. Convinced that the only solution to the five-year-old war was the liberal one of having Algerians – both European and Muslim – decide their own future in a referendum, he has never dared to take the necessary measures against both Army and settler plotters to ensure that this policy could be applied without touching off an explosion in Algeria.

For months past his Governor-General in Algeria, M. Delouvrier, has been steadily warning him of a developing plot against his régime in Algeria and of the growing anti-de Gaulle feeling inside the Army.

It was not until the last three weeks that de Gaulle began to take these warnings seriously. Before that he disbelieved them and thought it inconceivable that anyone, especially Army officers, should intrigue against him.

It is exasperating to most Frenchmen to reflect that in the weeks that followed General de Gaulle's return to power he could have posted General Massu out of Algiers and rounded up the half-dozen or so extremist civilian leaders for deportation to France without risking any serious trouble.

De Gaulle obviously prided himself on his cunning in handling both the Army and the settlers.

In fact his opponents have shrewdly understood that the only possible outcome of his Algerian policy was finally the creation of an independent Algerian state.

Whatever illusions they might have had in the past, these were dealt a heavy blow by de Gaulle's September 16 announcement supporting self-determination in Algeria and were finally shattered by his policy in 'black Africa', where he has swiftly granted independence in one form or another to some six former colonies.

Now the challenge of a test of strength between Paris and Algiers has to be faced.

The big question still remains – will the Army or a large section of the Army side with the settlers? Almost certainly if the uprising spreads there will be defections in the French Army's ranks. The crucial element in this situation are the junior officers and the NCOs. They are even prepared to envisage Algeria's secession from France and to use the blackmail of the Sahara oil against Paris. The French Army has now 'colonised' Algeria to the point where it sees its own future linked with the future of that country.

Even if the present revolt is crushed, it will regain even greater force once de Gaulle reaches the penultimate point of having talks, even if they are only strictly cease-fire talks with the Algerian rebel leaders. While the Algerian war continues, de Gaulle's régime remains in deadly peril. Ironically enough, if he were to solve the Algerian war his power would be menaced because he would have served his purpose. And if he doesn't solve it his power is menaced because he will not have served his purpose.

Evening Standard
Tuesday, January 19, 1960

MASSU: 'I'M LOYAL'
But will de Gaulle be satisfied?

A curiously worded and somewhat impudent communiqué was issued by General Jacques Massu after a fifteen-minute interview today with the French Minister of Defence, M. Guillaumat, in Paris.

The Minister recalled General Massu from Algiers yesterday to explain an interview given to a German newspaper in which he is quoted as making a violent attack on President de Gaulle's Algerian policy.

Massu, France's top paratroop general who commanded in Algiers almost from the start of the rebellion five years ago and who played a leading part in the 1958 revolt which brought de Gaulle to power, is alleged to have stated in the interview:

'Our greatest disappointment has been to see General de Gaulle become a man of the Left. De Gaulle was the only man available in May 1958. Perhaps the Army made a mistake. We no longer understand his policy.'

Massu's communiqué after the interview with M. Guillaumat carried no reference to the alleged interview, the authenticity of which is not doubted by anyone in Paris despite a denial on Massu's behalf by the Commander-in-Chief in Algeria, General Challe.

Massu makes two main points in the communiqué:

*　　　*　　　*

1–'I am convinced that President de Gaulle's efforts to end the war in Algeria have enabled him to retain the confidence of the great mass of Muslims.

2–On the question of uneasiness in the Army in Algeria, Massu denies any wish to become a spokesman for this discontent. He goes on: 'General Challe's authority is not challenged by anyone in Algeria. I myself and my troops without any intellectual reservations are behind the C-in-C, whose loyalty to the President of the Republic cannot be held in doubt.'

*　　　*　　　*

M. Guillaumat is understood to be satisfied with Massu's statement. It now remains to be seen whether it will satisfy President de Gaulle, who has made no arrangements so far to discuss the matter with Massu.

But de Gaulle will be seeing Massu on Friday when he opens a conference of military and civilian chiefs in Algeria on the situation there.

The summoning of this conference has created great uneasiness among the Army and Europeans there because they fear a further initiative by de Gaulle to bring the five-year-old war to an end on the basis of his self-determination offer. Certainly if Massu were removed from his post at this moment the reaction in Algeria would be violent and possibly dramatic.

Meanwhile the news from Algeria continues to be grave. Correspondents of Paris newspapers there speak of 'an atmosphere heavy with plotting', and never since the revolt of May 3 has the situation been more menacing.

There are insistent demands by settlers that they be given arms to meet the new wave of terrorism that has broken out in the countryside around Algeria. The settlers attribute the fresh outbreak of terrorism to de Gaulle's 'soft' policy.

In fact the new terrorist outbreaks in the region of Algiers are due largely to the fact that the bulk of the Army is now operating in the mountains in an effort to clean out rebel strongholds. In this atmosphere extremist organisations have multiplied their membership, in some cases twenty-fold in the last few weeks.

Evening Standard
Wednesday, January 20, 1960

MASSU SACKED
He must not go back to Algeria

General Massu's days of power and glory as military and civil governor of Algiers are definitely over. The famous paratroop general has been removed from his post and an official communiqué on the subject is expected hourly.

Meanwhile Massu finds himself in Paris barred both from a top-level conference on Algeria presided over by General de Gaulle and from returning to Algiers – even to pack. He is to be posted to a minor post in one of the more obscure French colonies. President de Gaulle has acted with deliberation and ruthlessness following an interview given by Massu to a German newspaper attacking de Gaulle's self-determination policy for Algeria. The President acted against the advice of many of his ministers, who were almost indecently in a hurry to declare the incident 'closed' after a vague and impudent declaration by Massu on the subject of his loyalty to de Gaulle.

De Gaulle's dismissal of Massu is the first major act of political courage by any French government to re-establish its authority over mutinous soldiers and settlers in the five years of the Algeria war. Furthermore, in an open act of defiance of mounting anti-de Gaulle feeling in Algeria, the President has made a gesture of great personal courage. He has announced that he will make a tour of inspection in Algeria lasting several days beginning on February 5.

In short he is defying the European settlers to subject him to the indignities that previous French Prime Ministers have had to endure on Algerian soil.

Disciplinary measures taken against Massu are unlikely to stop there. It is pointedly hinted in Paris that General Challe, the Commander-in-Chief in Algeria and Massu's immediate superior, may also be removed.

An officer who enjoys General de Gaulle's full confidence, General Jacquot, is at present in Algeria conferring with the only other French general who is not present at today's talks – General Olie, who commands the Constantine area.

The move against Massu coupled with a ban on a proposed visit by the former Premier and Foreign Minister, George Bidault, foreshadows a tough crack-down on Right-wing extremists in Algeria.

The arrest and deportation to France of several European extremists is expected in the next few days,

Evening Standard
Friday, January 22, 1960

DE GAULLE AND MASSU FACE TO FACE

General Massu, removed yesterday from his post of Commander-in-Chief of the Algerian Region, was called to a face-to-face meeting with President de Gaulle at the Elysée Palace today.

Massu was in uniform and wearing his paratroop red beret. No doubt de Gaulle, among other things, discussed Massu's future. No new appointment has so far been announced for him. It must have been a moving meeting, because Massu has hitherto been a devout de Gaullist and is a member of de Gaulle's exclusive personal Order, the Companions of the Liberation. The get-together lasted twenty-five minutes, then Massu talked with other presidential officials. Afterwards he slipped away through a side door.

The meeting came as the first angry reaction showed up in Algeria where Massu is the hero of the Right-wing Europeans. Combat-armed French troops fanned throughout the city as a general protest strike spread. The strike began in the suburbs of Belcourt and Bab-el-Oued. Authorities reacted immediately and police and Army patrols were sent out. Vans stood at the big intersections and Army patrols wore steel helmets and combat uniforms.

Merchants banged down the steel shutters fronting their shops and knots of nervous people gathered.

In the Belcourt suburb, merchants said the strike order was passed by armed territorial guards – which is a militia of local citizens. In Bab-el-Oued young men and students spread the word.

College students – a volatile lot – passed the word that some sort of action was expected later. Earlier today a dramatic 'keep calm' appeal was made in a broadcast to the people by M. Paul Delouvrier, the French Government's Delegate General in Algeria.

In a reference to the decision to replace General Massu by General Jean Crepin as Commander of French troops in Algiers, he said:

'A fortuitous incident led to General Massu's departure from Algiers. I know what he meant for you and I know what he meant for myself. I wish to pay a tribute to him and to his discipline in accepting the decision.'

M. Delouvrier then gave a warning that 'the authority of the State must no longer be questioned'.

After his address, Algiers Radio broadcast an appeal by General Maurice Challe, Commander-in-Chief. He asked French forces in Algeria to maintain their unity. cohesion and discipline.

In reference to General Massu's replacement, General Challe told his troops to 'refrain from unconsidered reactions which would play into the enemy's hands' and said, 'You can rely on me to keep up the fight'.

Evening Standard
Satuday, January 23, 1960

DEBRÉ SPEAKS
'We will restore order and stand by a policy of self-determination'

The French Prime Minister, M. Debré, who returned to Paris this morning after all-night talks with military leaders in Algiers, is to broadcast to the nation this evening. He will reaffirm the Government's determination to restore order in Algeria and continue the policy of self-determination for the country.

The text of M. Debré's speech was made public soon after he reported on his mission to President de Gaulle.

M. Debré begins his broadcast with the words: 'The riots have already done too much damage to France.'

He reaffirms de Gaulle's intention to broadcast to the nation next Friday and to go on a tour of inspection of Algeria after that.

He continues: 'President de Gaulle's policy has the support of Parliament and the nation. It aims at showing the world that the object of the Algerian war is to give to all Algerians, Europeans and Muslims, the chance of deciding freely on their future.

'This free choice is the true hope of France. French policy cannot have any other basis than the free choice of men and women as to whether they wish to be French.

'But before there can be a free choice there must be peace. It is to establish peace that the Army is fighting against terrorism in Algeria.'

M. Debré, seeking to reassure the insurgent settlers, said all those in Algeria who are French and wish to remain French will be considered as such whatever settlement is reached, not only for this generation but for generations to come.

'France will never forget the Algerians who have been loyal to her and justice and reward will be given for their fidelity', M. Debré will tell the nation.

'France is not regarding the outcome of the Algerian struggle. Her interests and her honour are involved in Algeria. How then is it possible to even envisage the possibility of abandoning this country?'

M. Debré ends with the assurance that nothing will divert the Army and the nation from restoring France's authority in Algeria.

*   *   *

From Algeria today's big news is that a group of colonels commanding parachute regiments in Algeria have told the Commander-in-Chief Algeria, General Challe, that they are not prepared to open fire on settlers entrenched behind two barricades in the city centre. How far this disinclination to evict the rebels from their strong-points will affect the paratroopers of the Foreign Legion is not known. These troops, sixty-five per cent German, have largely taken over the task of guarding the two rebel strongholds.

The nonchalance of the troops yesterday has given place to a sterner attitude. Passers-by are not allowed to approach the rebels. The almost festive scenes of yesterday, with rebels' women-folk delivering picnic lunches over the barricades, have gone.

Paris newspapers, which yesterday were overwhelmingly optimistic, today reflect the growing anxiety.

The two rebel strongholds in the centre of Algiers, which have held out since Sunday night, are greatly reinforced. There are probably about seven thousand armed men holding them. They have been reinforced openly under the eyes of troops lining two perimeters only twenty yards away.

A disquieting feature is that both the Governor-General and General Challe continue to parley with the rebel leader, Joseph Ortiz. General Challe does not appear to be prepared to arrest him.

Press communications with Algiers are sporadic. Messages are heavily censored before being allowed through.

Tension is rising as demonstrators, defying the state of emergency decreed on Sunday, mass in the centre of Algiers. It was expected to reach its peak with the funeral of a civilian victim of Sunday's clash between Republican Guards and demonstrators.

A significant feature of the military censorship now being applied in Algiers is that the local Press is allowed to publish editorials praising the instigators of the uprising and messages from Algerian MPs in support of the rising.

The General Strike, which has paralysed Algiers, Oran and Constantine, has spread to Bône, the only other major city in Algeria.

Two more wounded died in hospital today. bringing the total number of dead to twenty-seven.

Evening Standard
Tuesday, January 26, 1960

DE GAULLE GETS SHOCK FROM MARSHAL JUIN

Seventy-one-year-old Marshal Juin, France's only living marshal, let it be known today that he has given General de Gaulle an ultimatum on Algeria. It is: 'If the Army moves, I go.'

The Marshal, who saw de Gaulle yesterday. is said to have told him that if the Army opens fire on the insurgents he will quit – and tell the nation why. According to friends of Marshal Juin, de Gaulle appeared to be 'very moved' by the warning.

According to Ministerial sources, de Gaulle intends to maintain his Algerian policy and to restore order.

And according to some Paris newspapers there is speculation about one prominent Cabinet Minister – Jacques Soustelle, who played a leading part in the 1958 uprising. It is said he has offered his resignation.

As the deadlock between Algiers and Paris entered its fourth day. tension in official circles became almost unbearable.

Premier Debré held a thirty-minute meeting with Jacques Chaban-Delmas, President of the National Assembly. and Pierre Guillaumat, Defence Minister, called at the office of de Gaulle.

A Cabinet meeting, presided over by de Gaulle, is to be held this afternoon.

One decision which he is reliably believed to have taken is to hold a nation-wide referendum within the next three weeks on his Algerian policy of self-determination.

In Metropolitan France he is assured of at least a seventy-five per cent majority on this issue.

The Centre-Right Union for the New Republic (UNR) political party which rode to power on de Gaulle's coat-tails has assured him ample votes in the National Assembly for his Algerian policies.

The UNR Assembly Steering Committee issued a statement which reaffirmed 'without reserve' its confidence in de Gaulle and the Prime Minister.

This will give de Gaulle great moral force in facing up to the Algiers insurrection. But it will not solve his major problem of overcoming what has now become the open defiance of the Army.

The calm that has reigned in Paris since the crisis began was broken today. Some thirty Right-wing students at the Law Faculty barricaded themselves in a section of the Law School while hundreds of Communists, many of them coming in from the suburbs, gathered menacingly around the building.

The mood in Paris now is one of grim apprehension.

When the Cabinet meets, it is reliably reported, its main task will be that of giving special powers to President de Gaulle under the Constitution to enable him to handle the Algerian challenge to his authority.

An MP, Maurice Schumann, who saw the President early today, said on leaving: 'De Gaulle will not give way or give in.'

Meanwhile something like a popular front is building up in France in support of de Gaulle. From the Communists on the extreme Left to Catholics and Conservatives on the Right messages and resolutions of support are pouring into the Elysée Palace.

A Committee for the Defence of the Republic has been formed and is likely to assume a national character in the next few days.

All three major trade union organisations – Communists, Socialists and Catholics – have pledged their support against what they describe as 'a threatened Fascist coup d'état'.

The very sections of the French nation which were most bitterly opposed to de Gaulle's return to power are now, it would seem, the most fervent in support.

De Gaulle's assumption of special powers will probably be announced by him when he makes his tensely awaited broadcast to the nation on Friday evening.

*   *   *

In Algiers paratroopers who have encircled the two rebel strongholds in the heart of the city are being reinforced by Marines and Air Force units – another ominous sign of the unreliability of the Army. Two tank regiments have moved up to the outskirts.

With the General Strike still complete, there are growing fears regarding the city's food supply.

The two rebel fortresses are organised on military lines. The defences are being strengthened every day under the tolerant eyes of the paratroop guards, and food and medical supplies, sufficient for several weeks, have been stocked.

Crowds gathered today to watch comings and goings. Many girls had a picture of General Massu pinned to their dress. They went from barricade to barricade chatting with the last-ditchers.

Evening Standard
Wednesday, January 27, 1960

DE GAULLE FACES HIS DAY OF DECISION
France waits for the big speech tonight

President de Gaulle now faces a decision every bit as momentous as the one he took in 1940 to leave France and continue the War from Britain.

His problem can be briefly summed up: Can he bring himself in tonight's broadcast to the nation to make the necessary concessions to a group of no more than thirty Army officers, most of them colonels, which will convince them that he rules out the possibility of an independent

Algeria? If he fails to make this concession, then Algeria is headed for secession from France and the country as a whole lies under the threat of imminent civil war.

De Gaulle is a considerable verbal acrobat and there may be lines in his speech which these Army officers will find a sufficient assurance. But his margin of manoeuvre even for so skilled a verbal gymnast is terribly narrow.

On the one hand he is committed to giving the nine-tenths Muslim population of Algeria a choice between integration with France, some form of dominion status, or independence. The Army insists that he rules out independence. The Army, and only the Army, needs to be won over. If it is, the armed civilian uprising in Algiers can be easily ended.

De Gaulle has a France united as it has rarely been in history behind his policy. To take the risk of compromising is to risk splitting the nation almost as fatally as if he faced the challenge from Algiers. Nobody who knows de Gaulle is in any doubt that he will stand firm on his Algerian policy.

A major mystery in Paris today is whether the Governor-General of Algeria, M. Delouvrier, and the Commander-in-Chief, General Challe, acted on Government orders to move their headquarters from Algiers to the airport base of Reghia, thirty miles east of Algiers. Certainly the majority of the Government was unaware of the inpending move. It is conceivable that the two men acted on their own initiative, fearing arrest if they remained in Algiers.

Great pressure has been brought in the last few days on General Challe by his fellow officers to take the leadership of the insurrection. Whether he reacted on de Gaulle's orders or not his departure from Algiers was certainly a way of both resisting this pressure and demonstrating his loyalty to the President.

As for M. Delouvrier, he is believed in Paris to be in the throes of a nervous breakdown. This is the only explanation for the hysterical and often contradictory speech he made last night. The Government is now considering replacing him.

In Algiers paratroopers occupied the principal Government building this morning on orders of a senior French general in the city, General Gracieux, who has been charged by General Challe with maintaining order there.

The insurgents are now in virtual control of Algiers and are in the process of setting up, with some Army support, a committee of direction for the insurrection. In the event of secession precipitated either by de Gaulle in his speech tonight or by the insurgents themselves this could be the embryo of a government of an independent French Algeria.

De Gaulle's speech is awaited with even more feverish impatience in

Algiers than in Paris. On both sides of the Mediterranean there are growing fears that this weekend will see a final break between Algeria and France.

Army chiefs in the other two most important Algerian centres – Constantine and Oran – are giving signs of their loyalty to de Gaulle. The civil and military commander of Constantine, General Olie, in a proclamation today declared: 'Not a second's hesitation is longer possible. We have ranged ourselves behind our chiefs – General de Gaulle, M. Delouvrier, General Challe.'

General Gambiez, commanding eastern Algeria, has issued a similar appeal.

The executive of the Socialist trade unions, meeting today, issued an order to its members to consider themselves in a state of alert to take appropriate strike action should events warrant it.

There are unconfirmed reports that General Ely. Chief of the General Staff, has flown secretly to Algiers to meet M. Delouvrier and General Challe.

Meanwhile an avalanche of messages of support is pouring into the Elysée Palace. Yesterday three hundred such messages were received.

Evening Standard
Friday, January 29, 1960

DE GAULLE IS GAINING THE UPPER HAND

There are growing signs that President de Gaulle is gaining the upper hand in Algeria following his grim speech to the nation last night, in which he called on the Army to obey him and restore order in Algiers.

The Governor-General, M. Delouvrier, and the C-in-C, General Challe, have now returned to Algiers following their flight from the city yesterday, when they established their headquarters thirty miles away.

A communiqué from the insurgents' headquarters issued today announces that the general strike in Algiers, which has lasted since Monday, is to be called off next Monday.

And from Oran, in eastern Algeria, where the strike has already ended, the Home Guard has submitted to the orders of the general commanding the Oran region, General Gambiez. The barricades are down.

In Algiers the Army has re-established its control over the city's radio station and re-established censorship over the local press.

Decisive conferences between the general commanding in Algiers, General Gracieux, and the colonels commanding regiments in the city are going on.

Orders have been issued to Home Guard units to hand in their arms and to return to work.

Huge crowds are gathering outside the barricaded headquarters of Joseph Ortiz following an announcement that he will reply to President de Gaulle's speech today. The crowd are maintaining a constant chant of 'Massu, Massu, Massu' and 'de Gaulle to the gallows'.

There were signs this morning that the insurgents were preparing for a long siege. As last night's torrential rain ceased this morning they started strengthening their barricades and unloading food supplies.

Reporters who visited the insurgents' headquarters this morning are unanimous that their morale appears to be lower and that many among the Home Guard are privately saying they wish to return home. The men appear to be worried and nervous. It is believed in Paris that General de Gaulle's orders to the Army do not exclude the use of force against the insurgents if they do not disperse within a limited period.

In an early morning broadcast the general commanding in Eastern Algiers, General Gambiez, said: 'M. Delouvrier and General Challe will be obeyed without hesitation by my entire army. Our ties with France and with General de Gaulle are indestructible.'

There is now widespread optimism both in Algiers and Paris that order will be restored in Algiers without bloodshed.

Evening Standard
Saturday, January 30, 1960

ALGIERS REBELS GIVE IN

The week-long insurrection in Algiers is now all over bar the shouting — and it was to shouts of 'Vive Lagaillard' that the bearded, handsome, former paratroop officer led some four hundred of his men from the barricaded building that they had occupied and surrendered to officers commanding a battalion of Foreign Legion paratroopers. As onlookers cheered Lagaillard many of the women in the crowd wept. The insurgents were led to Army trucks and driven off to Army headquarters. They marched out carrying their arms and bedding and preceded by a huge Tricolour.

The other leader of the insurgents, Joseph Ortiz, has not been seen this morning. It is believed he left his headquarters during the night.

The men in his redoubt located in a bank building have deserted in a steady stream throughout the morning and those who were left are now removing the barricade around their headquarters.

(Algiers Radio announced this afternoon that Ortiz had fled and that the insurgents will be sent to fight Muslim insurgents in eastern Algeria.)

Overhead, in the clear blue sky, two Army helicopters were attempting to force down a helicopter belonging to the insurgents from which they have been scattering leaflets.

Meanwhile, the Army order calling for an end to the week-long general strike was largely obeyed throughout Algiers.

In Paris there was a one-hour general strike as a gesture of support for General de Gaulle.

Buses and the underground railway came to a stop and offices and shops emptied, giving the city a holiday air as thousands of workers crowded into cafés.

President de Gaulle, it is known, is determined to bring the ringleaders of the rebellion to Paris to stand trial here on the charge of treason.

A Cabinet meeting is to be held today and it is thought that Parliament will be recalled to vote special powers for President de Gaulle under the Constitution.

Evening Standard
Monday, February 1, 1960

DE GAULLE'S GAMBLE: NOT SO RASH AS IT SEEMS . . .

General de Gaulle has now had almost as much time to settle the six-year-old Algerian war as did the preceding Force République and he seems no nearer to a solution. 'Seems' is the operative word, for in fact a solution is in the making and should be plain to all men of goodwill.

Next Monday de Gaulle gives one of his rare Press conferences at which he will carry his thinking on Algeria a stage further. There is no doubt now as to his aim – it is to create an independent Algeria under which the one million Europeans who have lived there for generations and who largely created the Algeria of today will have the representation to which they are entitled.

It is this Government which will carry on secret discussions and open negotiations with the rebels for a cease-fire. This is, of course, de Gaulle's great achievement – to remove the detonator from the Algerian bomb. Only a year ago any talk of an independent Algerian state would have provoked an Army uprising and all the preconditions for a civil war in France. Today this proposal will be accepted by the Army as a whole. How good are the chances of de Gaulle pulling it off? Time is against him, the United Nations may soon vote against him, the Foreign Office and the State Department are clearly impatient, and there is a rabid political fanaticism at home which goes close to preferring a de Gaulle failure to a humane and liberal solution of the Algerian problem. But the chances of his pulling it off are really much better than they seem.

Contacts with the rebels are now secret but close and continuous. A kind of forced feeding of democracy in Algeria has now produced something like a Muslim political élite which finds no difficulty in getting visas for regular visits to the rebel headquarters in Tunis.

A million of Algeria's nine million Muslim population now live in modern European-type flats, own cars and hold important jobs in the administration of the country.

The Army has been heavily purged of political officers and so have the police. European firebrands are being deported from Algeria at a fast rate, especially this weekend before General de Gaulle's Press conference.

No one doubts the honesty of de Gaulle's intentions nor of the cunning and the determination with which he pursues them.

The prospects could be bright. It seems a pity that so many people in France and abroad seem to prefer a Congo-like abandonment.

Evening Standard
Friday, September 2, 1960

DE GAULLE ATTACKS WESTERN RIVALRY
Congo chaos could have been averted, he says

General de Gaulle today bitterly attacked the lack of liaison between the major Western powers over the granting of independence to the Belgian Congo.

This lack of liaison, he said at a Paris Press Conference, had played into the hands of the Russians. The West, in the matter of colonial policy, not only failed to act in unison but 'often acted in rivalry'. Had the Western powers, especially the three chiefly interested in the effects of Congolese independence – Belgium, Britain and France – acted in unison, the present chaos could have been averted.

As it is, he declared, 'The prestige and cohesion of the West has been gravely damaged and has left the way open to the so-called United Nations.

'The real beneficiaries of Western disunity were the Russians, who aimed to make the transition from colonialism to independence, on which we were all agreed, a kind of chronic world crisis instead of the peaceful transition it could otherwise be.'

If the Belgians, the British and the French had simultaneously guaranteed the Congo's right to independence and assured it of the technical aid necessary to make this transition, the present chaotic situation would not have arisen.

General de Gaulle, relaxed and confident as ever, was speaking in a crowded chandelier-lit reception room of the Elysée Palace. It was his third conference since he came to power.

France, he said, was 'lucid and serene', decided on its own policy and was not impressed by the 'tumultuous threat and theatrical stage play of the totalitarians'.

They were having their own troubles 'in trying to impose a system contrary to human nature' and in coping with 'national rivalries which erupted despite common ideology'.

He considered it absurd and 'criminal' for the colonies to turn against the heritage that had been bestowed on them by the former colonial powers.

'Now', he added, 'Soviet and U.S. rivalry – the great product of the last war – is bedevilling what could be a smooth transition.'

Answering a question, General de Gaulle said that Algerian self-determination was the only solution to the six-year-old war. An Algerian Government could now be confidently envisaged. He cited crushingly convincing evidence of the fantastic growth in Muslim participation in the administration of Algeria. He cited, too, the vast scale of French state investments in the country.

Stating that the only question now was whether an independent Algeria would be pro-French or anti-French, he gave his reasons for believing that a future Algeria would be pro-French. Among these was the fact that one-fifth of the active male labour force of Algeria worked in France.

'Where will they go', he asked, 'if Algeria turns against France?' Then, with heavy irony, he added: 'To Cairo? To Saudi Arabia? To Moscow? To Peking? To New York perhaps?'

Evening Standard
Monday, September 5, 1960

BITTERNESS – THAT IS THE NEXT PROBLEM FACING FRANCE . . .

The imagined mists surrounding General de Gaulle's Algerian policy are fast evaporating in the Mediterranean sun which bathes this gleaming city.

Two years ago, immediately after the revolution which has brought him back to power, de Gaulle opened a speech to a wildly cheering mob here with the words: 'I have understood you.' This statement deserves to rank with Mark Antony's 'Brutus is an honourable man' as one of the blandest tongue-in-cheek remarks in history. By the time he had finished even the stupidest among his listeners began to have doubts as to whether in picking de Gaulle as the man to keep Algeria French they had not made a terrible mistake.

Slowly de Gaulle has led the French to accept the hard political fact that they cannot and should not hold Algeria.

Now de Gaulle's intentions are clear to all except the most bigoted of his Left-wing opponents at home and abroad: a phased French disengagement from Algeria leading to an independent Algerian Republic in which the rebel leadership which has fought this bitter six-year-old guerrilla war will have an essential and possibly dominant role.

Guy Mollet, the French Socialist leader, once called the French Right 'the stupidest in the world'. To do the French Right justice it realised de Gaulle's true intentions, right from the start.

Not so the French Left which continued to pour doctrinaire derision on every one of de Gaulle's Algerian moves. It was as though, impotent themselves to enforce an Algerian peace, they were determined to impose their own impotence on de Gaulle. As a result they have made their own unique contribution to prolonging a war and producing a civil war climate in France.

'It's a trap' – this was the warning publicly given by M. Mitterrand, one of Mendès-France's chief lieutenants, to the rebel leaders in Tunis when de Gaulle first invited them to come to Paris for talks with him over a year ago. The warning was heeded and the invitation ignored. It is a sorry story which will bear bitter fruit in the days to come. As the Fascist threat over Algeria grows in France so out of sheer self-preservation the Left will be forced to rally behind de Gaulle. Then we will have the edifying spectacle of people who a few weeks ago were advocating desertion from the French Army demanding loyalty to de Gaulle's orders from it.

As we found after the Boer War, a war of this kind leaves such an inevitable legacy of bitterness that the only way to win the peace is to throw away the fruits of military victory. The French who have, in fact, won the military side of the war realise this only too well, with the result that they are pushing even supporters of the rebellion into key administrative posts.

The French Government's view is that a moderate nationalist force will only emerge after a final peace with the rebels, and not before.

Evening Standard
Friday, November 18, 1960

ALGIERS TRIAL MEN FLEE FRANCE

France edged several inches nearer the precipice of civil war when it became known today that five of the ringleaders of last January's anti-de Gaulle insurrection in Algiers who were standing trial in Paris had mysteriously fled the country. They are believed to be in Spain.

Among the five is twenty-eight-year-old bearded Deputy and former paratrooper Pierre Lagaillarde, who commanded one of the two principal barricaded strongpoints in Algiers during the insurrection with the tacit approval of the Army.

The disappearance of these five – the other ten accused appeared in the box when the trial was resumed after a four-day adjournment today – has touched off the greatest post-war judicial scandal in France. It also confirmed fears that a new anti-de Gaulle insurrection may take place before or during the General's scheduled visit there on Friday.

As soon as the news of their flight was confirmed an enraged de Gaulle summoned his Prime Minister, M. Debré, to the Elysée Palace. It is believed Lagaillarde crossed the frontier into Spain this morning and that he has joined General Salan, the former Commander-in-Chief in

Algeria, in San Sebastian.

General Salan has come out in strong opposition to de Gaulle's self-determination policy for Algeria. He disappeared into Spain five weeks ago, allegedly for a few days' visit. This visit has been mysteriously prolonged and its prolongation has caused great disquiet here. The judicial scandal arises because all the accused, after spending eight months in prison awaiting trial, were released on bail shortly after the trial, by a military tribunal, started.

Furthermore, when the court made its four-day adjournment the accused men – who face charges of plotting the Algiers revolt – were not ordered to remain in Paris and report at least daily to the police. In fact, Lagaillarde spent the weekend in his family's house near Toulouse, only one hundred miles from the Spanish frontier.

When the trial reopened today counsel representing the missing men asked for an adjournment. This was opposed by the prosecutor, General Gardon, who said that the trial could continue in the absence of the five accused.

Maître Gallot, counsel for Lagaillarde, spoke with deep emotion about his client and at the end of his brief statement broke into tears.

He said: 'I knew him as a child. I know his loyalty, his courage. I cannot believe that he has deceived the court. If he does not return within two or three days I, who love him, will not be able to continue with his defence.' To the astonishment of the court the civilian judge, M. Thiraet, who presided over this military court, rejected a prosecution request that the trial should continue and ordered a further three-day adjournment.

The sinister feature of the flight of Lagaillarde and his companions is that the case was going well for them. Until now they have had the best of the argument against an incompetent prosecution. If they fled it could not have been out of fear of the Court's verdict, but because they had more important business elsewhere.

Their escape spotlights the notorious existence of a secret network and a secret escape route which has succeeded in the past in getting Ring-wing extremists, in trouble with the authorities, out of France. The escape route leads through Spain and Spanish Morocco into Algiers.

Lagaillarde's principal colleague in the January conspiracy, Algiers café proprietor Joseph Ortiz, who mysteriously failed to be arrested when the insurrection collapsed, is known to be in Spain. The network which looks after these people in Spain is composed not only of French Fascists but of an international gang of Fascists who have taken refuge in Spain since the War.

Evening Standard
Monday, December 5, 1960

ALGERIA: THE DRAMATIC LAST APPEAL
De Gaulle: Vote 'Yes' or it's Chaos

General de Gaulle today made a final appeal to the French nation to give him a massive majority in the referendum on his Algerian policy.

A six-minute nationwide broadcast shortly after six bomb blasts had added to the rising tension in Paris revealed de Gaulle in his most icily aloof and arrogant mood. It was a 'take it or leave it' speech with no concessions to his critics on the Right, clamouring for specific guarantees to the European population of Algeria, or to the Left demanding that he should commit himself to negotiate with the Muslim rebel leadership in Tunis. Instead, with icy disdain, de Gaulle told the French nation: 'This is a matter between you and me. It is to me you will be replying. I am appealing to you over the heads of all intermediaries' – a clear and contemptuous reference to Parliament.

He made two points clear however – that if he obtained his majority then 'in the quickest possible time' a conference would be called 'representing all tendencies involved in the Algerian issue'. And that this was France's last chance to settle the six-year-old Algerian war itself before it became an international issue. He spoke of the need to create an independent Algeria to replace 'a system that is absurd and out of date'. He described a vote against his proposals of giving Algeria immediate Home Rule followed by a referendum when peace was restored to enable the population to choose its own political status as 'choosing chaos and national degradation'.

He added: 'We have paid dearly for our differences in the past. I ask for a majority that is equal to the great issue involved. I appeal to you as I appealed to you twenty years ago'.

The speech, which was clearly deliberately vague, is calculated to infuriate still more French politicians by its almost imperial tone. This was de Gaulle the monarch addressing his nation. Behind it lurked the threat that de Gaulle would resign if he did not receive what he considered to be a substantial vote of confidence. This is a possibility not entirely ruled out.

For example, if he gets a majority of those actually voting but a minority due to abstentions from the vote of the total electorate, de Gaulle may well consider himself to have been defeated. Estimates of his majority vary from as little as 52 per cent to 75 per cent. A great deal depends on the number of abstentions which de Gaulle will lump with the NO vote as a vote against himself.

A Right-wing communiqué is asking people to vote NO in next Sunday's referendum because Communists, who are also advocating a NO vote, are only seeking to drive anti-Communists into voting YES.

This illustrates perfectly the mental and moral confusion that reigns in France on the issue involved in the referendum. The question to which voters will be asked to reply with ayes or noes is whether they approve de Gaulle's policy of creating an embryo independent Algerian Republic, pending a free vote by the Algerians themselves to decide whether they wish to remain a part of France, or secede entirely, or remain loosely linked with France.

The object of the exercise is of course to break armed settler opposition to de Gaulle's policies to end the legal fiction that Algeria is as much a part of France as, say, Normandy. It is also to ensure that when a settlement with the Muslim rebel leadership in Tunis is finally reached a strong Muslim administration will already be in place to make possible a smooth, rather than a bloody and chaotic, transition to independence.

Six weeks ago when the projected referendum was announced there were serious fears of a military plot against the régime and the referendum was welcomed as a means of showing the Army that the nation was behind de Gaulle. Since then, as fears of a military revolt have receded, the confidence of the politicians has returned. Communists will be joining with Fascists, so-called Liberals with Conservatives, M. Mendès-France with M. Soustelle, in voting NO. They will be doing so for precisely the opposite reasons, with the result that if the NOES win confusion will be complete with de Gaulle forced to resign, but with no alternative Algerian policy emerging from the victory of his opponents.

But of course there is no danger of de Gaulle being defeated and that is why so many politicians long discredited can afford the luxury of, as it were, washing their soiled political consciences in public.

M. Mendès-France, for example, in the course of an interview in which he advocated a NO vote, was asked whether a NO victory would not produce chaos in France, with a danger of civil war and of military dictatorship. His reply was: 'But there is no likelihood of a NO majority'.

In short, Mendès-France feels free to advocate a dangerous course only because he is sure the electorate won't follow him. De Gaulle has said many harsh things about French politicians and political parties. It is hard in the light of M. Mendès-France's reply not to feel that these harsh judgments were justified up to the hilt.

Evening Standard
Friday, January 6, 1961

THE ALGERIAN LEGEND IS DEAD
Newsflash – pickaxe mob marches

More than two hundred Muslim demonstrators carrying pickaxes, spades and rebel flags sacked houses and damaged cars in Batna today. Each time police broke it up the mob reformed and marched again.

General de Gaulle's three-to-one victory in yesterday's referendum – far bigger than even the most optimistic of his supporters expected – means that a course has now been set which can only end in Algerian independence. It marks the end of the 'Algeria is French' legend and as a political factor this slogan is now as dead as the dodo. It also marks the end of persistent nightmare threats of a military coup against the régime, for who can now possibly hope for such a coup to succeed against a régime and a policy so solidly backed by public opinion?

The real purpose of the referendum can now be clearly seen – it was to reinforce de Gaulle's authority at home and abroad so that he can now proceed with the next and final phase of his Algerian policy.

From now on events will move swiftly. De Gaulle's first move will be the creation of an Algerian Parliament overwhelmingly Muslim in numbers reflecting the nine-to-one proportion between the Muslim and the European populations.

There will also be an Algerian executive, which in effect will be a provisional Algerian government pending settlement with Muslim rebel leadership in Tunis.

De Gaulle is expected to fulfil the promise he made in his last election address of seeking a round table conference 'of all tendencies' involved in the Algerian question.

The result of the referendum is a humilating defeat for most of the established political leaders who opposed de Gaulle, and especially M. Jacques Soustelle, the bulk of the NO vote having been supplied by the Communists.

In short, the Right-wing Nationalist opposition to de Gaulle is unmarked as being an insignificant minority.

Even the Communist voters refused to follow the party line and either abstained or voted YES.

The scale of de Gaulle's victory can only be measured if it is realised that if the voters had followed the advice of party leaders then, according to the last election results, he would have been heavily defeated.

He faced the opposition not only of the Communists (four million voters) but of the Right-wing politicians who technically commanded nearly five million votes.

Only four of the red belt Communist suburbs of Paris provided NO majorities – and slight ones at that – and all other Communist strongholds in Paris and elsewhere returned YES majorities.

In Algeria the Muslim peasantry provided de Gaulle with a majority over the virtually unanimous European vote against him.

The heavy Muslim abstentions in the big cities like Algiers, Oran and Constantine can be explained by Muslim fears of threats against them, both from the Muslim Nationalist side and the Europeans.

To sum up: de Gaulle's referendum victory does not of itself provide a solution to the six-year-old Muslim rebellion, but it does provide the necessary condition for a solution.

Final official returns gave de Gaulle a 75.25 per cent majority in Metropolitan France and 64.5 per cent in Algeria, where he carried every district except Oran and Algiers.

Evening Standard
Monday, January 9, 1961

THE GENERALS GRAB POWER IN ALGIERS

Four retired French generals, backed by Foreign Legion paratroops and other Army units, seized control of Algeria in a bloodless pre-dawn coup today.

The generals – all bitterly opposed to de Gaulle's Algerian policy – declared that they had 'saved French Algeria' and warned: 'All resistance will be smashed, wherever it comes from'.

But the generals' claim to have taken over the rest of Algeria and the Sahara was strongly denied by the French Government, which said that 'the mad team in Algiers will remain confined to Algiers'.

Official sources in Paris said the generals commanding the Oran and Constantine areas had rejected an ultimatum issued by the rebel leaders demanding that they join the rebellion. But an official report reaching Paris says that other parachute regiments are leaving their posts in the interior and moving towards the cities of Oran and Constantine.

The French Government cancelled leave for all French servicemen, officers and other ranks. Extra guards were put on key installations and arms depots.

Algiers Radio broadcast a proclamation signed by the four rebel generals which said civil and military representatives of the 'regime of treason' had been arrested and that all power had passed to the leaders of the revolt.

General de Gaulle was woken with the news of the revolt at 2.30 a.m. He is reported today as showing signs of fatigue. But he is going through with an official programme of receptions for M. Senghor, President of Senegal, whom he received for lunch at the Elysée Palace with full military honours.

It is believed that the Government had received some information of the plot and that was the reason why General de Gaulle cancelled last night a provincial tour he was to have begun on Monday. An emergency Cabinet meeting has been called for this afternoon.

It was after a telephone conversation with de Gaulle that M. Joxe, Minister for Algeria, took off by air for Algiers, empowered to act as he thinks fit to cope with the situation. M. Joxe was accompanied by six members of his staff.

The next few hours are likely to be decisive. The Government is anxiously waiting word as to what will be the fate of M. Joxe when he and his party land in Algiers.

Evening Standard
Saturday, April 22, 1961

INVASION THREAT — IS ARMY LOYAL?
French troops in Germany and France remain confined to their barracks

Algiers Radio today denied that an order for the landing of troops in France had ever been given, as claimed by the Paris Government last night.

General Maurice Challe, one of the leaders of the revolt, in a broadcast today, said that no personal or political ambitions prompted it. The sole aim was to save Algeria from the grip of the Muslim rebellion and to hand over a pacified Algeria to France, he said.

*   *   *

Despite today's anti-climax to last night's high drama there is little doubt that an invasion from Algiers and an attempted coup d'état will be made in the next few days.

The alternative for the mutinous generals is certain defeat by blockade from Metropolitan France.

The mutineers now control virtually the whole of Algeria including all its seaports and airfields. Only small pockets of the 350,000-strong French army there have shown a will if not to resist at least not to co-operate.

The brutal and appalling fact remains, however, that the French Republic appears to have been deserted by the bulk of the Army. This is not only the case in Algeria but it is also indicated by the fact that the Government is showing no inclination to use for its defence its 60,000-strong Army in West Germany.

As to the reliability of the Air Force, this is compromised by the fact that two of its most illustrious officers, General Challe and General Jouhaud, are among the four military leaders in command of the rebellion.

The Navy is notoriously and traditionally anti-de Gaullist.

There are 160,000 troops in France excluding the 60,000 in West Germany, the overwhelming majority of whom are conscripts undergoing preliminary training. This figure also includes 11,000 paratroopers, most of them stationed in south-west France.

All these troops remain confined to barracks and the Government has at its disposal at the moment, in addition to the normal police force numbering 18,000 men, 14,000 members of the para-military riot squads.

As against these shock troops alone the military junta in Algiers can put into action 15,000 paratroopers.

The military correspondent of the influential Paris newspaper, *Le Monde,* evaluating the military situation that came to a showdown between Algiers and Paris, writes: 'It is clear that the Government has hesitated to call into action the troops it has at its disposal in France and West Germany'.

He points out that the French Army in West Germany is composed of some its best-trained infantry troops and a superb fighter air force. It is clear from his analysis that if the French Government could safely call on these forces the possibility of a coup d'état in Paris would melt like snow under an African sun.

He also points out that the army in Algiers will find itself desperately short of petrol in two weeks and that therefore everything points to an attempt to seize power in Paris at the earliest possible moment.

His view is reinforced in an editorial by the editor of *Le Monde,* who also argues that the rebel generals must act in the next few days.

It is tempting, in view of the overwhelming support that General de Gaulle enjoys in the country, to consider such an invasion attempt as the wildest folly.

It remains a fact, however, that all the reasons which produced the strongest scepticism of a possible coup d'état in Paris apply equally to the actual coup d'état in Algiers, and the position of the rebel generals can be summed up in the saying 'if you strike at a king, you must strike to kill'.

Evening Standard
Monday, April 24, 1961

BLOOD MAY FLOW TOMORROW — DEBRÉ
My plans to break mutiny — De Gaulle

French Premier M. Debré told an emergency meeting of the French Parliament today that blood has not yet flowed in the Algerian revolt 'but it may flow tomorrow'.

His dramatic statement to a packed chamber followed the reading of a message from President de Gaulle in which he outlined his plans to break the mutiny.

Only a few hours before, *Les Paras*, the 'blooded' soldiers, the veterans, started the first fighting by trying to take the naval base at Mers el Kebir. A warship fired a blank — and they fled. Only a few hours before, General de Pouilly was arrested in Algiers after rebel leader ex-General Challe broke a promise. And only a few hours before, French armoured units in Western Germany were recalled to Paris.

The message from de Gaulle was read to Parliament by M. Chaban-Delmas. It said:

*   *   *

'The mutiny of certain Army chiefs and the events in Algeria which have flowed from this plot against the State, encouraged as it is by certain elements in France itself, produces a heavy and immediate threat to the independence of the nation.

'In accordance with the Constitution and after consultations I have decided to apply Article 16 of the Constitution and to take the necessary measures.' (Article 16 of the Constitution lays it down that the President can take over full powers if the independence of the country is menaced.

'On the other hand this will not interfere with the activities of Parliament which will still continue to exercise its legislative rights and to supervise the affairs of State. Parliament is thus called upon to continue its task. In this hard and unhappy test that France is undergoing today let me tell you that I count on your support to help me fulfil my duties'.

Premier Debré said:

*   *   *

'The object of the Algerian coup d'état was not and is not simply Algeria. It was, and remains, to spread to Metropolitan France in trying to impose mutiny on certain units and on certain army corps stationed in France or stationed near France.

'To occupy the heart of Paris was, and remains, without any doubt, one of the objectives of the rebellion. I must not hide from Parliament that the State of Emergency is not ended.

'The ringleaders of the rebellion cannot stay where they are. They must go all out for a political success. They have taken upon themselves a great responsibility. This responsibility will carry them as far as bloodshed.

'The Navy fired on the rebels at Mers el Kebir today and what happened there may soon happen here. I trust Parliament understands fully that under present conditions those responsible for the Algiers plot may soon provoke civil war here.

'If the plotters do not quickly withdraw it's civil war. I do not wish to hide from Parliament the seriousness of certain measures which will be revealed shortly nor the firmness with which I will act without consideration of any legal niceties.

'How could it be otherwise? One cannot reply to flagrant illegality by sticking to legality'.

*   *   *

When Les Paras attempted to storm the naval base of Mers el Kebir, they were met by a blank cannon shot fired from the cruiser *Marille-Breze* in the naval flotilla commanded by Admiral Querville, while five other warships trained their guns inland. Then *Les Paras* withdrew . . . to the hills. Should they attempt to return and take the base Admiral Querville had these orders: Open direct fire.

As this, the first known shot in the revolt, was fired, there was the news of the arrest of General de Pouilly, the only important general believed to be still loyal and the man who represented the last official contact with Algeria.

According to a Paris statement by the Minister of Information, M. Terrenoire, General de Pouilly went to Algiers to discuss technical details with ex-General Challe, the rebel leader, on a promise that he would be allowed to return to his base in the interior where he moved after paratroopers took over Oran.

Challe 'broke his word'. General de Pouilly has played a curious role since the mutiny broke out last Saturday, obviously attempting to act as a go-between between Paris and Algiers. Radio Algiers claimed that General de Pouilly went to Algiers on a personal mission on behalf of de Gaulle. Whatever the explanation, his disappearance is clearly a heavy blow to Paris and can only have a troubling if not actually a demoralising effect.

Radio Algiers also announced that troops in the Sahara commanded by General Jacquiet have gone over to the insurgents. This news is serious because it means that the rebel generals will now have access to Saharan oil

The first of the military decisions today was the recall to France of three armoured regiments from the 60,000 strong army stationed in and around Baden-Baden in Western Germany. The regiments crossed into France last night and are now waiting at Strasbourg to catch trains for Paris. The decision to move them – it followed a declaration of loyalty to de Gaulle by the C-in-C in Germany, General Crepin – came as a surprise. The French Army in Western Germany has long been the dumping ground for mutinous officers in Algeria who have been removed from their commands because of political unreliability.

The second important decision was that the French Mediterranean Fleet at Toulon be put under orders to sail for Algerian ports today. Its task will be to complete the blockade of Algeria by taking up positions overlooking every port in rebel hands on the Algerian coast.

There remains an element of mystery regarding the arrival of the West German troops in France. The Paris newspaper *France Soir*, reporting on their movement before the official announcement, said: 'According to Government circles in Paris, the concern that one might have concerning the reliability of the troops in Germany has now been removed. News of their arrival in Strasbourg is considered here as a reassuring sight'.

A series of arrests of senior officers in Paris and the provinces has been carried out in the past twenty-four hours. Among those arrested are General Allard, former C-in-C Germany; General de Beaufort, a former military aide of General de Gaulle; and Colonel Dufour, who commanded the first Foreign Legion paratroop regiment which led the Algiers swoop, and who was removed from Algiers several months ago to take command of a crack infantry regiment stationed in Germany.

Three other generals whose names have not been disclosed are also known to be under arrest.

Evening Standard
Tuesday, April 25, 1961

CHALLE IN PARIS FACES DEATH
Army court will try him, may send him to a firing squad

Maurice Challe, ex-General, leader of the Algiers mutiny which collapsed so ignominiously last night, arrived at the military airport of Villacoublay today – under arrest.

He was immediately whisked off to the Santé prison to be charged with organising an armed uprising, a charge that carries the death penalty. Quickly will follow a military trial. And then all that is left to do as far as the Government is concerned is for the firing squad to begin its work. There is virtually no doubt that Challe will die.

Meanwhile Paris exalts at the victory over the mutineers; Algiers is calm, but crestfallen at the disappointment of its hopes; and the Stock Exchange in Paris experienced an unprecedented boom.

From M. Pinay, the Conservative leader who remained silent during the crisis, came these words: 'I rejoice that the Algerian adventure has been ended and that the authorities of the State have been restored'.

The fate of Challe's comrades – ex-generals Salan, Zeller, Jouhaud and ex-colonels Argoud, Godard and Lacheroy – is still unkown. But M. Terrenoire, the Minister of Information, said an aeroplane carrying 'accomplices' of the rebel leaders had landed at Gibraltar. Their identity was not known. [The French Consulate at Gibraltar has told Paris that it knows nothing of such an arrival.]

M. Terrenoire revealed that during the first hours of the insurrection France was in mortal peril.

'The State risked being abandoned, it is certain, by those whose duty it is to support her,' he declared. 'This must not happen again. The State must be strong, solid. It must not be at the mercy of subversion, of any sort'.

He also confirmed that the rebellion had been staged by three units, regiments of the general reserve, which in French military terms means striking forces – paratroops and the Foreign Legion.

'The rebel generals ran from one side of the country to another trying to establish their authority', he said, 'but this was in vain because it met with resistance of loyal troops'.

He added that de Gaulle would probably report to the nation on 'the consequences and the lesson of recent events'.

Telephone contact between Paris and Algiers has now been restored. First reports indicate that the force of 200,000 conscripts played a vital role in frustrating the mutiny. It was obvious that they were not prepared to fight on the side of the rebels or to disobey Government orders.

Some 5,000 arms are reported to be missing from a major arms depot in the city and what is even more disquieting, one ton of plastic charges have been removed.

M. Jacques Soustelle, a most noted civilian sympathiser with the rebels, has disappeared. It appears certain that he skipped France the moment news reached him that the Government had decided to arrest him.

It was authoritatively learned here that the date of the mutiny was advanced by several days by the plotters because some of the most prominent officers in Algeria who were to have taken part in it were in imminent danger of being removed from Algeria.

Government circles are convinced that a parachute landing on Paris was imminent on Sunday night. It is believed it was abandoned or postponed because pilots of the transport planes to be used refused to take part in the operation.

The signal for the collapse of the mutiny seems to have been the blank shot fired by the cruiser lying off the naval base of Mers el Kebir as paratroopers invested the port. This was a signal that whatever the Army might do the Navy was prepared to obey all orders to fire on mutinous troops.

When the generals quit Algiers they took a number of their paratroopers with them. Behind them they left thousands of sullen, dispirited supporters, and the notorious Colonel Godard, who was in charge of security. He was most dispirited of all. 'The only thing left for me to do is put a bullet through my head', he said.

Algiers reports said thirty-five people, in civilian and military clothes, accompanied Challe, Salan and Jouhaud. More tried to, but a paratrooper lieutenant in charge of loading the trucks said: 'Brass hats only, the others can fend for themselves'.

Several minutes later flames could be seen through a window in the government delegation building where, it appeared, officials were burning documents.

Wild scenes took place when the end was announced over Algiers

Radio. Mobs hurled abuse at paratroopers quitting the city, which was taken over shortly before midnight by marines, gendarmes, riot police and a regiment of Zouaves consisting largely of conscripts.

Armoured cars and half-track vehicles patrolled the streets.

Within hours not a vestige of the uprising flickered. Those imprisoned by the military junta were freed, including M. Morin, the government representative in Algeria, and General Gambiez, the deposed Commander-in-Chief.

The total casualties involved in crushing the mutiny: three slightly wounded gendarmes, fired on by snipers.

The crumbling of the generals' dream came suddenly.

Mobile gendarmes loyal to de Gaulle sped into Algiers in a well co-ordinated strike. Armoured cars and half-track vehicles appeared at strategic spots. A jeep convoy converged on Algiers Radio.

In front of the Hotel Aletti in central Algiers, the gendarmes ran into paratroopers. Both sides opened fire. The gendarmes pulled back with some wounded, carrying them into the hotel lobby.

The loss of the 'Battle of the Aletti' was temporary.

More gendarmes swarmed through the city. An insurgent radio programme was in full swing when the gendarmes burst into Algiers Radio. The shocked announcer looked up and shouted into the microphone: 'Everyone to the forum'. The forum. Scene of so many of the recent dramatic events in Algerian history. A crowd of some fifty thousand Europeans gathered as rumours spread that de Gaulle's men were retaking Algiers.

Challe, Salan, Zeller and Jouhaud listened with despair as the news poured in. Oran and Constantine, once in insurgent hands, had surrendered to Government forces. So the game was up and the generals, professional soldiers long used to evaluating their power, knew it.

Challe and Salan attempted one last gesture. They went to the balcony overlooking the forum, the same balcony where Challe on Monday told a cheering crowd of a hundred thousand that they would fight to the death.

Now Challe looked down on the angy mob and tried to speak even as the first shots rang out from the clashes between paratrooopers and gendarmes. But the microphones were dead. His words were lost in the tumult of wild shouting that welled up from the forum.

Challe, Salan and Jouhaud left, climbed into trucks and departed. All but Challe were broken men. Challe just laughed – and smoked his pipe.

Evening Standard
Wednesday, April 26, 1961

IT'S NOT OVER YET . . . 'LES PARAS' MAY FIGHT ON
Tanks close in on Legion camp

The dramatic events in Algeria are not ended. There is a serious danger that paratroopers and Foreign Legion regiments are preparing to carry on a guerrilla resistance. And the place where the trouble is likely to start is Zeralda – base of the men who spearheaded the revolt. A large force of riot police surrounded Zeralda. French Army tanks blocked the road leading to it.

Then a Foreign Legion sergeant pointed to two teen-aged National Servicemen about twenty yards from his stronghold and said: 'We're not frightened of kids like that'.

Contemptuously he added: 'They've sent these kids down here to keep an eye on us. But it takes more than that to scare us. This is a real unit'.

The four rows of medals glinted on his chest and the corporal by his side turned his cheek, a cheek disfigured by a three-inch scar.

As they were talking, their commander, Colonel Giraud, was in conference with M. Pierre Messmer, the French Minister of Defence. What they discussed was not revealed.

Meanwhile, units of the French Fleet remained at anchor opposite Zeralda. They are led by the aircraft carrier *Arromanches* which has its guns trained on the Foreign Legion base.

The correspondent of *Le Figaro*, Serge Bromberger, who has been in Algiers throughout the mutiny, states that the three missing generals who led the mutiny have taken refuge with foreign legionaries at Zeralda. A spokeman at Zeralda denied that any generals were there. But authorities in Algiers and Paris are convinced that they have not succeeded in leaving Algiers.

Another general who joined the mutiny after it broke out – General Gardy – is also missing. So are several colonels who played a prominent part in the revolt and who are now believed to be with missing paratroop regiments.

Meanwhile, in addition to General Challe, who gave himself up yesterday and who is now incarcerated in the Santé Prison in Paris, three other generals – Bigon, Petit and Gouraud – have also been removed to Paris where they are under arrest. So is Colonel de Boissieu, who brought a letter from Challe to de Gaulle before Challe gave himself up. The colonel is a distant relative of de Gaulle by marriage.

The Communist newspaper, *Humanité*, and a fellow-travelling newspaper, *Libération*, were seized today for carrying a resolution of the

Central Committee of the French Communist Party which charges de Gaulle's government with complicity in the revolt.

The first steps were taken today to dissolve the Foreign Legion with a government decision to close recruiting bureaux for the Legion throughout France.

De Gaulle has made it clear to his ministers that he intends to retain the dictorial powers given him under Article 16 of the Constitution for some time yet, for an indefinite period.

De Gaulle intends using Article 16 not only to carry out a thorough-going purge of the Army but also to institute basic changes in its structure which he now considers inevitable. These include the dissolution not only of the Foreign Legion but also of the paratroop regiments.

Some changes are likely to be made in the French police force and in the security service.

De Gaulle also intends to change the political structure in France by having a Vice-President elected who will automatically replace him in the event of death or incapacity.

He plans that both his own office and that of the Vice-President should become elected offices after the American model. He intends to reform and broaden his Government and certain ministers are likely to disappear.

De Gaulle subjected his ministers to a severe test during the crisis. When the mutiny broke out he called them in one by one and said: 'This looks like the end, doesn't it? What do you think?' Some of their replies may have lacked the necessary resolution.

Hundreds of arrests continue to be made in Paris and the provinces.

Ex-General Challe will be questioned by an examining magistrate today at the Santé Prison. He will not be tried by a court martial but by a civilian court set up by the Minister of Justice, M. Micheler. Proceedings against him will be speeded to such an extent that his trial is expected to take place in ten days time.

Challe faces the death penalty. At the same time a special court has been set up to deal exclusively with those charged with organising or participating in the uprising. Four generals who went over to Challe after the revolt broke out have been flown to Paris and are now under arrest. At the same time hundreds of arrests continue to be made.

*   *   *

Admiral Jean-Marie Querville today told correspondents how he kept the French Navy and Marines out of the Algerian insurrection.

He said: 'The insurgents wanted us to intercept all French warships trying to leave Algeria for France. I refused and an ultimatum was sent to the Naval base at Mers el Kebir, which the insurgents then threatened to occupy with two paratroop regiments if it did not comply.'

He slipped away from Algiers with an hour to spare before the time-limit fixed by the insurgents for him to accede to their demand to bring the Navy under their control.

Evening Standard
Thursday, April 27, 1961

DE GAULLE STARTS PURGE — FIVE GENERALS HELD
'Les Paras' disbanded — judges, police are sacked

General de Gaulle is to broadcast to the French nation on May 8, it was announced in Paris today. He wil give a detailed account of the measures he has taken to restore discipline in the Army and of the constitutional changes he will propose to make as a result of this week's events.

General de Gaulle is also expected to announce the opening of peace talks with the Algerian Muslim Nationalists.

At the same time in Algeria the first Foreign Legion paratroop regiment has been dissolved and its officers taken into custody.

A ruthless purge of the civil service in Algeria is being carried out on the spot by the Minister for Algeria, M. Joxe. Hundreds of civil servants have been dismissed, not only for collaborating with the mutineers but also for not defying their orders. The dismissed civil servants include judges, magistrates, mayors and high police officials.

Hundreds of civilians and army officers are under arrest. It was announced in Algiers today that five generals had been arrested and sent home to France. The number of arrests in Algiers alone, and not only for civilians, amounted to more than five hundred.

Street scenes in Algiers are marked by furious quarrels between officers who took opposite sides during the mutiny.

The French Government today named the judge who will preside over a mixed civilian and Army court which will try General Challe within a month. The court will be presided over by M. Maurice Patin, a senior judge and a noted Liberal.

*   *   *

Political dissension has broken out here on the subject as to how long General de Gaulle should retain the almost dictatorial powers granted him under the constitution in the event of a national emergency.

In some quarters it is thought that General de Gaulle is intent on keeping these powers until peace is restored in Algeria.

There has been a shameful aftermath to the Algiers mutiny in Paris. The Paris newspaper *Le Monde* yesterday published in an editorial a rumour which has been circulating in Fascist and Communist circles that General Challe received promises of support for his rebellion from the US Central Intelligence Agency. Today *Le Monde* claims that this information comes from official sources.

The rumour received widespread circulation earlier, as a result of astonishingly crude editing in *Le Figaro* of a column by the famous American commentator, Mr Joseph Alsop.

Mr Alsop referred to these rumours, then added a comment to the effect that anyone who could believe that could believe anything.

Le Figaro cut out the comment and presented Mr Alsop's column in a manner which clearly implied that Mr Alsop himself believed these rumours. *Le Monde* is a pious and honest newspaper but it never misses an opportunity to indulge in its favourite sport of Washington-baiting.

Many harsh things have been said about the US Central Intelligence Agency but it has not yet deserved a reputation for being quite as undisciplined as the French Army.

Evening Standard
Friday, April 28, 1961

THE BIG DEBATE: WOULD DE GAULLE LET CHALLE DIE?

A fascinating debate is going on here about whether General de Gaulle would allow fifty-three-year-old ex-General Maurice Challe to be executed for his part in the recent Algiers mutiny.

A sentence of death on a 'Guilty' verdict is inevitable at his trial that opens at the end of this month. Would de Gaulle let the sentence stand or would he use his presidential powers to commute it to, say, life imprisonment? The answer to that question would not only be important politically, but would also provide a new insight into de Gaulle's character.

There is, here in Paris, a poignant pointer to what de Gaulle's decision would be. It is in the person of Mme Pétain, widow of the late Marshal Pétain, Head of State during the occupation. Now eighty-four, crippled with arthritis, she continues to live in a modest Paris flat on her widow's pension. A pension which by an administrative irony – because her husband was sentenced to death and the death penalty was never carried out – became payable to her during her husband's lifetime. The execution was not carried out only because of Pétain's great age. Had he been a few years younger his fate would have been the same as that of Laval. Instead, he was sentenced to life imprisonment on an island, where he died and where he is buried. His last wish was that he should be reburied in France.

Mme Pétain has made two requests that his last wish might be carried out. The first was to M. Mendès-France when he was Prime Minister and M. Mendès-France placed the request before Parliament, which rejected it. The second was in a personal appeal to General de Gaulle after he returned to power. He replied through an official to her lawyer. The reply was a firm 'No'. In short, Pétain dead remained as much subject to the full rigour of the law as Pétain alive.

One theory as to why de Gaulle could show clemency to Challe is that de Gaulle failed to condemn the main 1958 mutiny – as a result of which he came back into power. The parallel is false. De Gaulle failed to condemn the 1958 mutineers because the Government itself failed to condemn them. General Salan remained throughout the May events the accredited miliary and civil representative of the Government.

De Gaulle accepted power not from the generals but from Parliament. Had the generals usurped power in Paris and then offered it to de Gaulle, I am convinced he would have rejected it. De Gaulle was not brought to power by a military coup d'état – he averted one.

Evening Standard
Friday, May 12, 1961

ALGERIA: DE GAULLE SAYS 'CEASE FIRE'

The French Government today announced a unilateral cease-fire in Algeria from five o'clock tonight. An official statement said the truce was for a month, but could be suspended or prolonged, 'according to how the situation develops'. The announcement, which coincides with the opening today of peace talks with the Algerian Nationalists to end the six-and-a-half-year-old Algerian rebellion, has raised the tension in Algeria to a point of acute crisis.

The cease-fire move, though expected, is bitterly resented by the French Army and the European settlers.

Tension is all the greater because two of the generals and five of the colonels who led last month's military uprising are still at large in Algeria. Their whereabouts appear to be known but the Government has failed to enforce stringent orders for their arrest. The result is that fears of a new coup in Algeria are now extremely great.

With the truce, France also announced easier detention conditions for Mohammed Ben Bella and other captive insurgent leaders, and the release of six thousand political prisoners. Ben Bella and two other rebel leaders were flown today from an island fortress off the Atlantic coast to a residence about one hundred and twenty miles from Paris.

Ben Bella, a vice-premier in the insurgent 'government', and his aides were captured by the French in 1956. Their plane, flying from Rabat to Tunis, was forced down at Algiers. Mostofa Lacheraf, a former Algerian teacher who was also on the plane, was released immediately from Fresnes prison, near Paris.

In Paris, there is intense concern for the personal safety of General de Gaulle and of possible assassination attempts against him and members of his Government. General de Gaulle today left for a week-end visit to Chancellor Adenauer in Bonn, and vast security measures have been taken by the West German Government to protect him.

In Evian, where the peace talks opened today, the city is almost in a state of siege, with some twenty thousand riot police patrolling its streets and guarding both the residence of the French delegation and the Hotel Duparc where the talks are being held.

In Geneva, where the nine-man Algerian rebel delegation led by Belkacin Krim, 'Foreign Minister' in the provisional rebel government, is quartered, similar security measures have been taken by the Swiss Army.

The Algerian delegation flew by helicopter this morning from its Geneva residence to the Hotel Duparc, on the French side of Lake Geneva, for the talks.

The French delegation is being led by M. Joxe, former French Ambassador in Moscow and Minister for Algeria in the de Gaulle Government.

Every detail of protocol for today's meeting was carefully studied by the French Government beforehand. The French fetish of hand-shaking presented a particular problem. This has been overcome by the provision of an especially large table across which it would be impossible for the rival delegations to even attempt to shake hands. Instead French delegates stood up when the rebel Muslims entered the conference room and nodded to them across the table.

The conference opened with an exposition by M. Joxe of General de Gaulle's views on the future of Algeria. These can be summarised as an unconditional offer of independence to Algeria with the hope that commonsense and self-interest would lead the Algerians themselves to choose a free association with France, amounting to a kind of dominion status.

The major point at issue will be a settlement which will guarantee lives and property of the 1,200,000 European settlers in Algeria.

The first session lasted an hour and forty-two minutes. The next one will be on Tuesday.

The unilateral cease-fire announced today really consolidates an already existing military situation. On the principle that nobody likes risking death in the last fifteen minutes of a war, the military effort of the Nationalist rebels has been virtually non-existent for several months.

It is in this paradoxical situation of almost total military victory that the French are conferring the status of victors on the Tunis-based Muslim rebels.

De Gaulle's views on this point are clear: Military victory is insufficient and a political settlement giving the nine million Muslims in Algeria the right to decide their own destiny is essential to eradicate the certainty of a much more massive Muslim revolt in years to come.

The issues being discussed in Evian are of incalculable importance to both the future of North Africa and of France itself. The failure of the talks would mean the firm implantation of Communism throughout North Africa and would produce a dangerous drift to chaos in France.

Evening Standard
Saturday, May 20, 1961

NEW PLOTS

The sombre French treason trials arising out of last April's Algiers mutiny go on with guillotine-like regularity. Except that this time the guillotine never falls. Instead, long sentences are handed down on the mutinous generals, ensuring live martyrs instead of dead ones. In the process, the French have made another noteworthy contribution to jurisprudence: henceforth *le crime patriotique* like *le crime passionel* is immune from the death penalty.

Meanwhile, one wonders if the mutineers had succeeded would they have recognised the patriotic motives of those who opposed them. The outlook is as gloomy as the weather. New plots to overthrow General de Gaulle are now definitely under way.

This noble man, whose honest anti-colonial intentions are now recognised even by the editor of *The Economist,* is now engaged in peace talks with the Algerian Muslim rebels.

Their response, even while engaged in peace talks and even as six thousand terrorists are in the process of being freed, is to step up terrorist attacks in Paris.

One would have thought in those circumstances that leading figures of the French Left, who have great influence with the rebel leaders, would now be seeking to persuade them to caution and moderation. Not a bit of it. They are as silent now when de Gaulle is trying to make peace in Algeria as the leaders of the French Right were silent when de Gaulle set about crushing the military revolt.

Evening Standard
Friday, June 9, 1961

THE GULF

I wish I could like de Gaulle less and the French more. Here are a few pointers to the normal gulf that separates him from many of his countrymen.

*　　　*　　　*

POINTER ONE

Peace talks with the rebels are about to recommence. They were broken off last month on the issue of the rebel claim to sovereignty over the Sahara. The claim is baseless ethnically, geographically, politically and morally.

What is even more important, however, is that the claim is opposed by all newly independent African states bordering on the Sahara. They favour the French plan of a seven-nation partnership to exploit the Sahara's wealth.

At this point when negotiations are about to resume, M. Mendès-France writes an article in which he says: 'The French Government knows full well that there is no way of avoiding Algerian sovereignty over the Sahara.'

In short, he is telling the rebels to stick to the maximum demand with an assurance that the French Government knows full well that it will have to be granted. Charming!

*　　　*　　　*

POINTER TWO:

General de Gaulle is being violently attacked for clinging to the special powers under Article 16 of the Constitution which Parliament accorded him at the time of the last Algiers' mutiny. The powers are not being used and are clearly held in reserve for the next Algerian blow-up.

At the time of the last mutiny de Gaulle was bitterly criticised for not putting suspects into preventive custody before the mutiny broke out.

The argument seems to be that it would have been acceptable for de Gaulle to have acted unconstitutionally before the last mutiny, but unacceptable for him to act constitutionally at some future time of great danger.

*   *   *

POINTER THREE:

For weeks now words like 'patriotism' and 'honour' have been foaming from the mouths of mutinous officers like saliva from Pavlov's dogs.

A foreign military attaché here gives me the other side of the picture. He tells me of his positive embarrassment at the confidence showered on him by French Army officers regarding their future plans to overthrow de Gaulle. All this is accompanied by bitter personal attacks on de Gaulle.

My military attaché friend commented: 'They do not find it in the least unseemly to talk like that in front of a foreign officer'. Charming!

Evening Standard
Friday, June 30, 1961

SO MANY MEDALS, NEVER A BATTLE

It is, of course, in a sense tragically appropriate that the most decorated general in the French Army should never have fought a battle. What kind of a man is General Raoul Salan who now commands the secret army organisation in Algeria?

I can only report my first impression on seeing him in Algiers four years ago when he was Commander-in-Chief. He looked like an actor playing the role of a general. His deadpan face, glazed eyes, a fixed and crooked smile, his pallor, the elegance of his uniform and the depth of his decorations, all combined to give him an air of baffling unreality. It is only fair to say that others – especially women – have been bowled over by his personality, with its overtones of subtlety and self-control.

His military career has been a bureaucratic one, mostly to do with Intelligence and mostly to do with the Far East – which has clearly marked him. It has provided him with his two Army nicknames of 'the Mandarin' and 'the Chinese General'. His last-war record was a non-committal one – he took an appointment from Vichy and French West Africa but never joined de Gaulle until after the Liberation.

As Commander-in-Chief both in Indo-China and Algeria he became notorious for a monumental operational laziness and lack of aggressiveness. This apparent lack of character, and indecision combined with his snowballing decorations and his evident popularity with the politicians in Paris, all combined to make him intensely disliked in the French Army officer corps. This dislike still persists, to the point where Salan's leadership of the secret army is the secret army's major weakness.

His indecision became evident during the May 1958 revolt when he created the impression that he did not know which side he was going to be on but implying that whichever it was it was going to be the winning one.

The mystery, however, is how the time-serving general that Salan clearly was can be transformed into the desperado and outlaw he is today.

Salan, accustomed to the respect and importance he enjoyed in the Fourth Republic, was shaken and finally demented by de Gaulle's jibes and carefully calculated patronising insults. For example, Salan was removed as C-in-C in Algiers on the promise that he would be given the specially created and all-important post – so he was told – of Inspector-General of the Army. He returned to Paris to find a magnificent apartment, made available to him at the Invalides, but no job and no access to de Gaulle.

He did, however, receive yet another decoration, this time France's highest, the *Médaille Militaire,* usually awarded for courage in the face of the enemy.

The job of Inspector-General never materialised. Instead, he was given the purely honorific post of Military Governor of Paris. His complaints met with taunts from de Gaulle on the rare occasions he could get to see him.

It may be that these final indignities heaped on a man who was convinced he was responsible for bringing de Gaulle back to power finally proved too much for his pride.

Evening Standard
Friday, October 13, 1961

PARIS SWOOP UNCOVERS KEY OAS RIOT PLAN

The French Ministry of the Interior claims to have struck its heaviest blow to date against the OAS Organisation in France with the arrest of three Army officers and a lawyer in Paris last night.

The arrested officers includes retired Colonel de Seze, who was adjutant to the French forces in Korea, and Major Casati. The third officer has not been named. They were all arrested at a conference with the lawyer Maître Jean Pirche.

The group of arrested men is said to have been acting on direct orders from ex-General Salan, transmitted by a deserter from the French Army, Captain Sergeant, for whom police have been searching for the past eight months.

Police found important documents both in Maître Pirche's flat and the homes of the other arrested men, including many coded messages. They also claimed to have discovered a detailed plan for OAS subversive acts to coincide with an uprising in Algeria.

As a result of the documents seized, the entire Special Branch of the Paris police has been mobilised to carry out further arrests and searches. It is strongly hinted here that many senior officers are implicated as a result of a study of the seized documents.

The news of the arrests hit Paris, calm and unruffled, as it awaited General de Gaulle's broadcast to the nation tonight with an inward awareness that it would open a historic phase in the future of France and Algeria.

De Gaulle's speech will be made as the Algerian rebel leaders meet in Tunis to decide whether they will accept the terms agreed at secret negotiations to end the seven-year-old Algerian war.

Their answer – or a strong indication of it – is expected by Wednesday. The problem for them is to agree on overall acceptance of terms to which they have already largely agreed in detail.

There is no chance that General de Gaulle will announce a rebel acceptance of the peace terms tonight. In the first place, their answer will not be ready in time for his broadcast, and secondly de Gaulle has made it clear that he will not personally announce the ceasefire. It will be in the form of a government statement.

Nevertheless, he is expected to give a strong indication of his personal optimism regarding the outcome. He is also likely to make bitter references to attempts by political leaders to exploit the present situation in order to undermine his authority.

In Algiers today European gunmen machine-gunned a train carrying

Government employees, wounding five people.

An officer attached to the Algerian Affairs Ministry and an Italian-born barrel-maker were killed by two gunmen in an Algerian street.

Evening Standard
Friday, February 5, 1962

'YES'. . . AND DE GAULLE GOES STRIDING FORWARD
The next move may be an election

The French nation, in yesterday's referendum on General de Gaulle's settlement of the Algerian war, gave him sweeping powers to implement it in the next few months. It was a landslide victory with more than seventeen million voters, representing 90·7 per cent of the votes cast, responding 'YES' to de Gaulle's double request for approval of his action and for special powers to deal with it.

The increase of over a million YES votes over last year's referendum on Algeria is no doubt due to the fact that the Communists who voted NO last year voted YES this time.

There was a slight increase in the number of abstentions. Many Communist voters could not bring themselves, despite Party orders, to vote for de Gaulle and preferred to abstain.

Whatever interpretations are placed on the final figures one conclusion is inescapable: it is a most impressive victory for de Gaulle and will have immediate and far-reaching consequences.

As a result of the referendum figures General de Gaulle may be tempted to dissolve Parliament a year ahead of time and hold an early General Election.

There is also some speculation that if he decides against early elections the present Prime Minister, M. Debré, will resign to enable General de Gaulle to re-form the Government.

The question of an early dissolution will be decided by de Gaulle this week.

Five points are clear from yesterday's result:

1–France voted by overwhelming majority not for any kind of peace in Algeria but for the peace that was negotiated with the Algerian

Muslim Nationalists which provides guarantees for France and promises a future of close Franco-Algerian co-operation. No such overwhelming approval would have been given for a peace which represented simple abandonment of Algeria.

2—The overwhelming YES vote will reinforce the loyalty of the French Army to the State by revealing to it the insignificance of opposition in France to de Gaulle's Algerian policy.

3—It will have a sobering effect on the European population in Algeria and will speed their disillusion with the OAS.

4—It will greatly enhance de Gaulle's prestige at home and abroad.

5—It will confirm de Gaulle's determination to go ahead with his plans for root-and-branch reforms of French institutions, and in particular to make the election of the President a matter of a national vote instead of, as it has been in the past, by a restricted electoral college.

*   *   *

The victory confirms de Gaulle's faith in the efficacy of the referendum as a political weapon. No Parliamentary vote on such an issue would have given such a clear-cut and impressive result.

For example, if the Algerian treaty had been subject to a Parliamentary vote, the consequence would have been a turbulent debate and a final vote which would not have reflected with any accuracy the country's feelings.

Evening Standard
Friday, April 9, 1962

ANTI-DE GAULLE PLOT BY ARMY
Generals held for questioning

French military security have discovered a serious anti-de Gaulle plot in the ranks of the 90,000-strong French Army in West Germany. Its importance may be judged by the fact that thirteen officers, most of them of field rank and including two generals, are at present being held for questioning.

The authorities stumbled on the plot as a result of information that ex-Colonel Antoine Argoud, one of the six colonels leading the OAS, had completed a tour of Army units in Germany last week.

There is now no doubt that, in fact, Argoud, considered one of the most dangerous and ruthless of the OAS conspirators, did, in fact, visit Army units in Germany and that his movements were known to senior officers, many of whom saw him.

As a result of Argoud's 'tour of inspection' at least one senior officer has been posted as a deserter.

Argoud is now also known to have made his way through Toulon to Metz, where he was received by paratroop officers stationed there and on to Strasbourg, where he was also received by officers in that region, and finally to West Germany.

Argoud is one of the OAS chiefs who took refuge in Spain and was later moved by the Spanish authorities to the Canary Islands. He escaped from the Canary Islands three months ago.

An intensive search for him is now under way in France but it is thought that he may have succeeded in crossing into Switzerland with false papers.

Argoud's main task, it is thought by officials here, was to reorganise the badly shattered OAS underground in Metropolitan France.

Evening Standard
Monday, May 7, 1962

DE GAULLE: BIG NEW HUNT FOR SQUAD OF KILLERS

French security officials believe they have completely dismantled an OAS killer squad which was to have assassinated General de Gaulle in Limoges in Central France. All sixteen members of the gang, including a woman, are under arrest and being interrogated.

There are, however, strong grounds for fearing that parallel squads of killers may be still at large. Today, security worries centred on tomorrow's State visit of the President of Mauretania, M. Moktar Doddah.

De Gaulle is scheduled to make several public appearances during the day. It was also learned today that he intends to undertake another of his provincial tours early next month.

The attempt on the President's life was to have been carried out either when he arrived at or left Limoges Cathedral. The weapon: a telescopic rifle.

The leader of the gang, whose name is given as Blanchy, was arrested in his Paris flat on Sunday morning after police had lost track of him for a nerve-racking twenty-four hours.

Blanchy, an insurance agent, is the only one of the sixteen arrested who was born in France. Police say that he was paid £21,000 to carry out the assassination.

All sixteen plotters were sent from Algeria. The woman among them is reputedly well known in Algiers society.

Police were put on their track when a notorious OAS gunman, François Leca, was arrested in Algiers a week ago. Under round-the-clock questioning he revealed that he knew of an OAS squad which had either just arrived in France or was about to leave for France and which had been given the mission to assassinate de Gaulle in the course of his tour of central France.

With the details he supplied, police, both in Algiers and Paris, were able to trace their movements. They learned that Blanchy and another member of the gang, whose name is given as Slebodia, had arrived in Limoges two days before the General's visit to reconnoitre the area.

They were watched, but the increased security precautions and possibly the suspicion that they were being followed led them to abandon their attempt and they left for Paris. At that point police lost contact. Twelve hours later Blanchy was spotted and arrested. In his car were several bottles of highly explosive butane gas.

Evening Standard
Tuesday, May 22, 1962

DE GAULLE SAYS 'NEW MEASURES' AFTER THE SALAN SHOCK

The French Government and especially General de Gaulle are not going to take lying down the astonishing sentence of life imprisonment passed on OAS leader ex-General Salan last night.

This was made clear today by M. Alain Peyrefitte, the Government's spokesman, after a Cabinet meeting.

The meeting, presided over by General de Gaulle, considered the implications of the sentence – a stinging slap to de Gaulle.

M. Peyrefitte was asked point-blank if the Government considered taking any measures to reverse it. He replied: 'There is no comment at the moment.'

He went on: 'The Cabinet has considered the possible consequences of this verdict on the security of the State, on the maintenance of its authority and on public order.

'Certain new measures will be taken very soon on this subject, notably as it concerns the judiciary and particularly to ensure the effective repression of subversion and crimes.

'These measures cannot be revealed at the moment, but they may become known at the end of the week.'

M. Peyrefitte also said that M. Joxe, Minister of Algerian Affairs, had spoken on the deplorable effect the Salan sentence could have on those charged with maintaining order in Algeria.

It is thought that the military tribunal specially created to try cases of high treason may be disbanded and that special tribunals may be set up in their place. M. Peyrefitte indicated that some important initial changes were being contemplated.

It is being suggested in some quarters that General de Gaulle, enraged by the Salan trial and fearing the serious political consequences it may have both in France and in Algeria, may decide to execute ex-General Jouhaud, Salan's second in command, and condemned to death only five weeks ago by the same tribunal which last night spared Salan's life.

One explanation for the sentence that is being given is that one member of the tribunal which condemned Jouhaud was replaced by another who may have given the casting vote which has saved Salan's life. The tribunal, composed of four generals and five judges, was otherwise precisely the same as that which condemned Jouhaud. The only change was a replacement in the ranks of the generals.

Salan was moved in secret at dawn today from his cell at the Paris Law Court to Fresnes prison. He may be moved later to an island prison off the French Atlantic coast.

This morning's Le Figaro writes: 'It is to be hoped that the verdict will be taken as a gesture of reconciliation rather than a sign of weakness.'

It is a pious hope. The exact opposite is certain.

The news that Salan's life was spared has been greeted with joy and exultation by the European population in Algeria. From now on the lowliest OAS killer can feel the rustle of legal mercy at his side.

The trial and the verdict disclose vividly the appalling moral climate that exists in France. The trial itself was rich in perjury, melodramatics and open sympathy for murder as a political weapon. A serving general and a serving admiral saluted Salan in court before they gave evidence.

Nevertheless, in fairness, it should be made clear that the judges were under enormous emotional pressure.

Among all the false emotion there was one plea which got straight to the heart. It was made by the Russian-born barrister Maître Goutermanoff who has lived for twenty years in Algiers and who was one of the defence counsel.

He pointed out that for seven years the entire Algerian population had been mobilised for war against the Muslim nationalist 'outlaws'.

'Now', he said, 'the same outlaws are to return to Algeria as commissars, Ministers, and judges'.

General de Gaulle heard the news of Salan's sentence at a State banquet for the visiting President of Mauretania. There was general astonishment at the verdict, which immediately became the main subject of conversation.

The court's verdict will enrage the French Left, which is already alleging that Salan's life was spared by agreement so that he would not reveal secrets embarrassing to the Government. This rubbish will be widely believed. If the trial proved anything, it proved the independence of the court from the Government. An excellent thing normally, in this particular case it shows the fragility of the régime and the power of entrenched opposition to de Gaulle within the French establishment.

The immediate outlook is depressing.

Evening Standard
Thursday, May 24, 1962

THAT 6ft 4in TARGET CALLED DE GAULLE: WHAT A HEADACHE IT IS TO PROTECT HIM

The question of assuring as near to total protection as possible from assassination for General de Gaulle is now easily the most urgent issue in France. With his immense height – he is 6ft 4in – and his zest for hand-shaking and mingling in crowds, he is for a man marked down for assassination a peculiarly vulnerable target.

He towers over his numerous guards like a tall poppy in a field of corn stubble. In addition to his frequent provincial tours scarcely a week passes without his entertaining some African or Arab dignitary to a State visit.

The official portrait of General de Gaulle taken when he became President of the Republic on 21 December 1958.

General Salan greeting de Gaulle on his arrival in Algiers on 5 June 1958, just after the General became Prime Minister on 2 June.

'*Je vous ai compris . . .*' (I have understood you). The famous speech in Algeria during his June 1958 visit.

De Gaulle salutes at the Oran War Memorial. Behind him (left to right) are Colonel de Bonneval, M. Jacquinot, M. Guillaumat and General Salan.

General de Gaulle, the newly elected President, on the steps of the Elysée Palace with M. Coty, the outgoing President, in December 1958.

Army tanks on the streets of Algiers in 1960 when the tension in Algeria was at its height, with de Gaulle's self-determination policy splitting the country.

De Gaulle continued to travel throughout Algeria, however, visiting the smaller towns – here he is at Orléansville – where he was shunned by the Europeans but greeted enthusiastically by the Muslim population.

The General's car after the attempt on his life in 1962 by the OAS. Twelve bullets from tommy-guns struck the car — this picture shows three of the holes and the flattened back wheel.

This did not prevent the General from travelling around France campaigning for the 1962 General Election. Here he is seen at Velleminfroy.

Harold Macmillan and de Gaulle in the grounds at Rambouillet in 1962 after talks over British entry into the Common Market.

Harold Wilson with de Gaulle on his first visit to Paris in April 1965, when the breakthrough hoped for in the deadlocked EEC negotiations did not materialize.

The General casting his vote in the Presidential Elections in 1965.

Pompidou, Wilson and de Gaulle.

De Gaulle and George Brown deep in conversation during the 1967 summit, but
de Gaulle's answer was still 'No'.

Every time there is a State visit he uses the main entrance to the Elysée Palace, which fronts the exceptionally narrow Rue Faubourg St Honoré. The driveway is only a little longer than a cricket pitch and as he gets out of his car and slowly mounts the steps he could be hit by a pebble thrown from the gateway. The distance from any of the innumerable windows overlooking the Palace steps would be, as a bullet flies, about fifty yards. Needless to say a regular security check is made on all the occupants of flats and shops in the vicinity. A close check is also maintained on all those who book in at the two big hotels, both on the opposite sides of the Palace. This of course, with a floating population involved represents a more difficult task.

But the most serious fear is the obvious one: that any of the occupants of the flats overlooking the Palace might open the door to someone who wishes to take forcible occupancy of the flat for the necessary time. This possibility represents a serious gap in the security precautions.

As a result I learned that General de Gaulle is being strongly urged to move from the Elysée Palace to one of the government-owned châteaux near Paris. The pressure on him to do so is unfortunately unlikely to succeed.

Evening Standard
Friday, May 25, 1962

DE GAULLE SETS UP WAR-TIME COURTS
They may sit in secret

The French Government has decided to set up virtual courts martial – the proceedings of which may take place in camera – to try captured OAS leaders.

This was announced this afternoon following a Cabinet meeting presided over by General de Gaulle.

The decision to set up these courts follows the verdict last Wednesday of the high military tribunal which sentenced ex-General Salan to life imprisonment instead of to death as was generally expected.

A Government spokesman said these special courts will function 'as they would in war-time'.

The courts will be composed of a presiding officer and four officers or non-commissioned officers and two magistrates will assist them but they will most likely be magistrates from the Judge Advocate's office.

Meanwhile, it was learned that there is no question of a re-trial of Salan or the carrying out of the death sentence on ex-General Jouhaud. Jouhaud's execution had been ordered following the verdict in the Salan case but I understand that the Prime Minister, M. Pompidou, successfully intervened with General de Gaulle and the execution was cancelled.

It was also announced after the Cabinet meeting that General de Gaulle would make a nationwide broadcast on Friday week. Such broadcasts are only made on occasions when grave national issues are involved.

Apparently at the conclusion of today's Cabinet meeting General de Gaulle made a vigorous statement in which he promised that no matter the dismay created by recent events – in Algeria and in particular by the Salan verdict – he was determined to apply his Algerian policy to its very limit. At the same time he would protect the Republic against all seditious attempts.

Evening Standard
Wednesday, May 30, 1962

AFTER THE BLOODBATH
Can friend and enemy live together?

The tumult and the shouting die, the Colonels and the legionaries depart. Or if you prefer it the OAS has ended 'not with a bang but a whimper'.

Listen to the whimper. It comes from Jean-Jacques Susini the civilian head of the OAS in a pirate broadcast this week. He said: 'Those Europeans who have gone must return. Those who remain must stay. Muslims and Europeans must shake hands, forget the past, and together build a new independent Algeria'.

Strange words from the twenty-eight-year-old failed medical student who only three weeks ago gave the order that Muslim women were to be shot down in the street as ruthlessly as their menfolk. Those were the days when Bab-el-Oued braves, many of them in their early teens, would walk into a bar, order a drink, then, seeing a Muslim walk by, would step out, shoot him down and walk back to finish their drink.

Two weeks ago Susini called off terrorism in Algiers on the promise, never endorsed by the Algerian Provisional Government, that the amnesty already contained in the Evian agreement between the French and the Algerian nationalists would be extended to cover the period of the last three months of OAS terrorism.

The ex-colonels in Oran called off the fight without even getting this assurance. Will Susini follow his own advice and remain in Algeria after next Sunday? Ironically, he cannot emerge from hiding while French sovereignty lives out its last few hours, for the French are not bound by the new amnesty agreements. But he has let it be known that he intends to stay. We shall see, but personally, after so much vainglorious boasting by OAS leaders, I doubt it.

The ex-colonels have of course all fled, some to Spain or to Switzerland or Belgium on forged passports. So have the Foreign Legion deserters. So too have the locally recruited killers of the so-called Delta Commandos. Many of them have gone under the guise of refugees to France itself.

The actual active membership of the OAS was remarkably small. It never amounted to more than 45 officer deserters including three ex-generals, 144 NCO deserters, most of them drawn from the Foreign Legion, and fewer than 1,000 of the Delta Commandos. Its strength lay in the total support it received from the million Europeans and its wide network of complicity inside the Army and the administration.

In fact its methods were both cowardly and stupid. It forgot that whereas terrorism may pay off in the case of a majority seeking to overthrow minority rule, it is doomed to failure in the reverse circumstances. Perhaps the shrewder OAS leaders thought that by terrorism they could sow such panic in Paris as to force de Gaulle's resignation or overthrow. There they had some grounds for their illusions, for they received encouragement from important political, social and financial circles. But in this they were up against the majestic figure of de Gaulle himself, who judged them at their true value.

For example, three months ago the chaos in Algiers and Oran was such that de Gaulle was urged on all sides to postpone the date of the Algerian self-determination vote. Instead of postponing it he advanced it by two weeks. He knew that the sooner Algerian independence approached, the quicker the OAS would collapse. His judgment and all it implies in contempt for the courage of his opponents now stands vindicated. Where now are the Budapests they threatened, the scorched earth they promised, the blazing oil wells of the Sahara and all the rest of the apocalyptic future for Algeria if Paris did not bow to their will?

It now remains to estimate the damage the OAS have done to the chances of the two communities working together in an independent

Algeria. Certainly they have rendered the future more difficult for the Europeans who remain. However, the Europeans here have lived with the Arabs for over 130 years, and if they have influenced the Arabs, the Arabs have also influenced them.

Paradoxically, a man like Susini, whose family has lived here for five generations, has more in common (including a taste for cruelty) with the Arab Nationalists' leader than with, say, a Paris Liberal.

Furthermore the French still hold excellent cards: the 400,000 Algerian workers who live in France, the massive economic aid France will continue to pour into the country under the Constantine plan, Algerian wine (which constitutes fifteen per cent of the country's economy and for which France is the only customer), and finally the natural gas of the Sahara, much more important than the petrol for which the Common Market nations provide the only profitable outlet.

There is of course, as far as France is concerned, a continuing menace of the OAS being transported to France and operating from the probably irreducible base of some four hundred thousand embittered refugees. The booming French economy can not only absorb but positively benefit from this additional labour force. Can it, however, absorb it politically? On the face of it the refugees will make a ready-made clientèle for the parties of the extreme Right. Electorally they may prove dangerous, but it is unikely that they will remain for long a homogeneous political entity. Many of them are likely to turn to their former political allegiances on the Left and the extreme Left.

In any case the OAS in France will not operate with anything like the same immunity it enjoyed in Algeria. Now not only will it be rigorously hunted down, but the population itself will react with vehement hate against those who threaten its present unprecedented prosperity.

It is not the least of the OAS crimes that the detestation it arouses will to a large extent include its principal victims – the Europeans of Algeria. They do not deserve it. Ever since the Algerian rebellion broke out eight years ago, their fears have been relentlessly exploited by political adventurers from Paris.

What emerges from the whole Algerian tragedy is its disclosure of the moral squalor in France. This is at the root of the French sickness which now dates back to the end of the First World War. How else explain that generals and politicians of distinction should launch themselves on adventures of which the only successful outcome would be civil war? How else explain that politicians of Left and Right hoped that the OAS would prove to be the battering ram which would dislodge their chief enemy, de Gaulle? How else explain the 'Bravos' that went up in Paris when Salan was not sentenced to death?

Having dragged France screaming into the second half of the

twentieth century, de Gaulle's principal task now is to ensure that there will be no return to the bad old ways.

Evening Standard
Friday, June 29, 1962

3

The Sixties

DE GAULLE SHOCK — 'I QUIT, UNLESS . . .'
Vital vote tonight

General de Gaulle, in a televised speech to the nation today, threatened to retire if he did not get 'massive' support for the October 28 referendum to reform the French constitution.

The poll will give the answer to de Gaulle's request that his successor as President of the Republic should be elected by universal suffrage instead of as at present by a restricted electoral college of 80,000 'notables'.

The President's proposal has plunged France into the most serious political crisis since he took over in 1958. Parliamentarians have accused him of a breach of the Constitution. De Gaulle, by resorting to a referendum, has deliberately by-passed Parliament.

The French National Assembly met today to debate the issue and to vote on a motion of censure against the Government. This vote, it appears, is certain to be carried, with the result that the Pompidou Government is expected to fall some time tonight. In that case de Gaulle will order a dissolution and a General Election one or two weeks after the referendum. His aim in seeking that his successor should be elected by a vote of the nation is designed primarily to give the future president a stature which he might otherwise lack.

De Gaulle is not affected by the proposed change in the Constitution. All he wants to do is enhance the prestige of the office which inevitably will fall to a man of lesser national standing. His broadcast, advanced seven hours so that it could be made before the Assembly met, made no concessions to the Parliamentarians. On the contrary he seemed to go out of his way to pour scorn on them.

In a key passage he said: 'It will be your reply on October 29 which will tell me if I can or if I should continue my task in the service of France.'

Characteristically he added: 'I consider it necessary that a massive vote of the nation bears witness that at this moment the nation does not wish that after de Gaulle the state should be delivered over to the political practices which would bring it to an odious catastrophe.'

Evening Standard
Thursday, October 4, 1962

WHY DE GAULLE WELCOMES THIS HEAD-ON CLASH WITH PARLIAMENT

There is something positively awe-inspiring about the apparent wilfulness with which General de Gaule has provoked the present crisis in France.

A most immediately striking feature of his proposal to change the Constitution, so that his successor will be elected by national vote instead of, as now, by a limited electoral college largely controlled by the politicians, is its seeming disinterestedness; it will not affect him, but only his successor. It is an attempt to force greatness on his successor, who will certainly lack de Gaulle's stature and prestige.

What is wilful is his manner of going about it. He refuses, as the Constitution clearly demands, that the proposal should first be submitted to Parliament, not because he is afraid that Parliament would reject it, but because he is convinced it would reluctantly accept. He is by-passing Parliament because he wishes to establish that the present reform, once passed by referendum, can only be changed by referendum. In other words he knows that if Parliament passes such a reform today it would be only to eager to revoke it after his disappearance from the political scene.

The politicians are determined now that de Gaulle has got them out of the Algerian mess, to return to the political ways of the past; he is equally determined to ensure that there can be no return. That is why he welcomes this head-on clash and will seek to make it the occasion of a devastating defeat for the political parties.

It is difficult not to feel sympathy for him. Twice he has picked France up out of the gutter, brushed her down, and made her presentable again.

There is a significant passage in Volume II of de Gaulle's *Memoirs* in which he speaks of the evident eagerness of the members of the provisional parliament in Algiers to return to the old parliamentary system once France was liberated.

De Gaulle writes: 'Probing their souls I reached a point where I asked myself if among all those who spoke of revolution I was not in truth the only revolutionary'.

Of one thing de Gaulle is absolutely certain: The quickest way to Fascism in France is via a return to the political practices of the past. And, as he said in his broadcast yesterday, next time there may not be a de Gaulle around to save the situation.

Evening Standard
Friday, October 5, 1962

DE GAULLE SHRUGS OFF THE GREAT CRISIS
'Do not disturb me' says the President

President de Gaulle is treating with magnificent disdain the political crisis provoked by his demand for a change in the Constitution to allow the President of the Republic to be elected by universal suffrage.

He left today for Army manoeuvres in the champagne country without even waiting to receive his defeated Prime Minister, M. Pompidou, whose Government was overthrown on a motion of confidence in the early hours of this morning. Indeed, it is now learned that de Gaulle left strict instructions to his staff that he was not to be disturbed with the result of the vote.

Attending the Army manoeuvres (where, incidentally, the Blues are supposed to defeat the Reds commanded by, of all people, General Massu, a central figure in the 1958 uprising in Algeria which brought de Gaulle to power) gives today's crisis the not unexpected touch of a squire attending a point-to-point while newspapers are screaming that his daughter has run off with a butcher's delivery boy.

De Gaulle will receive his defeated Prime Minister possibly this evening but more probably tomorrow morning. He will then confirm him in his post until General Elections are held early next month.

Optimism is running high in de Gaullist circles that the President will obtain a crushing victory both in the referendum on his proposals to be held on October 28 and in the General Elections which will follow.

In those circles de Gaulle's challenge to the political parties is seen as a master stroke, the outcome of which will be that they will be routed and the political map of France drastically redrawn as a result. It will be shown – so de Gaullists claim – how little the traditional parties really count in the country.

More objective observers, however, consider that while de Gaulle will win the referendum he will lose on the elections. In other words, what the electorate will concede to him with one hand they will take away with the other when it comes to elections for the National Assembly.

This is, of course, the essence of the gamble. It will do de Gaulle little good to win the referendum only to find himself saddled with a Parliament resolutely hostile to him. In those circumstances, to twist the historic 1940 declaration of de Gaulle's, he will have won a battle and lost the war.

Evening Standard
Friday, October 5, 1962

NOW DE GAULLE'S PROBLEMS START

There is virtually no doubt that General de Gaulle will consider the 61 per cent majority he received at yesterday's referendum a sufficient vote of confidence to enable him to remain in power. The 61 per cent represents a sharp drop in support for the General compared with previous referenda. For the first time he polled less than an absolute majority of registered voters.

Also for the first time, entire departments, including virtually the whole south-west of France, voted against him. He was defeated too in Marseilles, and his majority in Paris was a narrow one. The fact that the south-west went against him is not surprising. Most of the 700,000 refugees from Algeria are concentrated in that region.

De Gaulle's performance after four years in power is an impressive one. In the two previous polls – in 1958, and April 1962 on Algeria – he enjoyed, in the case of the first, the support of all the political parties except the Communists and in the second the support of all the political parties including the Communists.

In yesterday's referendum on his proposal to change the constitution so that his successor as President should be elected by universal suffrage, he faced the bitter opposition of all the political groups. He took them on and defeated them. Furthermore he was opposed by virtually the entire French Press, including the extremely influential provincial Press, and all the administrative, legal and trade union forces.

To show how poorly France's traditional political parties fared it is only necessary to deduct the 20 per cent Communist poll from the total to show that the Socialists, Catholics, Radicals, and Conservative Independents polled seven million votes.

Their normal combined voting strength, excluding the Communists, is seventeen million and, had the electors remained loyal to their political parties, de Gaulle's project would have been massively rejected. Nevertheless, the results give little ground for complacency, General de Gaulle's real difficulties are now about to start. In three weeks' time Parliament, which was dissolved after the overthrow of the Pompidou Government, will face a General Election. The results of the referendum indicate that almost certainly the result of the Election will be a hostile Parliament. This is clear, both from a study of the electoral map and from the twenty-four per cent abstentions in the referendum.

General de Gaulle will be backed in the election by only one party, the Union for the New Republic which emerged as the biggest single group in the 1958 election. But the Union is unlikely to increase its representation and may even find its representation reduced by more than a third. Its fate is largely in General de Gaulle's hands. If de Gaulle descends into the political arena and campaigns actively for this party then it may hold its own. However, the General will almost certainly refuse to do this and will leave it to fight its battles alone.

Evening Standard
Monday, October 29, 1962

DE GAULLE WINS THE REVOLUTION
Ambition achieved and rivals crushed

General de Gaulle's landslide victory in the first round of the French General Elections yesterday means he has achieved his primary political ambition – a total revolution in French political habits and practices.

The victory, greater in extent than even his victory in the 1958 General Elections, has shown the bankruptcy of the traditional French political parties who held almost uninterrupted political sway in France for the past fifty years.

The Radicals, for example, the lynch-pins of almost every government during the Third and Fourth Republics, have virtually disappeared from the political map. The traditional French Socialist Party and the so-called Conservative Independents have suffered losses on such a scale that it is difficult to see how in their present decrepitude they can survive the ensuing five years of solidly based de Gaullist power. For the Socialists the outcome of the Elections is dramatic: they now look like being little more than an appendage of the Communists in the new Assembly.

M. Guy Mollet, the virulently anti-Communist Socialist leader, is fighting for his political life in Arras. His survival is entirely dependent on the Communists transferring their votes to him in the second ballot.

There is scarcely a well-known political leader among the traditional parties, with the exception of the Communists, who have not either gone down in humiliating defeat or who will not be at the mercy in the second ballot of Communist or an agglomeration of opposition votes going to him.

The second round of voting will take place next Sunday for all those candidates who failed to gain an absolute majority in their first round.

The parties have to decide by midnight on Tuesday which of their candidates they will withdraw in favour of better placed ones whose election they favour in preference to a common enemy. Whatever agreements the parties may reach among themselves the de Gaullist victory can only be amplified as a result of next Sunday's voting.

One clear lesson of yesterday's vote is that the traditional parties have lost virtually all authority over their one-time followers. The greater part of the large abstentions are due to this fact and at public disgust over alliances made by traditionally opposing parties simply in order to defeat the de Gaullist candidate.

For once the logical French have been ruthlessly logical. Having voted YES in the referendum they voted massively for de Gaullist candidates.

The defeat of M. Paul Reynaud, the veteran French politician and Prime Minister at the time of the French collapse in 1940, is dramatically symbolic. It was Reynaud who led the attack against de Gaulle and it is he, more than any other politician, who epitomises in his own rejection by his electors the electorate's rejection of all the politicians who symbolise the political chaos of the inter-war and post-war years.

The result gives a political stability to the country which it lacked even in the 1958 triumph.

There is now only one imponderable on the political horizon: Assassination.

*   *   *

The Ministry of the Interior announced the complete results for candidates elected in the first round of balloting:

UNR 45 seats, MRP 14, Pro-Gaullist Independents 12, Communists 9, Indpendents 7, Left Centre Parties 6, Radical Socialists 2, Socialists 1. Total 96.

The Ministry also announced the number of votes cast in all the 465 constituencies of Metropolitan France:

Registered voters 27,535,019. Actual voters 18,931,733 (68.79 per cent). Valid ballots 18,329,986.

*   *   *

President de Gaulle returned to Paris from his country home at Colombey-les-Deux-Eglises by air today. He called a meeting with M. Pompidou, the Premier, to discuss the results.

Evening Standard
Monday, November 19, 1962

DE GAULLE GETS FREE HAND TO RESHAPE FRANCE

The results of the second round of voting in the French General Elections yesterday confirmed those of the first – a landslide victory for de Gaulle. As a consequence, the French political map has been radically re-drawn and the old multi-party system has been cast into limbo.

Most observers agree that the most important consequence of the de Gaulle victory will be the emergence of something like a two-party system in France – which is what he intended.

The major feature of the election results is that for the first time in French political history a single political grouping has an absolute majority in Parliament. This assures de Gaulle of an unprecedented political stability for the remaining three years of his mandate, which are likely to see an avalanche of constitutional, judicial and social reforms, including abolition of the Senate as it now exists.

General de Gaulle is expected to announce this afternoon that M. Pompidou, whose defeat as Prime Minister last month provoked the present elections, will be re-confirmed as Prime Minister.

A striking feature of the result is that the extreme Right, associated with the OAS, has been completely wiped out. Furthermore, the Right-wing party, the so-called Independents, which was the second largest party in the last Parliament with more than a hundred seats, has been reduced to a mere eighteen.

The Left-wing parties slightly increased their gains, largely because of Communists switching their support to Socialist and Radical candidates. The Socialists were the chief beneficiaries of Communist support – M. Mollet, their leader, owes his survival entirely to this factor.

Now Socialist representatives in the new House will be sixty-six – twenty-five higher than the Communists with forty-one. Communist gains are not viewed with undue alarm in official circles here.

The large Communist vote, already an anachronism in the France of today, is likely to decline in the future as prosperity grows in France and as a new generation of voters comes into being.

Another striking feature of the result is the Gaullist gain in Paris itself. For the first time in French political history, a single party has captured all the thirty-one Paris seats.

The results are likely to have serious international consequences. De Gaulle, flushed with victory, will be more unbending in seeking to achieve his diplomatic aims.

The victory is entirely his own and, almost alone, he foresaw it – at a time when it was generally believed that his power was on the wane. He has once again shown his uncanny grasp of the realities of French political life.

Evening Standard
Monday, November 26, 1962

WHAT MAC TOLD DE GAULLE
The Paris Story

General de Gaulle has expressed to close associates 'great pleasure' at the outcome of his week-end talks with Mr Macmillan. As a result of these talks the General has now dismissed from his mind lingering suspicions that Britain was adopting Trojan horse tactics in seeking entry into the Common Market. He has given associates the clear impression that the talks came as something of a revelation to him of the Prime Minister's state of mind.

Thus, whereas de Gaulle was once convinced that Britain would never pay the full price for admission to the Common Market, he is now satisfied that she is indeed prepared to do so. The General, until this week-end, never really believed that Britain was prepared to throw in her lot fully with Europe. He took the view that in the final analysis Britain would not be prepared to trade her position as head of the Commonwealth for admission to the Common Market. He is now certain that Mr Macmillan has undergone a great conversion.

'Britain is now prepared to be a good European' is how one associate sums up de Gaulle's impression of the talks. General de Gaulle was also favourably impressed by the fact that Mr Macmillan did not argue Washington's thesis and offer criticisms of France's determination to go ahead with its own atomic striking force. This was a piece of Macmillan tact which greatly impressed de Gaulle. Furthermore, Mr Macmillan did not echo Washington's concern that the Europe envisaged by de Gaulle would seek to be a 'Neutral bloc' between the United States and the Soviet Union.

The diplomatic correspondent of *Le Monde,* which reflects the views of the French Foreign Office, writes in connection with Mr Macmillan's week-end talks with General de Gaulle:

*   *   *

'It appears clear from the talks that England once and for all has "chosen Europe".

'This was the essence of what the Prime Minister had to say to General de Gaulle.

'He amplified very emphatically the scale of the revolution that has taken place in British thinking on the subject.

'He made it clear that this was in substance an irreversible choice and that the efforts of the Dominions could not reverse this decision.

'Mr Macmillan showed irritation on this subject at the criticisms made by Mr Menzies.'

Evening Standard
Monday, June 4, 1962

HOW ON EARTH DID MAC AND DE GAULLE FIND TIME TO TALK?

I am vastly intrigued by last weekend's Macmillan-de Gaulle talks. What intrigues me is not what they talked about but how they found time to talk at all. A weekend with de Gaulle is not a weekend à la Windsor or Sandringham: it is a one-night, not a two-night stopover.

The Macmillans arrived at five-thirty. Dinner was at eight. Given half an hour for an exchange of greetings and small talk and three-quarters of an hour to change for dinner, that would leave only an hour for pre-dinner talk.

At dinner they were joined by M. André Malraux, the Minister for Culture. M. Malraux is a man of towering erudition. He is coming more and more to be General de Gaulle's secret diplomatic weapon — he saves the General's breath.

After dinner, M. Malraux showed a new French film. After the film, M. Malraux explained that bedtime for two such elderly gentlemen can be reasonably fixed at eleven-thirty.

On Sunday morning de Gaulle went to Mass. He returned at eleven-thirty. The eight lunch guests began arriving shortly after twelve. After lunch, there was a walk in the park and then return to the Château for tea and farewells.

When de Gaulle gets together with Adenauer, no such distractions as Mass or M. Malraux are permitted. Small wonder the French are enthusiastic regarding the outcome of the talks; I almost doubt if there were any.

Evening Standard
Friday, June 5, 1962

THE MAN WHO MAKES IT TOUGH FOR MR HEATH

If Mr. Heath occasionally has nightmares over Britain's negotiations to enter the Common Market, the face that must loom most terrifyingly in them is the handsome aquiline one of forty-nine-year-old M. Olivier Wormser.

M. Wormser, head of the Economic Section of the French Foreign Office and chief French negotiator at Brussels, exercises a snake-like fascination on our delegation there. He inspires in them a condition of mingled awe and terror.

It is generally believed that M. Wormser's task at Brussels is to apply General de Gaulle's policy of excluding Britain from the Market while, at the same time, not making it obvious that this is, in fact, his dedicated purpose.

No better man could have been chosen for this task. M. Wormser is a superb negotiating machine equipped with a fabulous memory, unshakable tenacity and stamina which makes him brush off an all-night session as though it were an interlude in an otherwise leisurely day.

Tall, thin, with an elongated thin nose, he speaks in a rasping voice and is always concise and to the point. A belief has grown up in some quarters that he is an Anglophobe of the peculiarly dangerous kind — the kind who cannot forgive his bad luck in not being born English. This seems highly exaggerated and based on little more than his rarely-used but excellent English, and the fact that his two young sons are looked after by an English nanny.

The son of a distinguished Jewish banking family, Wormser has long been something of a legend in the French Foreign Office. His distinguished actor-like appearance, his detached and urbane manner, single him out in any company. His reputation is that of a man who is only interested in seemingly intractable problems. Certainly, no task could better match his talents than the one which de Gaulle has entrusted to him — to stall, to delay, to spring intricate points of difference, and all this without rousing the anger of those of the Six who wish to see us in.

The precise nuances of General de Gaulle's attitude to our application to join the Common Market can now be fairly clearly established.

He is still by no means convinced that our entry is inevitable. But even if it is, his attitude is: 'Let the British wait. I still have some consolidating to do in Europe.'

On one point he is adamant: If Britain comes in, the club will be closed after our entry. The Danes and the Norwegians, for example, will be left outside.

Recently de Gaulle said to the Canadian Ambassador in Paris, Mr. Pierre Dupuy: 'Britain may well marry into Europe, but the marriage will be a stormy one.'

*   *   *

This is Referendum Weekend in France and the issues are enormous for they concern either the disappearance or the consolidation of de Gaulle's régime. What de Gaulle seeks is that his successor be elected by universal suffrage instead of, as at present, by a vote of politicians, mayors and councils. The aim is to reinforce the authority of the President by giving him a national mandate.

The politicians are opposed because with Algeria out of the way, they wish to return to the old system of rule by party manipulators.

There have been some striking pieces of hypocrisy in the course of the campaign. For example, de Gaulle is accused of hogging the TV, which is something every government has done in the past.

The Socialist Government of Guy Mollet carried it to the point of recalling the TV correspondent in London because he gave an outline of Labour opposition in Britain to the Suez operation.

It is interesting to recall too that in 1958 M. Mendès-France attacked the Constitution precisely because the President was elected by a restricted electoral college. Oddly enough, he finds it equally undemocratic that the President should be elected by the people.

Evening Standard
Friday, October 26, 1962

DE GAULLE GO-SLOW ON THE TUNNEL
His reprisal for the Concorde decision

General de Gaulle has ordered a 'go-slow' policy on the Channel Tunnel as a reprisal for British withdrawal from the Concorde project. No public announcement to this effect will be made, but French policy on the Channel Tunnel will become clearly apparent in the weeks and months ahead. General de Gaulle's reasoning on the subject is that the tunnel offers greater commercial advantages to Britain than it does to France.

And he adds with considerable feeling: 'If Mr Wilson wants economies he can have them at the expense of the tunnel.'

The French Government does not intend to take any initiative in the matter of reprisals against Britain's three-shillings-in-the-pound import surcharge. It considers that this will not be a purely temporary duty, but will last for at least nine months or a year. The French have decided to leave reprisals, which they consider inevitable, to other nations and they will merely follow suit.

General de Gaulle is particularly bitter about recent changes in British policy, especially as regards the multilateral force, because he considers that over the past six months he has followed an increasingly friendly policy towards Britain.

He has ordered, however, that there should be no recriminations on a government level over the collapse of the Concorde project.

There are increasing signs that France is preparing to launch a major European crisis both over the Common Market and the NATO Alliance in mid-December.

The first clash is likely to come on December 15 at the ministerial meeting of the NATO Council in Paris. This was made clear to Belgium's Foreign Minister, M. Spaak, when he saw de Gaulle in Paris last week. M. Spaak, I understand, is now under no illusions as to the slim possibilities of averting an open split in the Western alliance.

General de Gaulle is particularly bitter about the multilateral force and the potential dangers of a German finger on the nuclear trigger in the present state of Europe. He considers that, just as the Soviet grip on Eastern Europe is loosening and there are nationalist stirrings within the Soviet empire, the effect of allowing the Germans a say in nuclear defence will be to scare nations like Poland and Romania into closer dependence upon Moscow.

The General does not plan any dramatic moves concerning Moscow. His line will be simply to play it smooth with the Russians. Despite his visionary air the General is not blind to the internal political advantages accruing to himself from steadily improving Franco-Soviet relations. Presidential elections are to be held in France next year and the five million Communist vote represents a serious factor.

If the Communists, for example, can be persuaded to put up their own candidate, then the Left-wing vote will be hopelessly split and M. Deferre, the major Opposition candidate, will probably finish with a vote lower than that of the Communists, thereby being defeated in the first round.

General de Gaulle, it should be added, is in excellent health after his arduous South American tour. This month-long journey left his staff exhausted, but he appears to have benefited from it as though from a holiday.

Evening Standard
Thursday, November 5, 1964

WHAT THE FRENCH THINK OF BRITAIN
'Market? You'll join in the end'

Britain's eventual membership of the Common Market is inevitable and desirable, a key member of the French Government told me in an exclusive interview on the eve of Mr Wilson's arrival in Paris.

'I am profoundly convinced Britain will be driven to go into the Market,' he said, and added that events were moving very quickly and that this entry would probably come about sooner than most people expected. He said that it was false that de Gaulle had always been unalterably opposed to British entry. And he claimed that, after the meeting between General de Gaulle and Mr Macmillan at the Château de Champs, in June, 1962, de Gaulle was convinced that Britain's entry was inevitable and he welcomed the prospect.

It was the subsequent Rambouillet meeting, however, which convinced de Gaulle that Britain's political and defence priorities, even after the Skybolt fiasco, remained overwhelmingly committed to the United States, he said.

He went on: 'The basic difference between the British and French views is concerned with the kind of relationship that Europe should have with the United States.'

He said that France wanted to forge an independent Europe which would be an ally of the United States, but capable of acting independently.

Britain, he claimed, wanted to transform the merging Europe into some kind of Atlantic community which would, in fact, be disguise for continued American domination of the Alliance.

He confessed freely that at present French and British views on this and other issues were irreconcilable, but he repeated that events were moving fast and Britain would finally realise that her true interests – political, economic and military – lay in Europe.

In any case, he considered that if Britain re-applied to join the Common Market on the basis of total acceptance of the Rome Treaty a second veto was virtually inconceivable.

He frankly admitted, however, that the present improvement in Anglo-French relations was partly due to the fact that the Labour Government had not been involved in the disastrous negotiations in Brussels and showed no desire at present to re-open them.

But the great turning point, in his view, was marked by the British decision to go ahead with the Concorde project.

He reverted once again to the Common Market issue by saying emphatically that 'It is in France's and Europe's interest for Britain to make a clear-cut choice in favour of joining Europe'.

The war in Vietnam will figure largely in Mr Wilson's two days of talks in Paris. On this subject General de Gaulle's views are now profoundly pessimistic. He believes that the moment for negotiations has passed and will not recur again soon – possibly not for several years. It is in China's interests now, according to him, to keep the Vietnam war going.

Britain's initiative in despatching Mr Gordon Walker on a fact-finding mission to the Far East is not viewed with any optimism in Paris. The British delegation is, however, expected to ask the French to facilitate through their mission in Hanoi a visit by Mr Walker to North Vietnam.

Sterling will be a key subject for discussions here and there is no point in disguising the fact that the French are frankly pessimistic regarding its future. Devaluation is not thought here to be a satisfactory solution, for either it will be a modest devaluation, in which case it will be ineffective, or it will be a severe one, in which case it will be met by devaluation of other currencies. In the French view only a policy of limited austerity can restore Britain's economic situation.

Mr Wilson was to see President de Gaulle for two hours this morning. He will have a further meeting with him tomorrow morning. Later today he and the Foreign Secretary will meet with members of the French Government, including the Prime Minister, M. Pompidou. This is the first top-level diplomatic meeting between the two countries in two years.

Mr Wilson's fifty-minute meeting with General de Gaulle in London during Sir Winston Churchill's funeral left the French President deeply impressed.

For Mr Wilson the two days of talks will give him an opportunity to explore further the well-stocked and highly original mind of the French President.

Mr Wilson, it is understood here, will ask General de Gaulle to ease France's present policy of converting dollars into gold – at least over the next few months – because it is indirectly damaging sterling. The French, on the other hand, will propose to Mr Wilson an extension of present aircraft construction co-operation between the two countries to the construction of military aircraft.

Evening Standard
Friday, April 2, 1965

IT'S A SOFT TOUCH FOR MR WILSON
IN PARIS TODAY . . .

Now that Mr Wilson is visiting Paris today it is touching almost to the point of tears to recall earlier meetings between Mr Wilson's predecessor, Mr Harold Macmillan, and General de Gaulle. The most striking difference between the current talks and earlier ones between the British Prime Minister and French President is that Mr Wilson is being spared what can only be described as the 'château treatment'.

He little realises, I have no doubt, how lucky he is or that a subtle compliment is being paid to him in this regard. Not for him, lucky man, the Château of Rambouillet or Champs and all they entail. And what they entail chiefly is the presence at de Gaulle's dinner table of M. Malraux, the immensely erudite French Minister of Culture.

M. Malraux is a brilliant but compulsive conversationalist, and in his presence de Gaulle is spared all need to conduct any of the conversation himself. In short, on those occasions, M. Malraux is a useful diplomatic gadget which, if the General were deaf, might be dispensed with in favour of a hearing aid, which can be switched off.

Both Mr Macmillan and General de Gaulle are, of course, superb actors, and their meetings often struck observers as great histrionic occasions. They delighted, figuratively speaking, in weeping on each other's shoulders, telling each other their woes and troubles.

There was one occasion which future historians will cherish and which is recorded in both the French and British minutes of the talk. It occurred at Buckingham Palace during General de Gaulle's State visit to London in 1960.

Mr Macmillan was telling the General of Britain's economic difficulties, and when he had finished de Gaulle made a suggestion. He said: 'Why don't you join the Common Market?' Mr Macmillan's reply was 'Unthinkable.'

Right up to the final veto on Britain's Common Market bid, Mr Macmillan was under the illusion that his arguments and appeals were swaying de Gaulle. The shock and dismay at the final outcome was all the greater because of that.

One of Mr Macmillan's principal illusions was that a Briton of his education did not need an interpreter in conducting talks with de Gaulle in French. It was a small vanity which produced considerable misunderstandings. It was characteristic of their stage-like relationship that Mr Macmillan should have sent de Gaulle in 1962 an inscribed photograph of himself. De Gaulle, one of his aides has since told me, received it with bewilderment. I have made inquiries about the photo, but its exact whereabouts now remains a mystery.

Evening Standard
Friday, April 2, 1965

WHEN DE GAULLE FORGOT TO MENTION BRITAIN
What a testing time it was for his staff

Just as some men subject themselves to physical tests to see how age is catching up with them, so General de Gaulle gives himself regular and rigorous memory tests. Memory has always been a quite phenomenal attribute of this phenomenal man. All his speeches are memorised and so are the answers he will give to half a dozen questions at his bi-annual Press conferences.

Recently, however, there have been lapses amounting in most cases to only slight divergences from the distributed text. The most serious lapse of memory occurred at his January Press conference, when he had to be reminded by an aide that he intended to make a reference to Britain.

The whole question of memory is crucial with him, for it is well-known that it is mostly on the basis of his own testings of his mental alertness that he will decide whether or not to stand at the end of the year for a second term as President of the Republic. These self-imposed memory tests have now become a daily feature of life at the Elysée Palace and they add considerably to its strains. The tests take the form of recapitulation in the greatest detail of talks or reports days or weeks old.

The unhappy partners in this matching of memories are members of his staff. Knowing that economic and financial matters interest him least, it is precisely these fields in which he prefers to test his memory. The question of whether de Gaulle will stand again is now virtually the only political issue in France.

Pending his answer to this question, which he is unlikely to give before October, everything else remains in a state of suspended animation. The electoral miracle cannot be effectively plotted until the answer is known, nor can the full list of candidates be known.

There is, for example, a favourite dark horse in the person of their former premier, Antoine Pinay, a long-standing hero of the French middle-classes. He has said that he will not stand, but everyone reads into his statements the implication that he will not stand against de Gaulle. He would prove, however, a strong candidate against de Gaulle's most likely successor, the present Prime Minister, M. Georges Pompidou.

If I were a betting man I would at this moment, on my present siftings, be inclined to bet against de Gaulle standing for a second term.

Evening Standard
Friday, May 14, 1965

THAT VETO

Now that three years later the question as to what provoked General de Gaulle to veto Britain's entry into the Common Market has become something of an election issue, it is worth noting the latest researches on the subject.

It now seems clear that originally the veto was provoked on economic and not political grounds. In other words Macmillan's Nassau agreement with President Kennedy was an irritant but not, as Mr Wilson claims, a basic cause of the veto.

Tracing the history of the negotiations in the calmer atmosphere that prevails now, it appears clear that the agriculture issue was the main obstacle to Britain's entry. There had been a mounting clamour among French agricultural experts who claimed that Britain's entry into the Market before an agricultural Common Market had emerged would result in an Anglo-German line-up against France.

The argument went that both Britain and Germany had a vital interest in preventing the development of an agricultural Common Market as both were overwhelmingly consumers of agricultural products and their interest was always to get foodstuffs from the cheapest sources.

The French situation was unique among the Common Market nations and France's main interest in the Common Market as such was not industrial but agricultural.

The fatal mistake made by Britain occurred on the night of August 4, 1962. By then London, on information provided by its Ambassador, had become convinced that there was a serious possibility that de Gaulle would lose the forthcoming French General Election. In anticipation of this as a strong possibility the negotiating pace was slowed down by the British delegation instead of being hastened. In the event, of course, the General won an absolute majority in the French Parliament.

Evening Standard
Friday, March 25, 1966

DE GAULLE INVITES THE QUEEN

The French Prime Minister, M. Pompidou, flies off to London today for two days of talks with Mr Wilson with an invitation for the Queen to make a State visit to Paris in his pocket. The invitation is in the form of a warm personal letter from President de Gaulle to the Queen which M. Pompidou will hand to her when he is received by her tomorrow.

This, unfortunately, will be the outstanding feature of the visit. Apart from that, the outlook in Anglo-French relations is bleak.

On the central issue of Britain's possible entry into the Common Market, the French attitude is that it is not an immediate problem. Both M. Pompidou and the French Foreign Minister, M. Couve de Murville, take the view that Britain can only seriously envisage entering the Market when it has set its financial house in order and taken steps to prepare our British agriculture for the 'painful' shift in agricultural policy that entry into the Market would involve.

The French, therefore, consider that the issue will not be ripe for serious discussion for at least another two years. On the other hand, they have made it clear in private talks here that there can be no question of a second unilateral French veto on Britain's entry. They claim their view of the conditions for Britain's entry is shared by most of their Common Market partners.

M. Pompidou and M. Couve de Murville are going to London with their minds tinged by the prevailing bitterness in Paris over certain British attitudes. Apart from Mr Healey's unfortunate recent remarks concerning President de Gaulle, which are more easily swallowed than forgotten, there is a whole range of grievances agains Mr Wilson's Government.

They include the latest example of the British protest against French atomic tests in the Pacific which was more vehement in tone than even the Washington protest.

Then there is the lead taken by Britain in organising opposition to France in Europe against France's NATO policy.

The French speak with some bitterness over the alleged hypocrisies involved in both attitudes.

The British, it is pointed out, have their independent atomic striking force and have made no effort to share it.

As for French withdrawal from the integrated NATO command, it was pointed out here that only the British forces in Germany are integrated in NATO while the rest are not.

The persistent British view that what should be good enough for France is not good enough for Britain is a constant irritant here.

In M. Pompidou and M. Couve de Murville, Mr Wilson and Mr Stewart will be dealing with two of the coolest cucumbers in the business. For the first time in living memory, a French Prime Minister will be going to London with a stable government and a stable currency behind him.

Far from Mr Wilson doing most of the probing into French intentions, it is the French who are likely to cross-examine him closely regarding most aspects of British foreign policy and on Britain's financial and economic situation.

Apart from a sterile discussion on their differences, there is likely to be some solid achievement in the field of technical co-operation.

Evening Standard
Wednesday, July 6, 1966

AN ABSENT FRIEND — BY ORDER OF THE GENERAL
A slap from de Gaulle as Wilson and Brown prepare for market talks . . .

The hand that General de Gaulle will play when he meets Mr Wilson and Mr Brown for two days of intensive diplomatic poker next week in Paris has now been carefully arranged between himself and his Foreign Minister, M. Couve de Murville. The Prime Minister, M. Georges Pompidou, has been significantly excluded from these preparations.

This is bad news for Britain's bid to break into the Common Market. M. Pompidou is opposed to a second French veto of Britain's entry and is publicly and privately committed to the view that if Britain signs the Rome Treaty and the existing agricultural agreements between the Six, then no political considerations should be used to block it.

This is not the General's view, nor is it that of M. Couve de Murville. They consider that Mr Wilson will succeed in vetoing himself by inability to accept the agricultural agreements as they stand without seeking either significant changes or a seemingly over-long transition period, or both. In anticipating this, General de Gaulle has already secured a promise from the West German Chancellor of Bonn's 'neutrality' if it comes to a clash between France and Britain on agriculture.

But what happens if Mr Wilson decides to sign both the treaty and the agricultural agreements and asks for only a modest transitional period of, say, five years? In that case the General will retreat to prepared positions. He will raise new issues and new conditions ranging from sterling as a reserve currency to Britain's military and political ties with Washington.

That does not mean that this week's talks will end in a brutal 'No' from General de Gaulle. On the contrary, they are likely to be apparently inconclusive with the French doing as much probing as to British intentions as we are as to the French.

How, for example, does Mr Wilson intend to 'safeguard the essential interests of Great Britain and the Commonwealth' in the light of Common Market obligations?

In the last analysis, the full French case against British entry will be presented by de Gaulle himself to the other Five at the Common Market Summit in Rome next spring. By that time it is hoped that a sufficient degree of scepticism will be engendered among at least some of the Five to ensure that France does not stand alone. But if France has to act alone in imposing a second veto then it will do so.

De Gaulle's view is that Europe is evolving towards a considerable degree of financial, military and diplomatic independence of the United States and that this evolution would be compromised by Britain's entry into the Common Market.

To ensure that this tough line remains in force in the event that he does not complete the remaining six years of his presidential term, he is considering changing Prime Ministers after the General Election next March, replacing M. Pompidou with M. Couve de Murville.

Evening Standard
Friday, January 20, 1967

'NON' — AND CRASH GO MANY ILLUSIONS

General de Gaulle's second 'No' to a British effort to join the Common Market shatters some interesting historical and political illusions. The first is one encouraged by Mr Wilson himself when he began his first approaches to the Market.

It is that a piece of alleged double-dealing by Mr Macmillan at Nassau when he arranged to buy Polaris missiles from the US was directly responsible for de Gaulle's first veto. This is now shown up for the nonsense it always was.

In fact the Polaris deal as an alibi for the veto was a de Gaulle afterthought and the veto was decided upon before and not after Mr Macmillan's meeting with President Kennedy.

A second illusion shattered by this week's Press conference is that de Gaulle, because of his political difficulties at home, would be forced to accept the British application. In fact nothing of the kind happened. De Gaulle's declaration was every bit as unbending and harsh as the one he made in 1963.

A further illusion is that it would allow negotiations to open and drag them out into an interminable marathon. This one has not yet been shattered, but it will be. If negotiations do open I believe they will be brief and end with the French delegation being withdrawn.

This was the tactic adopted in 1963 when M. Couve de Murville, the Foreign Minister, was ordered by de Gaulle not to attend the Brussels meeting of the Six conducting the negotiations with Britain. It will if necessary be used again and this time, in the French view, with a show of support from West Germany and possibly Italy.

The question of British entry was largely discussed at last week's meeting of the French Cabinet with de Gaulle asking each minister to state his views while keeping his own to himself. It is a bizarre procedure used by de Gaulle on rare and important occasions.

A good third of the Cabinet was in favour of British entry, arguing that if Britain's so-called evolution towards Europe was to be encouraged and speeded up the best way was to allow her to come in. Rejection would only drive her back into America's arms.

A point at issue was whether in the event of an Asiatic war Britain's entry would help to keep Europe out of it or have the opposite effect.

In fairness to the French, the agricultural issue worried a majority of the Cabinet who felt that British entry would lead to a revision of the agricultural agreements so favourable to France which come up for review inside the Common Market in 1969.

The first the Government were to hear of de Gaulle's definitive views was at this week's Press conference. For many of them as for those observers who were at his 1963 Press conference it all sounded like listening to a worn and slightly cracked record.

*   *   *

Quote of the Week
General de Gaulle: 'Newspapers usually have some kind of a pasture to graze on.'

Evening Standard
Friday, May 19, 1967

WILL HE, WON'T HE?
The de Gaulle enigma

It is now election year in Paris, with presidential elections scheduled in December, and yet nobody, literally nobody, apart from General de Gaulle himself, knows if he will stand for a second seven-year term. Either way it will be a momentous decision. The fact is that at this stage no member of the French Cabinet knows what the decision will be. The subject has become a matter of lively debate within the Government, when its members are out of earshot of de Gaulle.

The Government is split on the issue almost fifty-fifty. The Foreign Minister, M. Couve de Murville, leads that half of the Cabinet opinion which believes de Gaulle will not stand for a second term.

M. Louis Joxe, Minister of State, leads the opposition to this view. The issue obviously hangs on de Gaulle's health, and this is now the major political preoccupation of the country.

This week the ferociously Right-wing and anti-Gaullist sheet, *Minute*, had as its main news story the claim that 'General de Gaulle's prostate has moved to other parts of the body'. It would be interesting to have some learned comment on this remarkable piece of levitation by the spokesman of the more disinterested British Medical Association. This could only happen in Paris, for only Paris could make such a deliberate attempt to mock the Establishment.

Evening Standard
Friday, January 29, 1965

DE GAULLE TO STAND AGAIN

General de Gaulle, it is now reliably learned in Paris, has decided to stand for a second term as President of the Republic in the French presidential elections to be held on December 5.

He has communicated this decision to his Prime Minister, M. Pompidou. He will announce it publicly in a nation-wide television broadcast on October 25.

The General's decision ends all hope of the French Opposition, both Left and Right, that M. Pinay, a highly respected former Prime Minister, may be induced to stand. It also considerably clarifies the electoral prospects and France's political future.

There is no doubt that with de Gaulle as a candidate his policies at home and abroad will be pursued with even greater vigour in the next seven years. Nobody doubts that General de Gaulle will be elected with a crushing majority. At the moment there are four candidates in the field against him. They are:

*   *   *

(1) M. MITTERRAND, who is backed by the Communists, Socialists and some Radicals.
(2) M. MARCILHACY, who represents the Centre-Right, but whose campaign so far has made little impression.
(3) M. ANTIER, who is seeking the peasant vote, but whose campaign also has failed to strike roots.
(4) MAITRE TIXIER-VIGNANCOUR, who has been waging a vigorous campaign but whose support is restricted to the extreme Right.

*   *   *

It will be seen from this list that the French Centre parties, whose hopes were fixed on M. Pinay, have so far failed to find a candidate, and it is unlikely that they will now present one.

M. Mitterrand's Left-wing support is at the moment divided, lukewarm and demoralised. Only this week the Socialist leader, M. Mollet, who is supposedly a backer of Mitterrand, made a public appeal to M. Pinay to stand.

As M. Piney represents financial orthodoxy and conservatism to the Left, M. Mollet's appeal dismayed the entire French Left.

M. Mollet made it clear that he himself thought de Gaulle would not stand for a second term and, therefore, M. Pinay had the best chance of beating the Gaullist candidate.

M. Mendès-France is expected to issue a lukewarm communiqué declaring his support for M. Mitterrand, but he plans to be absent from France throughout the election campaign and therefore will not campaign for Mitterrand.

As for the Communists, anything between one million and two

million are expected to vote for de Gaulle rather than Mitterrand.

Finally there is M. Tixier-Vignancour. He may not even qualify as a candidate at all. The reason is that under the Constitution, to discourage freak candidates, all those who wish to stand have to collect the signed support of one hundred elected dignitaries – either MPs, Senators, Regional Councillors or Mayors – spread over at least ten departments. However, through carelessness or inability to do so, M. Tixier-Vignancour has so far failed to line up these hundred signatories and in fact may fail to do so. In that case he will be automatically disqualified: a situation which he may not dislike, for in that case he will claim abstentionists as his supporters.

As for M. Marcilhacy and M. Antier, in view of the discouragements they have faced they may well withdraw from a campaign.

It becomes clear that next December's election will be largely a formality, with the size of de Gaulle's majority the only point of interest.

Evening Standard
Friday, October 8, 1965

THE THREE MILLION POUND PLOT TO DISH DE GAULLE

Now that General de Gaulle has publicly declared his intention to be a candidate in next month's presidential elections the full sordid story can be told of the methods used by a wide range of politicians to persuade the former Prime Minister, M. Antoine Pinay, to stand against him. These ranged from blackmail to an outright attempt at bribery.

M. Pinay is, after General de Gaulle, the most respected figure in French political life. He stood the best chance if not of defeating him at least of denying him an absolute majority and thereby involving him in the humiliation of a second ballot.

This was a calculation of politicians ranging from the extreme Right to the Socialist leader M. Guy Mollet. The objective – as M. Mollet made clear, stating that the Socialists would vote for M. Pinay, the Conservative, if a second ballot became necessary – was 'to have de Gaulle's skin'.

Earlier, M. Pinay had spoken darkly of being the object of 'threats, blackmail and calumny'. This week, to the consternation of his former supporters, he spelt out his charges. In an interview with the weekly *Paris-Match*, M. Pinay revealed that appeals to him to stand against de

Gaulle were combined with threats that certain 'revelations' concerning his private life would be circulated if he did not. This was put to him in the form that explanations would have to be given for his reluctance to stand.

M. Pinay alleges: 'An enormous sum was offered to me by way of election expenses'.

It should be noted here that basic election expenses of all candidates are paid for by the State. The sum involved in M. Pinay's allegation was, I understand, in the region of £3,000,000. This sum was raised by a group of leading French industrialists and financial figures, all bitterly opposed not only to de Gaulle's foreign policy but to his financial and economic policies at home.

As for M. Pinay's private life it is well known that some years ago he was the victim of a crude blackmail attempt by a young woman. All this as well as domestic tragedies in his life are now being aired in sections of the Paris gutter Press which previously supported him. It was a sickening episode only relieved by M. Pinay's own courage in revealing the methods used by his so-called supporters.

Evening Standard
Friday, November 5, 1965

SERIOUSLY – IS THERE ANYONE BUT DE GAULLE?

'On the whole, seeing around me these courageous colleagues of such goodwill, I felt myself full of esteem for all and of friendship for many. But also, probing their souls, I reached a point where I asked myself if among all those who spoke of revolution I was not in truth the only revolutionary.' – General de Gaulle's *Memoirs, Vol II.*

* * *

This reflection of de Gaulle's on the ministerial colleagues he was about to take back with him to liberate France is worth pondering today as France is about to go to the polls in a presidential election.

What de Gaulle meant was that, despite all the high-minded resolves made in the aftermath of defeat and disaster not to return to the bad old days of the Third Republic, this is precisely what his ministers intended to do once France was liberated.

When his forebodings proved accurate he quit, only to be recalled to power twelve years later by the same politicians caught up in the intractable coils of the Algerian war.

What is evident now is that the 1940 collapse marked the end of an era. The attempt after 1945 to govern France in the old traditional way was bound to cap tragedy with farce.

In 1940 the State abdicated in the face of German panzers; in 1958 it abdicated in the face of a handful of colonels.

Seven years after de Gaulle's accession to the presidency one thing is clear: the entire Opposition, ranging from extreme Right to Communist-backed Left, accepts – verbally at least – the broad outlines of the Gaullist Constitution.

Not only do they accept the Constitution as such but they also accept the amendment to the Constitution voted by referendum in 1962, in the teeth of their united and ferocious opposition, whereby the President of the Republic is elected by universal suffrage instead of by a restricted electoral college.

At the time this reform was proposed it was so savagely fought by the political parties that a government was overthrown and a new parliamentary election, giving the Gaullists and their allies a clear majority, had to be held.

Two points should be noted in this connection: this is the first time in the history of the Republic that a constitution has been universally accepted and it is the first time almost within living memory that there is a clear-cut majority in Parliament.

So unused are French politicians to the Anglo-Saxon idea of clear-cut parliamentary majorities that many of them regard this as the ultimate tyranny.

We now have to engage in a little of the 'soul probing' that the General permitted himself in his *Memoirs*: to what extent is a Mitterrand or a Lecanuet – despite verbal protestations that there can be no return to the bad old ways – either sincere or, even if sincere, capable of enforcing his authority?

Both, despite their relative youth, are old political war horses. Mitterrand, backed by the Communists, Socialists and some Radicals, was a member of eleven different governments of all political complexions in 13 years.

Lecanuet has a similar record, although as a member of the Catholic MRP he fought and finally helped to defeat the only hopeful government which those dismal years produced – that of Mendès-France.

These, apart from de Gaulle, are the only two serious candidates in the field. Both are backed by powerful party machines and plenty of money and Lecanuet in addition is receiving heavy clerical support in Alsace-Lorraine and Brittany.

Of the other three, one is a likeable crank, another is a club bore and the third is a man who in Britain would be unlikely to have a promising political future.

The almost certain second to de Gaulle is Mitterrand. The most likely to erode the Gaullist majority to the point where the General might fail to get an absolute majority on the first round and therefore face the humiliation of a second round between the two leading contenders is Lecanuet.

Imagine for a moment that Mitterrand wins the election. What conceivable hope has he of forming a stable government and obtaining a stable majority? There is no common ground between his Communist allies who will provide him with the bulk of his votes and his Socialist and Radical ones. Who will be his Minister of Finance, his Foreign Minister or his Minister of Defence? Can he put a Communist in any one of these key posts? Of course not.

What will happen is a repetition of the traditional pattern under the Third and Fourth Republics – the electorate will vote Left, but the parliamentary permutations will be such as to ensure a Centre or Centre-Right government.

Similar dilemmas would face Lecanuet. Once again the chief executive office – despite the new powers given it by de Gaulle's Constitution – will become the plaything of political cabals, each unable to rule but equally determined that no one else should rule in their place.

Here is the meaning of de Gaulle's phrase – 'Either me or chaos.'

The purpose of his Constitution was to end the confusion that had existed so long in France between the executive and legislative powers: the purpose of the reform whereby the President is elected by universal suffrage was both to give authority to the office and to force the French political parties to polarise and reform.

In the event, after seven years in the wilderness, the political parties appear to have learned nothing and forgotten everything.

This is best illustrated by the dismal affair of the candidature of the Socialist mayor of Marseilles, M. Deferre. He tried to form a broad Left coalition only to be finally scuttled by his own leader, M. Mollet, allegedly for going too far to the Right. No sooner had Deferre withdrawn and Mitterrand been chosen in his place than Mollet declared that his real choice was, of all people, the highly conservative M. Pinay. As someone remarked: 'If you have M. Mollet as a friend, you don't need an enemy . . .'

Oddly enough there is a staggering unanimity in the programmes of all the opposition candidates. All are for the Atlantic Alliance, all are for a Federal Europe, all promise to scrap France's deterrent, all are for a revision of aid to under-developed countries, all are for some form of amnesty to the 350 killers and their chiefs of the secret army still serving prison sentences.

The most glaring of the contradictions that leaps to the eye in all this is that the Communists by and large support de Gaulle's foreign policy whereas their candidate does not.

For de Gaulle this election must be an odd experience. Here he is at seventy-five with a career that has included first saving France's honour – what was left of it – and then saving it first from a Communist and then from a Fascist take-over, revealing himself for the first time as a political mortal.

This is the first time he ever stood for elected office and until recently the opposition insisted he would pull some trick both to prolong his rule and avoid fighting an election. Similar fantasies were spread about his electioneering intentions – for example, that the TV speeches of his opponents would be censored. Yet in fact the election has been the fairest I can recall in twenty years in France, with the Opposition hogging most TV time and supported by the overwhelming majority of the Press.

De Gaulle brings the Philistine out in all of us and we still tend to think of him in clichés. One of these is that he is a man of the Right – in fact, the French Right in all its manifestations, especially industrial and financial, detests him. No man was ever in a better position than de Gaulle to shackle France with a one-party State. He has done nothing of the sort.

Nor do I think that great international disasters will follow his victory. He is not out to wreck the Common Market – in fact, his quarrel with it will be settled within weeks of his re-election – and as for NATO, what will emerge after great debate is a stronger and more durable Western Alliance.

I am of course taking de Gaulle's re-election for granted: one would have to be 'bonkers' not to do so.

Evening Standard
Tuesday, November 30, 1965

WHY DE GAULLE FAILED

General de Gaulle has lost a battle but not the war. The causes of General de Gaulle's relative setback are not far to seek. The most important is undoubtedly the difficulty of a Government which has been in power for seven years to maintain itself at a very high level of popularity.

There were, however, other outstanding factors. On the Left there was serious dissatisfaction over housing, schools and pensions. On the Right, and especially too in the Centre, there was near panic about General de Gaulle's foreign policy.

De Gaulle clearly underestimated Catholic attachment to the Common Market and to the Atlantic Alliance. The Church, especially at the village priest level, campaigned heavily for the Catholic Lecanuet.

A final factor was that some thirty per cent of the electorate were under thirty-five. To them de Gaulle's name carries only faint recollections of the past and even of the recent past of eight years ago in the events which brought him to power.

De Gaulle refused to make any of the concessions an ordinary politician would have made, even before the campaign started. For example, it would have been easy for him to have patched up his quarrel with the Common Market before the election and thereby foiled a great deal of M. Lecanuet's campaign strength. Similarly he refused to ease his austere deflationary policy despite strong pressure from his Government well before the election. When the easing came it was too late for its full effects to be felt.

The deflationary policy brought him into collision with both the trade unions and big business. The ground swell of all these discontents brought to bear on him was too heavy for his absolute majority not to crack. His setback was not so much the work of the Opposition candidates – they became simply the focal points of these discontents.

Finally he refused to throw himself seriously into the campaign until it was too late and forbade his Ministers to take part in it until the very last few days.

His own television appearances were not always happy. He appeared aged, avuncular and spoke on a 'take it or leave it' basis. His first speech, with its famous 'chaos or me' line, struck an unusually high note of seeming arrogance even for him.

Yesterday's vote also throws into jeopardy the majority the Gaullists have in Parliament. Parliamentary elections are to be held in two years' time and if present trends are not arrested by then it may well be that this majority will be reversed.

In general, however, de Gaulle's achievement in polling nearly forty-five per cent of the vote after eight years of power and against five challengers remains an impressive one. He should have no difficulty in gaining a clear majority in the run-off fight in two weeks' time.

Like it or not, a further long period of de Gaulle rule appears assured.

Evening Standard
Monday, December 6, 1965

IT LOOKS LIKE DE GAULLE — THIS TIME

Three days before the final poll in the French presidential elections, General de Gaulle appears to be coasting towards a comfortable victory, according to most political observers here.

The run-off fight two weeks after the first round in the elections is between General de Gaulle and François Mitterrand, the Left-wing Communist-backed candidate.

General de Gaulle led on the first round with 44 per cent of the votes and M. Mitterrand was second with 32 per cent.

A public opinion poll taken late last week gives the General a 54 per cent majority on the second round. This, however, was taken before three highly successful appearances on television by the General in the course of this week. The general view now in Paris is that de Gaulle will now poll 58 per cent of the vote. In the opinion of most observers, had the General made the type of TV appearances two weeks ago that he has made in the current week he would have won an absolute majority on the first round.

The Gaullist campaign now is clearly based on a strong appeal to the Left. This has followed an order from the General himself that the bogey of a popular front should not be brandished before the electors.

There are sound electoral reasons for this policy. It is now clear that in the first round the General received ten per cent of the normal Communist vote. It is essential for him to hold this vote in the second round – and possibly increase on it. The possibilities of increasing on it are considerable. There is widespread unrest among the Communist rank and file, which provided M. Mitterrand with nearly sixty per cent of his vote on the first round, over his flirtation with the Right – and even the extreme Right – and his increasing vagueness on such key foreign policy questions as Europe and the Atlantic Alliance.

Furthermore, M. Mitterrand has not disassociated himself from declarations of support coming from the extreme Right, including former leaders of the secret army and such exiles as M. Soustelle and M. Bidault. This is seen here as a major tactical error. The extreme Right would have voted for M. Mitterrand in any case, on the principle that they would vote for the Devil himself in order to get rid of de Gaulle. At the same time if M. Mitterrand declared his distaste for such support he would have reassured his Communist following.

The pressures on M. Mitterrand coming from Left and Right have produced dissension among the members of his 'Brains Trust'. There are those who urge him to appeal for the votes cast on the first ballot for the

Catholic Centre Party candidate M. Lecanuet, and others who urge him to placate the Left.

M. Lecanuet himself, who polled more than three million votes, has already given the nod to his supporters to vote for M. Mitterrand and on the grounds that M. Mitterrrand's views on European integration approximate more closely to his own than those of de Gaulle.

It is expected that on the eve of the poll, M. Lecanuet will come out openly for M. Mitterrand. If he does not do so before the campaign ends on Friday it will be a clear sign that he considers that M. Mitterrand has no hope of toppling de Gaulle.

Evening Standard
Thursday, December 16, 1965

DE GAULLE TO SWITCH CABINET

General de Gaulle's return to power for a second seven-year term will mean no change in the basic tenets of his foreign policy but will involve a sharp switch to the Left in domestic affairs.

Substantial Cabinet changes are almost certain to follow, accompanied by a change of Prime Minister. The man most tipped to succeed M. Pompidou is Louis Joxe, Minister of State, a former diplomat and economist with marked Left-wing leanings.

Other changes are likely to affect the Finance and Foreign Affairs Ministries. It is expected that the Cabinet will be broadened to include some Radicals and Catholic centre party figures who supported de Gaulle in the current election campaign.

The next hurdle for the General is the Parliamentary Elections next spring. This may not prove a hurdle at all. Translated into Parliamentary terms the General's vote on the first ballot alone would assure him of a Parliamentary majority.

In the 1962 Parliamentary Elections a Gaullist vote of only 37 per cent was sufficient to give him a substantial Parliamentary majority.

Furthermore the General has returned to power at a time when a policy of strict financial austerity has laid the basis for a new period of rapid economic expansion. Then, too, the Common Market issue based on an essential French interest – agriculture – seems certain to be solved in the coming few months if not weeks and solved largely on de Gaulle's terms. This will bring enormous advantages to French agriculture and remove a major reason for his failure to get an absolute majority on the first round.

Two major features of yesterday's vote are:

*　　　*　　　*

1 – The refusal of the bulk of the three and a half million who voted for M. Lecanuet at the first ballot to follow his advice and vote against de Gaulle on the second round. This is a distinct setback to M. Lecanuet's political hopes and many observers in Paris believe that the promising political future of this staunch pro-European is now well and truly behind him.

2 – The inroads de Gaulle made in the traditional Communist vote. Ten per cent of the normal Communist vote went to him on the first ballot and he not only held it in the second but substantially increased on it. In that sense de Gaulle's victory is also a victory for the Left though not the doctrinaire Left. De Gaulle is the first French politician who has succeeded in eroding the massive French Communist vote. M. Mitterrand, the Communist candidate, polled best in the more backward regions of France south of the Loire where the vote of extreme Right and of former Algerian settlers was added to that of the Communists and Socialists. In the industrial north, however, especially in such cities as Lille, Arras and Cherbourg, de Gaulle won easily.

*　　　*　　　*

This has been a chastening experience for both de Gaulle and his followers. It is now clear that the régime cannot take the electorate for granted and that something more direct is needed in the way of communication between the Government and the nation than an occasional oracular statement by de Gaulle.

The Government went into the fight without any attempt at bribing the voters. It could, for example, have patched up the Common Market issue before the Election, and it could have relaxed financial austerity which aroused the resentment of both the trade unions and of the French equivalent of a federation of British industries.

The results also hold lessons for the leaders of French centre parties and the French Left. It is clear now that no stable centre party majority is possible without de Gaullists and no Left majority is possible until the French Communist Party transforms itself from a total allegiance to Moscow to something like an unmistakably French Labour Party.

The campaign was fought on an unusually high level and made nonsense of theories that after seven years of de Gaulle's patrician rule the French had lost interest in political affairs.

Evening Standard
Monday, December 20, 1965

THAT ODD BEN BARKA AFFAIR

The curious affair of the kidnapping of Moroccan Opposition leader Ben Barka in broad daylight in Paris a fortnight ago is now moving towards a climax.

This might well be a French decision in the next few days to break off diplomatic relations with Morocco. In any case a visit to Paris by King Hassan during which he was to see de Gaulle has been definitely cancelled at France's request.

De Gaulle's anger over the kidnapping has been made plain to the King and what the French are asking for now is first the extradition to Paris of a French gangster who was involved in the kidnapping and is now in Morocco, and secondly the dismissal of the Moroccan Minister of the Interior, General Oufkir. What de Gaulle cannot forget is not only the kidnapping itself but the fact that General Oufkir was on French soil at the time to supervise the details.

Meanwhile the King finds himself in a tricky situation: General Oufkir controls both the military and police forces of the country, and his dismissal would weaken the already strained props of the régime. But on the other hand a break in diplomatic relations would have serious financial consequences for the country, which is greatly dependent on French aid and at the time of the kidnapping was actually negotiating for further loans.

As for the unfortunate Ben Barka himself, there is now little hope that he will be found alive. In all probability he was killed in France and his execution was supervised by General Oufkir himself.

At present one thing is clear: that if France's two demands are not met the Moroccan Ambassador in Paris will be given his passport.

Evening Standard
Friday, November 12, 1965

WAITING FOR THAT LAST IRONIC TWIST IN THE BEN BARKA SCANDAL

Apart from the major scandal of the Moroccan Opposition leader Ben Barka, in Paris last October, with the connivance of French policemen and French security officials, there is almost as big a scandal concerning France's counter-espionage service, whose chief has just been retired by General de Gaulle.

This organisation which enjoys none of the favoured secrecy which envelopes Britain's MI5 and MI6 – its address is known, its chief is publicly named and its budget is regularly discussed in Parliament – is the direct emanation of the Secret Service General de Gaulle set up in London during the War. This is a considerable irony which will become apparent later. Known in London by the initials BACRA, transplanted onto French soil it became the 'Service of Documentation and Counter-espionage' (SDECE) responsible until two days ago to the Prime Minister after the manner of the British Intelligence services.

The original head of the organisation in London was the legendary Dewavrin, better known as Colonel Passy. A brave man, Passy insisted on making several parachute drops into Occupied France and was finally succeeded by the redoubtable Jacques Soustelle, now in exile and a deadly enemy of de Gaulle.

A former scholar and anthropologist, Soustelle took to secret service work like a duck to water. After the Liberation Passy resumed his post as Chief of the Service, but immediately became a political football. He was finally ousted by a compromise which gave the post to a Socialist and made his chief adjutant an anti-Gaullist colonel.

The significance of this chequered history of the Secret Service organisation will now become apparent. It has been riddled from the beginning with officers of strong colonial ties – officers who had served in all the former French colonies and especially Indo-China, Algeria and Morocco.

I am now revealing no secret when I revert to the irony I pointed out earlier in the fact that this organisation was founded by de Gaulle. At present its staff have a remarkably high proportion of anti-Gaullists who have never been able to forgive the General for his 'betrayal' of the French colonial empire.

Officers of this service have maintained close contact with the Moroccan Minister of the Interior, General Oufkir, who was the most loyal to the French cause when Morocco was clamouring for independence.

It is equally no secret that there have been steady leaks over the past few years from this organisation to the extreme Right wing French Opposition Press.

It may well be that when the full story of the Ben Barka affair comes to be revealed it will be found that this originally Gaullist Secret Service has been playing a remarkably active anti-Gaullist role.

Evening Standard
Friday, January 21, 1966

'CURIOUSER AND CURIOUSER' — THE BEN BARKA AFFAIR

One of the more bizarre aspects of the Ben Barka mystery is that the French Minister of the Interior, M. Roger Frey, should have thought fit to, as it were, confess himself on the subject to M. François Mauriac, the eighty-year-old Catholic novelist and Nobel prizewinner.

It is a little as though a British Home Secretary under fire in Parliament and Press, should have made a confidential report on a matter of urgent national interest to Mr Graham Greene. Be that as it may, what did M. Frey tell M. Mauriac? I can reveal a part of that and it concerns a central mystery in the case.

Two genuine French plain-clothes policemen took part in the kidnapping of Ben Barka on October 29. Their identity was known five days later, yet they were allowed to remain at liberty for a further eight days. Why?

In the meantime, General Oufkir, the Moroccan Minister of the Interior now wanted by the French police, returned to Paris on official business and attended a dinner given in his honour by the Moroccan Ambassador. The dinner was attended by high French police officials. It was only on the night of that dinner in the early hours of November 4 that the police began to have a clear picture of what had happened, and the full list of the people involved.

All that was unknown, and still remains unknown, is Ben Barka's ultimate fate. That same morning Oufkir took an aeroplane back to Rabat. Three Ministers were immediately informed: Pompidou, Frey and the Foreign Minister, Couve de Murville.

De Gaulle, at that precise moment, was not informed. Should Oufkir be arrested there and then? It was deemed unthinkable to take such an appalling risk at that stage of the investigations as to arrest a member of the government of a friendly nation. Furthermore, if Ben Barka was still alive, this was the one certain way of assuring his death.

Early that afternoon, it was decided to dispatch the Foreign Minister's chief aide M. Maleaud to Rabat. It was at this stage it was decided to keep secret the complicity of the two French policemen. It was considered that if it were made public it would weaken French diplomatic representations in Rabat. Four days later M. Maleaud and the French Ambassador in Morocco returned to Paris empty-handed.

All French hopes that they could secure the return of Ben Barka and the resignation of Oufkir were dashed. There was no longer any reason to hide French complicity and the two policemen who had been kept under discreet surveillance were finally arrested on November 11.

Evening Standard
Friday, February 4, 1966

AFTER BEN BARKA – THE HEADS BEGIN TO FALL

General de Gaulle at his press conference was a little premature in declaring that French complicity in the Ben Barka kidnapping existed only at a 'vulgar and subaltern level'.

In fact, even as he was speaking, a major shake-up was going on in the French counter-espionage services of which one member, Major Finville, is already under arrest on the relatively minor charge of failing to disclose to the authorities that a plot was afoot to kidnap the exiled Moroccan Opposition leader.

At least two hundred, out of a total staff of two thousand, of the French counter-espionage organisation (SDECE) are threatened with re-posting or outright dismissal. As a result of this shake-up three, and possibly four, fairly senior members of SDECE face charges connected with the kidnapping.

It is now known that as early as October 19 – Ben Barka was kidnapped on the 29th – a photographic report went to several leading members of the organisation announcing the plot to kidnap Ben Barka on French soil. It seems hardly likely in that case that the complicity or simply a laisse-faire attitude will not go beyond the level of Major Finville.

The General's eagerness to establish that the major responsibility for the kidnapping rested with Moroccans and that the Opposition French Press had shown a high degree of recklessness in its reporting of the case seems on reflection to have led him a little too far. To an independent witness he was clearly right in stressing that there was not a tittle of evidence to implicate any member of the Government or any member of his own staff. But this does not alter the strong possibility that complicity went higher than at the modest level he indicated.

Evening Standard
Friday, February 25, 1966

THE BEN BARKA AFFAIR (continued)

Immediately after General de Gaulle's Press conference last January I wrote in this column that he was sticking his neck out in describing French complicities in the Ben Barka kidnapping as 'vulgar and subaltern'.

Now this appalling affair, which involved the kidnapping, with the complicity of two French policemen, of the Moroccan Opposition leader in broad daylight on October 29 of last year, has taken a new and highly dramatic turn.

It is now clear that complicities on the French side ran well above the 'vulgar and subaltern' level at which de Gaulle placed them even before the judicial enquiry had been closed. It has been closed and now brusquely reopened.

Without going into the complicated details of this mystery, in a way much more complete and intriguing than the disappearance of Burgess and Maclean for nothing more than a presumption that Ben Barka was killed exists to this day, it is perfectly clear that two policemen and a French Secret Service informant were involved, on the safe assurance of higher – and possibly very high – protection.

So far only minor executants of the kidnapping are under arrest. The rest – the notorious French gangsters and high Moroccan officials – have all managed to make their getaway. The reason why the judicial enquiry has been reopened before the accused are sent for trail is allegedly new evidence indicating a remarkably high degree of intimacy between leading police officials and the gangsters named in the case. This is possibly part of the scandal.

The real scandal, however, lies with the French Secret Service. As I have written before, the real complicities lie there.

Evening Standard
Friday, April 15, 1966

THE FATAL MISTAKE . . .

The war of nerves between Rabat and Paris over the Ben Barka case is fascinating to watch. Roughly, what it amounts to is this: The Moroccans have delivered Major Dlimi, one of the two principals (the other is the Moroccan Minister of the Interior, General Oufkir) accused of kidnapping the exiled Moroccan Opposition leader, with two objectives in view.

The first is to buy time, the second is to blackmail. If both Oufkir and Dlimi had been tried and condemned in their absence Franco-Moroccan relations would have been broken off.

By producing Dlimi the Moroccans have succeeded, at least for a time, in postponing the ugly consequence of a trial. At the same time, this delay will be used to try to persuade the French to be more reasonable about the affair and, in the last resort, to threaten that Dlimi will make revelations implicating high French officials.

It is a fatal mistake and one which could lead the Moroccans to a shattering solution. What they have failed to realise in their desperate efforts to escape the full diplomatic consequences of the kidnapping is that if the French had been susceptible to blackmail on the score of alleged high French complicity in the kidnapping they had an easy way out. This was to have observed the letter of the Franco-Moroccan judicial treaty of 1957 under which both countries agreed that neither could try the nationals of the other outside his own country. In other words, a Moroccan considered guilty of a crime in France would be handed over to the Moroccans, and vice-versa.

It is this treaty which the Moroccans have pressed to be applied, but in vain. In the circumstances of the present case, it would have provided the French, if they were anxious to suppress some hidden domestic scandal, with an opportunity to have observed the treaty by sending the dossier concerning Oufkir and Dlimi to Morocco. After that, it would have been up to the Moroccans to decide whether the dossier was sufficient or not. In short, observance of the treaty would have provided the French with a perfect let-out, without risking further scandal in France, and without risking a break in Franco-Moroccan relations.

Instead of that, General de Gaulle quite deliberately, and knowing full well the consequences, decided that Oufkir and Dlimi should be tried in Paris even if it meant trying them in their absence. This invited an open breach between the two countries and the threat that the Moroccan Secret Service, which has worked closely with the French for several years, would produce evidence compromising the high French officials and embarrassing to the Government. In short it is difficult to avoid the conclusion that the Moroccans are making an appalling mistake in holding the threat of revelations over de Gaulle's head.

Meanwhile, Dlimi's own line of defence is becoming crystal-clear. It is that a secret meeting for political talks with Ben Barka was arranged with the cover of the French Secret Service. Dlimi will then claim that by some unforeseen accident Ben Barka died on the day of his kidnapping —

October 29, 1965 – and that he was already dead when he and Oufkir arrived in Paris on the 30th.

Evening Standard
Friday, October 21, 1966

VIETNAM – AND THE SECRET INTERVENTION OF DE GAULLE . . .

General de Gaulle is preparing to make a personal bid to provide the basis for a settlement of the Vietnam war. The bid is highly secret. It will be vehemently denied but it is nonetheless a fact.

De Gaulle has so far disdained the role of a possible peacemaker, feeling a gloomy certainty that the war must now run its futile course for the next several years. The resumpton of US bombing, however, has jolted and angered him.

He has also now had time to study fully the reports brought back from a recent visit to Pekin and Hanoi by his top diplomatic emissary, the former French Ambassador in London, M. Jean Chauvel.

His initiative was taken two weeks ago. It took the form of a detailed outline of possible cease-fire and peace terms which he considered would be acceptable to Hanoi if not necessarily immediately to Washington. These were sent to the French Delegate-General in Hanoi, M. Francois de Quirielle, with instructions that they should be submitted directly to President Ho Chi Minh of North Vietnam. M. de Quirielle was asked to tell the North Vietman Communist leader that General de Gaulle hoped for an answer to his proposals before February 21. The date is important – on February 21 General de Gaulle gives one of his biennial Press conferences.

The details of the General's peace plan are not known but they will of course conform to his conception of a neutralised unified Vietman from which all foreign interference has been eliminated.

This de Gaulle initiative has been accompanied by what may be considered as a mild rebuff to Britain. The General does not hide from intimates his contempt for Britain's attempts to act as peacemaker in Vietnam while supporting American policy in the air.

The British Government has recently asked France to join with it in an attempt to persuade Moscow to reconvene the 1954 Geneva Conference on Vietnam, of which Britain and the Soviet Union are co-chairmen. The

French have refused to do this on the grounds that the resumption of US bombing has made any such attempt futile.

At the same time Britain was not and has not been informed of de Gaulle's approach to Hanoi.

Evening Standard
Friday, February 11, 1966

DE GAULLE FLIES INTO MOSCOW

President de Gaulle flew into Moscow today in the presidential Caravelle on a visit which he hopes will improve East-West relations within Europe. With him was Mme de Gaulle, Foreign Minister Couve de Murville and top-ranking diplomats. He was welcomed by President Podgorny and Premier Kosygin.

General de Gaulle arrived in Moscow this afternoon on a twelve-day State visit which, despite careful preparation, still leaves a large margin for surprises. This explains a certain edgy nervousness noticeable among both French and Soviet diplomats.

Broad political outlines of the talks that de Gaulle is to have with the Soviet leaders are known, but the Soviets have been unable to pin General de Gaulle down on any serious agreement with their views on the central issue of Germany.

Furthermore there is a certain apprehension as to what the General will say in his many major speeches in the Soviet Union.

In view of the delicate relations that exist between Moscow and some of its satellites, General de Gaulle's views on national independence are likely to strike a discordant note. And according to French diplomats here General de Gaulle not only sees himself as the spokesman for the satellites but also to a large degree of West German aspirations for reunification and even of the West as a whole.

One of the intriguing mysteries of the trip is the impact de Gaulle's personality and manner will have on the Soviet crowds. The twenty-five miles from Vnoukovo Aerodrome to the Kremlin is lined with French and Soviet flags as from today and the crowds along the route are expected to be large. Schoolchildren are to be given a half holiday and one in three factory workers in the Moscow area are to be detailed for the welcome.

The General will stay four days in Moscow before flying to Siberia, Kiev, Volgograd — formerly Stalingrad — and Leningrad. He will be staying in the Kremlin in a five-room suite which was once the residence of the Grand Duke Michael, the uncle of Russia's last Tzar, Nicholas II. There are no pictures on the walls and the curtains are dark and heavy as there are no shutters on the windows to keep out the bright sun. This suite overlooks the Moscow river and ironically enough the Avenue Maurice Thorez, named after the former French Communist leader.

There was a problem set over the way to make the General and Madame de Gaulle's beds. It was undecided whether they should be made up in the Russian fashion or the Western. De Gaulle settled the matter himself with a crisp reply: 'As I am receiving the hospitality of this country I shall abide by its usages'.

Tonight there will be a massive Kremlin banquet in his honour. One important aspect of the talks will concern Franco-Soviet technical and scientific co-operation and a possible space project. I gather that the technical co-operation aspect has already been settled and will take the form of a graduated co-operation at all levels of French and Soviet industry.

The space project issue, however, has met with a certain amount of resistance from General de Gaulle. The Russians are pressing the French to join in a joint space project but de Gaulle insists on waiting to see how ELDO turns out.

So all is set in Moscow for the welcome — slogans, flags and crowds at the ready. The Russian population were only yesterday aware of de Gaulle's arrival today. Up to then they did not know the exact date of the visit and they still have not been told the itinerary.

In fact the build-up for the visit in the Soviet Press has been remarkably muted. Whatever the outcome of the visit one will once again marvel at the de Gaulle phenomenon — a combination of pride, stubbornness, rhetoric and stamina.

Evening Standard
Monday, June 20, 1966

WIN OR LOSE, IT'S THE GENERAL . . .

What will happen if General de Gaulle's party loses its present absolute majority in the French elections which will be finalised after two rounds of voting in two weeks' time?

Will the Government thereby fall? Will the General call on an opposition leader to form a government? Or will he continue as before? The answer came in categoric terms this week in a statement clearly authorised by General de Gaulle himself and stating that even if his party loses its majority, the Government will continue exactly as before.

This sounds at first glance like a monstrous defiance of the electorate's will, and has driven opposition political leaders into frenzies of denunciation. Yet it only requires a few moments' reflection on the meaning of the Constitution, which General de Gaulle introduced when he returned to power in 1958 and had ratified by an overwhelming majority in a referendum, to realise precisely the meaning of his declaration.

The whole point of the new Constitution was to break with a past, in which Parliament dominated the executive, and to establish a clear separation betwen the legislature and the executive power.

De Gaulle himself derives his authority from the fact that he is the popularly elected head of State. Under the Constitution executive power is firmly derived from him. Parliament legislates, but does not rule. The whole purpose of the reform was to wrest power from the political parties which overthrew governments at will and to vest effective power in the President of the Republic.

In the present circumstances it would be clearly absurd for de Gaulle to call on someone opposed to his policies to form a government. This would entail a reversion to precisely the practices of the past, when the executive, in the shape of a government, was the helpless instrument of the contradictions between rival political forces.

In the actual state of French party political life none of the Opposition leaders would be capable of forming an alternative government. M. Mitterrand, for example, the leader of the Left-wing Coalition, including, in a marginal sense, the Communists, could not form a government with the Communists, nor could he form a government without them. But that is not really the point. The point is whether the Elysée remains the centre of power or hands back its responsibility to Parliament.

Clearly, however, the results of the parliamentary elections, which promise to be exciting, will have their effect on the presidency. If, for example, de Gaullists lose their absolute majority, then it will be open to the Opposition to overthrow the Government by voting a motion of censure.

In that case, General de Gaulle will be forced to dissolve Parliament and order new elections. It has been widely claimed that he may resort to Article 16 of the Constitution which gives him powers to rule by decree in the event of a grave national emergency. But such a kind of emergency is strictly defined by the Constitution, and although the Opposition claims that de Gaulle may resort to it if he loses his majority, in fact nobody for a moment seriously believes that he will.

His course of action if he loses his parliamentary majority is clearly defined. It is to allow the present Government to continue until the various opposition parties who disagree on every aspect of domestic and foreign policy can agree on a common motion of censure.

This is a process which may well take the full lifetime – five years – of the next parliament. Apart from questions of principle, French MPs, once seated, are most reluctant to unseat themselves before the full term of their parliamentary life is completed.

It is, therefore, perfectly conceivable that General de Gaulle can continue to govern with a minority government. This may provide the Opposition parties with a constant sense of shock and outrage, but a solution will be squarely up to them.

Evening Standard
Friday, February 24, 1967

DE GAULLE: IT'S A GREAT VICTORY FOR THE FUTURE, TOO

General de Gaulle's supporters have swept back into power in the French General Election with almost the same landslide majority as they achieved in 1962.

The results in the first round of voting show that the de Gaullists will retain their absolute majority in the French Parliament, thereby giving the General an undisputed control of the nation's affairs for the next five years. To have achieved this result after nine years of office is a remarkable triumph for de Gaulle and his supporters. It is all the more remarkable as the vote was a record one, with eighty per cent of the nation voting. And the electorate included two million new voters for whom the memory of the political chaos which reigned in France before de Gaulle must have been a dim one.

The voting for 486 seats is in two rounds. On the first round only those with an absolute majority are elected: on the second round a simple majority suffices.

De Gaullists have already won sixty-four seats outright and a combined Opposition is trailing with only five. The percentage of the national vote for the Gaullists runs to nearly thirty-eight per cent – almost the percentage they polled in 1962. Among the sixty-four Gaullists already elected are eleven Cabinet Ministers, including the Prime Minister, M. Pompidou.

The runners-up are the Communists, who emerge as the major Opposition party. To everyone's surprise their total vote was some three per cent higher than that of the non-Communist Left led by M. Mitterrand. This is not so frightening a situation as it may seem. The 'cold war' is over and the French Communist Party has changed greatly and will continue to change greatly with the changing international situation. There is no reason why, in the future, they should not provide France with the basis of a French Labour Party.

The great loser of the election is the Centre Party leader, M. Lecanuet, who hoped to be the arbiter of the final outcome and who has in fact been eliminated as a serious political force in France.

It is clear that right across the nation the French showed their appreciation of the Gaullist Constitution by voting decisively for or against the Government and eliminating all parties which would have served to confuse the issue.

The record turn-out at the polls makes nonsense of a widely-held belief that General de Gaulle had 'depoliticised' the country.

The most interesting individual battle still left unsettled until next Sunday is M. Mendès-France's fight in Grenoble. He is trailing behind the de Gaullist candidate but is well ahead of his Communist rival. If the Communist stands down in the second round, as seems almost certain, M. Mendès-France should on paper win by a few hundred votes.

In Paris the Foreign Minister, M. Couve de Murville, is having a tough fight but is certain of victory in the second round.

The extreme Right suffered disastrous defeat throughout the country, with the exiled M. Soustelle being badly beaten at Lyons. And other prominent Right-wing figures are suffering the same fate throughout the country.

The results clearly eliminate as future political figures of stature both M. Mitterrand and the veteran Socialist leader, M. Guy Mollet.

The non-Communist Left will have to re-group around new leaders, and M. Mendès-France's probable election in Grenoble provides them with a potential leader.

As for the Government itself, its policy on domestic issues will certainly move to the Left as a result of this Election.

The result marks the end of vast illusions, both in France and abroad, regarding the future of Gaullism. It reveals that hopes in many foreign capitals, especially Washington and London, that de Gaulle's reign was coming to an end were hopelessly wide of the mark.

He emerges from this test with an even greater strength than he has enjoyed throughout his nine-year-reign.

Evening Standard
Monday, March 6, 1967

DE GAULLE WINS — BY A WHISKER
Now the General faces a tough situation after a major upset at the polls

General de Gaulle faces a tough but by no means menacing situation either now or in the immediate future as a result of his overall Parliamentary majority being slashed in yesterday's second round in the French General Election to a razor edge.

With 485 out of 486 seats declared, the state of the parties was:

*   *   *

Gaullists	244
Communists	73
Left-Wing Federation	116
Democratic Centre	27
Independent Conservatives	15
Other Left-Wingers	10

*   *   *

The final seat will be declared next Sunday when French Polynesia votes.

The salient fact about yesterday's voting is that the de Gaullist majority is the only one that exists, and there is no alternative. His nearest rival is the combined Communist and Socialist Federation bloc, which, with 180 seats, is sixty short of an absolute majority.

Furthermore, the de Gaullists are expected to draw support from some eighteen Centre Party MPs who owe their election to them. As for the Left-wing opposition, it still has to forge a common programme which because of its heterogeneous make-up — it includes some bitter anti-Communists — will be a painful process.

Its leadership problems will be complicated, too, by the re-entry of M.

Mendès-France into Parliamentary life. He is a powerful magnet for the non-Communist Left, but he is viewed with hostility by the Communists.

The Communists emerge as the major victors on the Left, collecting twenty-two per cent of the national poll in the first round – four per cent higher than the Federation's – and they were the major artisans of the gains on the Left as a whole.

They are, therefore, in a position almost to dictate terms to the Federation leader, M. Mitterrand.

Yesterday's results were a major upset of all predictions and to the trends shown in the first round of voting.

This appeared to assure the Gaullists of a comfortable majority.

The reasons for the surprising outcome are:

*　　*　　*

1 – The discipline of Communist and Federation voters who invariably voted in full strength for a Communist candidate when a Federation man stood down, and vice versa. It was not expected that Socialists would vote for Communist candidates at anything like full strength.

2 – Centre Party voters who found themselves without a candidate in the second round voted for the anti-Gaullist candidate even if he were a Socialist, or even a Communist.

The bulk of these votes were expected to go to the Gaullists in the second round.

3 – In many cases, especially in Paris, Gaullists faced an opposition ranging from extreme Left to the extreme Right, with the extreme Right either voting for a Communist, or Communists voting for a well-placed Rightist. This is dramatically illustrated by the defeat of M. Couve de Murville, the Foreign Minister, in the Seventh Arrondissement.

The Communists, who had only polled 3,000 in the first round, were eliminated, but it is clear from the result that the bulk of votes ensured M. Couve de Murville's defeat.

This is a situation rich in irony for M. Frédéric Dupont, who won the seat, for he is a man who has always operated on the extreme Right of French politics, whereas M. Couve de Murville was principal exponent of Gaullist foreign policy, which the French Communist Party finds 'positive'.

The Seventh Arrondissement also provides a microcosm of the hates which General de Gaulle inspires. It is similar to Belgravia, heavily populated by retired officers and civil servants, with the 'concierge vote' an important factor.

4 – The success of the Gaullists in the first round and the unanimous view of the public opinion polls that they would achieve a comfortable

majority in the second undoubtedly induced a lethargy in Gaullist ranks preceding the final vote.

This had serious consequences in the great number of seats that were wrested from the Gaullists by majorities of a few hundred, or even a few dozen.

*   *   *

The immediate question facing de Gaulle is whether to retain his defeated Ministers, as he is constitutionally entitled to do. It seems likely that he will retain two of his most important, M. Couve de Murville, and the man who symbolises the French atomic striking force and who lost his seat in Brittany, the Minister for the Armed Forces, M. Messmer.

The next question concerns the future of his Prime Minister, M. Pompidou. It was doubted even before the elections that M. Pompidou would remain in office.

There is no lack of candidates for his post, one of the most prominent being M. Giscard d'Estaing, whose party, the Independent Republicans, which forms part of the Gaullist majority, won ten seats at the elections. Another possibility is the former Prime Minister, M. Debré.

There is, however, no obligation on de Gaulle to change his Government, and it may well be that he will keep it as it is.

Many close observers here forecast that the Government will move sharply, even dramatically, to the Left in domestic policy. De Gaulle is known to be preoccupied with the problem of 'social reform' and ways by which the working class might be detached from their almost-automatic support of the Communists.

There is every reason to believe that projects for economic and social reform in France have been under consideration for some time and that de Gaulle is determined to use the remaining five years of his presidency to achieve a scale of social reform which, in the words of one of his Ministers, 'will astonish the world'.

*   *   *

Here are the percentages polled in the first and second rounds:

Gaullists: First round 38; Second round 43. Socialist Federation: First round 19; Second round 24. Communists: First round 22·46; Second round 21·55. Centre Democrats: First round 12·79; Second round 8·86. Oddments on the Left and Right: First round 8; Second round 2·57.

Evening Standard
Monday, March 13, 1967

HOW DID THE COMMUNISTS BECOME FRANCE'S SECOND PARTY?

Drive north out of Paris to Le Bourget airport or south to Orly, avoiding the auto routes, and you soon find yourself in a maze of streets bearing names like Rue Stalingrad or Rue Maurice Thorez.

These are parts of the Paris Red belt, which, with the heights of Belleville and Saint-Denis, have been revolutionary strongholds since the days of the Paris Commune and Communist strongholds almost from the year of the party's foundation in 1920.

Other areas of the party's basic strength are the mining areas of the north of France and the small peasant proprietors and small wine growers south of the Loire.

They have a tradition of voting as far to the Left as possible. In the Paris area this is true even of new dormitory suburbs which have nothing in common with the dilapidated hideousness of the classic Paris proletarian ghettos.

A suburb of Creuilly, for example, built on the fringes of the southern auto route in what was a wheatfield only nine years ago and which now has a population of 30,000 (one-third own their own cars), remains as stolidly Communist as, say, Belleville.

The answer is partly historic and the French Communist Party is part of that history. The French working class have always felt themselves a nation apart, defrauded of a revolutionary heritage, and they vote Communist as automatically as a miner in Wales or a worker in Stepney votes Labour.

Nor is there anything obviously alien about French Communism as there is for example about its British counterpart. The French party was founded not as a minority breakaway from the parent Socialist party, but as a majority one – in fact it was so much in a majority that it took over the main organ of the party. *L'Humanité*, which still bears under its masthead the boast that it was founded by the venerable socialist martyr Jean Jaurès.

The Communist vote may fluctuate but its limitations are clearly set. Its top poll was 6,000,000 after the liberation, 5,000,000 at the recent elections and just short of 4,000,000 at its lowest ebb. It lost 1,500,000 to de Gaulle after 1958 and now in the recent elections it has recovered most of those votes but remains a good million short of its postwar peak.

What is most intriguing about the French Communist Party is its dualism. It is at one and the same time both a dutiful agent of Moscow and a product of native revolutionary traditions. It is both Russian and

French. One of its current allies, the French Socialist leader M. Guy Mollet, once summed it up by saying: 'The French Communists are not on the Left, they are in Moscow'.

This dualism has, with a relaxation of the 'cold war', become less apparent in recent years, but it is none the less real. The French Communists are still tied to Moscow to a point which makes them seem backward compared not only with, say, the Italian party but even some parties like the Romanian and Polish in the East.

No word of enlightened comment on the Stalin régime has yet appeared in any French Communist journal and unlike the rest of at least the Western Communist world it never permitted itself a form of criticism of the recent savage jail sentences in Moscow on two non-conformist Soviet writers.

Part of the answer to the conformism of French Communism lies in the fact that its present leadership stems from a Stalin-appointed leadership, and therein lies the story in which farce and tragedy, iniquity and heroism blend themselves into an almost Renaissance-scale drama.

Ever since the majority of the French Socialist Party broke away to form the French Communist Party its history has unfolded in a melodramatic light, the best and worst in revolutionary movements. It has switched policies so often that reading its history is like riding a switchback railway.

Who will recall now without tears of rage that one year after Hitler came to power the French Communists were campaigning for the independence of – guess what? – Alsace-Lorraine?

The campaign showed how Stalin was thinking: If the West, as Stalin believed, was thinking of diverting Hitler against Russia then he, by using the French Communists, could tempt them to attack a softened-up France.

The French Communist leadership of the time was in the hands of Maurice Thorez, a former miner, a man of rhetoric and facility who had been groomed and selected for the leadership by Stalin personally.

Then came the switch and suddenly the French C.P. became the most patriotic party in France, singing the 'Marseillaise' as lustily as anyone and draping itself in the Tricolour.

In 1936 there came the great Popular Front victory ending four years later in the party being declared illegal by the very same Parliament whose election it had hailed as a triumph.

Stalin had signed a pact with Hitler without telling Thorez first. At first the patriotic line was maintained until the agent of the Communist International in Paris, a Czech who passed under the name of 'Clement', gave the word to Thorez: the war, which had already broken out, was an 'imperialistic' one.

Some Communists were arrested. Some, like Jacques Duclos, who is still in the leadership and who commanded the party's secret apparatus, went underground and remained hidden in Paris throughout the War. And some, like Thorez, on instructions from Moscow deserted their army units and fled to the Soviet Union. There was a brief period after the French collapse when the Communists tried to apply to the German authorities for permission to re-publish their newspaper. Permission was refused.

Then came the attack on Russia and the swift transformation of the War from an imperialist one into an anti-Fascist crusade. The role of French Communists in the Resistance is the noblest chapter in their history. They were quick on the political level to send a representative to de Gaulle in London.

They sought to create a revolutionary situation after the liberation but their troops were effectively integrated into the new French Army and de Gaulle refused them the three key posts they wanted in the Government — Interior, Foreign Affairs and the Army.

Thorez was allowed to return to France and after de Gaulle quit office in 1945 the Communists lingered on, only to be sacked by the Socialist Prime Minister, M. Ramadier, in 1947.

The party is now out of the political ghetto in which it has been since then, but it still remains far from effective power. Maybe it is only a matter of six or seven elderly relics from the Stalin period dying off before it becomes a perfectly respectable Left-wing party.

It once had nearly a million members. Its present membership officially is four hundred and thirty thousand. Unofficially, and possibly, more accurately, it is probably half of that.

Evening Standard
Friday, March 17, 1967

A MAN ALMOST ALONE — THAT'S DE GAULLE TODAY

What has happened in Paris as a result of the Middle East crisis is a political convulsion of major historic proportions.

On the face of it General de Gaulle's foreign policy is now supported only by a hard core of Gaullists and the Communists. On all sides and most markedly within the ranks of the Government's own majority the seventy-seven-year-old President's capacities, mental and physical, are being questioned with an unprecedented vigour and venom.

This week *Le Figaro,* organ of the French Establishment which has sided with de Gaulle in every crisis and whose criticisms of him have been timorous and equivocal, came out with a savage editorial attack on the General.

'Where is he leading us? By what path? Why this leap into adventurism?' it asked. The editorial amounted to a declaration of war on de Gaulle by French conservative opinion.

(It should be noted, however, that in sharp contrast to all this the latest public opinion poll taken after de Gaulle's first startling stand on the Israeli-Arab war gives him a popularity rating of 65 per cent, a rise of seven points in six months and his highest popularity rating since he wound up the Algerian war.)

Where then is de Gaulle going as his policies become more and more deliberately aligned with Moscow's? Basically de Gaulle's view is that the Middle East crisis was the outcome of the Vietnam war.

The Russian defeat in the Middle East only accentuates the need to wind up the Far Eastern war. The Russians cannot be expected to accept defeat at every confrontation, direct or indirect, with the US.

The Russians retreated over Cuba and over the Middle East, and the continuing mounting war in Vietnam exposes them to their worst humiliation yet. Somehow the equilibrium between the two super powers on which peace depends must be restored.

Otherwise the Russian military build-up in the Middle East will continue as it is continuing in Algeria, for example, where it is assuming such frightening proportions that Tunisia has secretely asked France for a military pact between the two countries and has been rebuffed.

The Russians have given their warning to Washington. They are prepared to wait only a few weeks, possibly no more than a month, for a sharp de-escalation in the war in Vietnam, beginning with an end to the bombing of the North.

As for Washington, its attitude to the Soviet warning should become clear in the next fortnight. Everything depends on whether President Johnson will accede to the army's request for reinforcements in Vietnam, amounting officially to 100,000 troops, but, in fact, to 200,000. If this is granted, then it means President Johnson has chosen escalation. If not, then the bombing of the North is likely to stop and the first steps can be taken towards a settlement.

Evening Standard
Friday, July 7, 1967

SWING OF THE PENDULUM

One theory that General de Gaulle's visit to Poland has 'kiboshed' is that the old boy is senile. After watching and listening to him in the past week all I can say is that if he is senile I would welcome a shot of some senility serum.

The whole senility theory launched by journals as reputable as *Le Figaro* and *Le Monde* and taken up with gusto by the entire French provincial Press has, in fact, boomeranged against those who launched it. The stormy uncertainties of the July days are now dissipated and the pendulum has swung strongly in de Gaulle's favour.

What the senility campaign has shown is the depth of hatred among the French Right and Left for what *Le Monde* called 'this intolerable old man'. It is a hatred born out of frustration, for both, in fact, in their various ways would have dearly loved to have been the architects of Gaullist foreign policy.

De Gaulle's impact on Poland was such that it is safe to say that the country will never be quite the same after his visit as it was before. His speeches were superb in style and rich in intellectual content. The fact that he was allowed to address both the Polish Parliament and the Polish nation on television broke new ground for those who are striving for greater freedom in Poland.

Physically he has lost weight and I have never seen him look better.

I particularly remember him at Auschwitz. There, in the grim setting of the former concentration camp, with Mme de Gaulle near to tears, the General did not speak a word while he listened to the guide until the very end, when he said: 'You must leave it exactly as it is.'

Then there was his striking entry in the visitors' book: 'What horror, what disgust, yet despite it all what hope for humanity'.

Visiting Auschwitz was a harrowing experience for everyone, but all the horrors of the place were brought home in an agonising fashion when we realised that one of the French reporters there had lost both his parents in the camp.

The political aspect of de Gaulle's emphatic reiteration that Germany's eastern frontiers end at the Oder-Neisse line should not be underestimated.

In fact, the General's emphasis on this point was approved by the Bonn Government which dared not say so itself. It is perfectly happy, however, that de Gaulle should undertake the task of educating West German public opinion on the subject.

Evening Standard
Friday, September 15, 1967

DE GAULLE RETURNED TO POWER AN OLD MAN IN A HURRY

General de Gaulle is the bearer of a terrible plague – heresy. He is a heretic at home and a heretic abroad. At home he challenges political doctrines which have divided France since the French Revolution and abroad he challenges doctrines which have divided Europe since the War.

He may not, in Roosevelt's sneering term, 'consider himself Joan of Arc', but, considering the almost miraculous political life he has had, he would have some justification for doing so.

His very arrival on the world scene is something of a miracle. He would never have become the leader of the Free French if any of a dozen better known candidates for the post had heeded his example and followed him to London.

That his example and appeals went unheeded in the higher political, military and diplomatic echelons of France has produced in him an abiding contempt for the French Establishment.

Then again the combined opposition of Roosevelt and Churchill should have led to his political extinction first in Algiers and then in Liberated France. Instead he triumphed in both places.

Then came his voluntary retirement in 1946 provoked by disgust at the determination of the political parties to revert to precisely the same political system which produced the 1940 collapse. On the very eve of his return to power he seemed France's forgotten man. In the end the régime collapsed under the threats of a handful of colonels just as the previous régime had collapsed under the assault of German tanks.

De Gaulle returned to power an old man in a hurry. Since then he has lived dangerously. He should have been a dead duck physically and politically several times over. Yet he continues to flourish in intellect and determination unblunted and it seems more than likely that he will complete the remaining five years of his presidential term.

A reactionary to the Left, he is a revolutionary to the Right. One has to go back to the pre-war figure of Léon Blum, the Jewish Socialist leader of the Popular Front, to find a man so pathologically loathed as de Gaulle is in what were once France's ruling circles.

Yet on the whole de Gaulle and his Government have served the nation well. Rarely, in fact, has a government allegedly reactionary been so progressive in domestic and in foreign affairs and its allegedly progressive circles so fundamentally reactionary.

One of the charges most frequently brought against de Gaulle both at home and abroad is that of 'mystification', of never revealing his true aims and objectives. Admittedly the General is rich in wiles and ruses but in matters of long term policies he has stated his aims over and over again with unusual clarity and undeviating purpose. It seems to me that those who are 'mystified' by him are those who wish to be mystified.

In this case there is a parallel between his domestic opposition at the time of the Algerian war and foreign opinion today. At the time of the Alerian war, despite unmistakable proofs to the contrary, neither Left nor Right would acknowledge that his aim was to give independence to Algeria. Hence the legend that he was forced to change his views under pressure of events.

For the Left it was impossible to admit that de Gaulle might do what they themselves had never dared to attempt; for the Right it was essential to build up the legend that they had been 'deceived'. In fact de Gaulle was so determined to give Algeria independence that while the war itself was still being fought he gave independence at a stroke to fourteen French colonies, thereby ensuring that there would be no other Algerias for France.

Similarly today, in the field of foreign affairs, over and over again he has hammered the theme that Europe should become the third force, independent of both super powers. He said so in his memoirs, at Press conference after Press conference, and to a variety of international figures including both British and American.

He is opposed to a bi-polar world dominated by Washington and Moscow. Such a world would be dangerous in his view because it would consecrate the present division of Europe and of Germany. Such a world can be averted by a policy of détente and co-operation within Europe itself, carried out by the Europeans themselves.

It can only take form as it emerges from a Europe of nations and not a supernational Europe as conceived by doctrinaires in Brussels. A Europe thus reconciled and united on both sides of the former Iron Curtain would provide a balance between the two super powers. It would also serve as a pole of attraction for the entire Third World, anxious to avoid satellisation by either of the hegemonies.

In those circumstances nationalism, far from being an outdated conception, is a revolutionary force greater in its liberating potentialities than it has ever been since 1848.

It is this insistence on nationalism as a mainspring of liberation from the two hegemonies that explains de Gaulle's stand on the Vietnam war, which he views as a national struggle; his recent Middle East stand; and then his speeches in Quebec.

Finally, détente in Europe cannot come about by agreement between the two super powers if only because whatever agreements they may enter into to avert mutual atomic self-destruction they will still remain in a state of dangerous rivalry. In those circumstances the Russians could easily produce a revival of the cold war in Europe, and a divided Germany could become a permanent threat of a European Vietnam.

De Gaulle has a remarkable record as a long-range prophet. He foresaw the end of the 'cold war' almost as it started and based his policies on that assumption. He foresaw the crack-up within the Communist bloc. He foresaw the inevitability of a China-Russia split. He also foresaw, to the scorn of both President Kennedy and Dean Rusk in 1962, that the American commitment in Vietnam, then restricted to a few hundred military advisers, would grow into a full-scale American war in South-East Asia.

He now sees the Soviet Union, weakened by enormous internal problems, reduced greatly in stature as compared to the United States. Furthermore, it is the power most directly threatened by the Chinese. In those circumstances he envisages the possibility of Russia, which is not in his view a super power in the American class, facilitating the emergence of a Europe 'from the Atlantic to the Urals'. As de Gaulle himself said many years ago: 'It will not be any European statesman who will unite Europe; Europe will be united by the Chinese.'

We now come to the basic problem of understanding de Gaulle as revealed in his reaction to British attempts to enter the Common Market. It would appear evident that, while Britain retains her close military and economic ties with the United States, and while she, for example, retains US nuclear armed submarines at Holy Loch, Britain is not able to follow a policy of independence of Washington which, for the General, is the basic political commitment.

In those circumstances de Gaulle thinks that Britain inside the Common Market would inevitably strengthen US political influence in Europe. Last year a British Minister told me that Britain's major political interest in joining Europe was to check what the British Government regarded as dangerous third force tendencies. This, of course, is to state for him de Gaulle's argument for keeping Britain out.

Recently, when Lord Chalfont visited Paris, the same basic political difference emerged. Lord Chalfont told the French Foreign Minister, M. Couve de Murville, that Britain's main interest in joining the Market would be to ensure for Europe a stronger voice within the Atlantic Alliance. But there is the rub.

France has already left NATO and will leave the Atlantic Alliance itself before 1969. As M. Couve de Murville pointed out to Lord Chalfont, France is not interested in a Europe which can influence the Atlantic Alliance; it is interested in a Europe which is ready to opt out of it.

Evening Standard
Tuesday, September 19, 1967

HOW THE GENERAL REHEARSED THREE MONTHS FOR THAT FAMOUS PRESS CONFERENCE

Two splendid sporting jousts in Paris this week – the France-All Blacks rugby match and General de Gaulle's Press Conference. Both left me a little lacerated, but the General's boisterous performance had a spine-chilling effect.

This was the de Gaulle his intimates know well but the public rarely sees. Gone were the ambiguities of language and the elaborate courtesies to vanquished foes – this time the language was correct and for once its meaning was unmistakable.

All this was flavoured by a salty humour and tremendous high spirits. The message was that the US was today the most aggressive of the two super powers and France would fight it on all fronts and on all issues – in its backyard through French-Canadian nationalism; in the Middle East by supporting the Arabs; in the Far East by supporting Hanoi; in Europe by blocking British entry; in the economic field by challenging supremacy of the dollar.

These are the objectives – to cut the US down to size while a third force 'from the Atlantic to the Urals' emerges in Europe. Unhappily for the General there is still no sign of such a force emerging.

So far all the indications are that his five Common Market partners will not follow him. Eastern Europe won't follow him and even the Arab world on which oil deals and aeroplane deals have been pressed unavailingly won't follow him. So it's France versus the rest and that, judging by de Gaulle's exuberance at his Press Conference, is the way he likes to play it.

There is probably no other head of state in the world who can allow himself the luxury to think aloud as de Gaulle did at his Press Conference. Some of his needling remarks, as, for example, in relation to Israel, seemed perfectly gratuitous – as though little more than an opportunity for showing off his very profound knowledge of the Old Testament, which is his favourite bedside reading.

No one else enjoys such absolute power. His Ministers had no inkling of what he would say and even on the day of his conference his Press Secretary was deliberately misled as to the subjects he would deal with.

The General prepares his Press conferences with the care and study a historian would apply to a volume. He begins work on each of his bi-annual conferences three months before they are scheduled, drafting them in longhand, endlessly crossing out version after version until he finds the correct one which he then reads out aloud and commits to memory.

It is fascinating when the final product is distilled to watch the sagging faces of Ministers seated on his right as one after the other realises that the glosses he has put on the General's intentions in the past are ripped away like so many gauze bandages by some ruthless and fairly sadistic surgeon.

What makes men like Pompidou, Couve de Murville and Debré take it? Take Couve de Murville, for example, with his famous statement that there is no objection 'in principle' to British entry and his promise to the British Ambassador that whereas negotiations on British entry could not begin before the end of the year a definite decision that they should start would be taken in December.

All three are honourable men, highly able and, for politicians, remarkably disinterested. The answer is faith. They go along because of de Gaulle's personality and the knowledge that he has been proved so often right in the past.

Some day the Emperor will emerge either fully naked or fully clothed. There is no mini-solution.

Evening Standard
Friday, December 1, 1967

4

May 1968

STUDENTS HURT IN NEW CLASH

Three students were injured when violence erupted in Paris again today. It happened as the Latin Quarter — site of Sorbonne University — simmered ready for another clash between students and police. Thousands of police armed with rifles, tear gas and water-hoses took over the Quarter to try to stop a banned demonstration by 160,000 students. The flare-up came when students gathered in groups. Police began throwing tear-gas grenades and charged. A paving-stone was thrown at them.

In another incident, a police first-aid car, carrying a traffic accident victim, was stopped and its windows broken.

But student leaders put back the demonstration until this evening and more violence is expected then.

One of the reasons for the demonstration is to complain at alleged police brutality in Friday's riots, in which 600 students were arrested. The police, too, are likely to be in an ugly mood because one policeman is still in a coma after those riots.

The demonstration — as similar ones throughout the country — was timed for the appearance of student leader 'Danny the Red' Cohn-Bendit, a West German, and four other students before a disciplinary committee of the Sorbonne for their part in Friday's riots.

The five, who arrived singing the 'Internationale', face expulsion.

They left after a few hours, again singing the 'Internationale'.

Tension eased slightly when it was announced that the committee's decision would be announced on Friday.

Two thousand police guarded the Sorbonne and only reporters, residents and students taking examinations were allowed through.

The students are also protesting against last week's closure of Nanterre University, outside Paris, the closing of the Sorbonne, and the fact that its Rector, M. Jean Roche, called in police last Friday to haul out students. They want M. Roche to resign. They are backed by university teachers who are also striking today in sympathy with the students.

Dr Grayson Kirk, president of Columbia University, New York, which has been closed for ten days because of sit-ins and fighting by students demanding more say in university policy, said on TV that he would not resign. 'That would be a victory for those who are out to wreck the University,' he said.

Evening Standard
Monday, May 6, 1968

PARIS MANS THE BARRICADES
15,000 students fight 8000 police

Thousands of Paris students fought a pitched battle with police and riot squads during the night. Fifteen thousand students, crouching behind fifty immense barricades of paving stones and overturned cars, held out for hours against massed charges by 8000 police hurling tear-gas and concussion grenades. As the police riot squads flung themselves at the barricades the screaming students threw Molotov cocktails and bricks.

Police chief Maurice Grimaud said the student revolt – which turned a square mile of the Latin Quarter into a battlefield – was a 'veritable guerilla action'.

He said: 'My men faced bands who can only be described as commando-style street fighters.'

And that was how the police dealt with the situation – smashing into houses to flush roof-top attackers from vantage points and pulling men and women from suspected houses and driving them away in trucks. The battle raged until dawn when a final charge by police, firing gas grenades point-blank into the student ranks, sent them reeling back.

Police said 367 people, including 102 students and 251 police, had been injured and 468 arrested in the eight-hour riot. The battle area was today a shambles of burning cars and broken glass. Fires burned in deserted shops. Radio stations appealed for medical aid. Taxi drivers were asked to help carry away the wounded. Flames threatened buildings and apartment dwellers dumped buckets of water down from balconies in an effort to control the fires.

The trouble began with a peaceful demonstration by students – some reports put the figure at 30,000 – who tried to mass in the Latin Quarter to protest at the continued closure of the Sorbonne.

As the students set out to march to the Latin Quarter and the Sorbonne police turned them off at the Boulevard St Michel without incident. Then a group of demonstrators marched to the Santé Prison demanding the release of students jailed in earlier protests about France's 'outdated' university system.

Quite suddenly the students took over effective control in the Boulevard St Michel between St Germaine and the Place Edmond-Rostand. They set up their own traffic control arrangements, spread into nearby streets, including the Rue Gay-Lassac, and built powerful barricades. A radio station established a link between one of the students' leaders and the Vice-Rector of the Sorbonne University.

The students demanded direct negotiations with Interior Minister Christian Fouchet. But this was turned down and the now angry students assumed complete control of the area, ripping up cobbles, tearing down hoardings, and manning their barricades.

At 2.15 a.m. the police were ordered to clear the streets – and the battle began.

The first police attack was repulsed by the chanting mob.

An eye-witness said: 'It was the ugliest, most frightening demonstration in Paris for many years. If you side with the protestors then you would consider their stand against the para-military CRS an heroic one.'

At one barricade on the west side of the Luxembourg Gardens the students held out for three hours.

It looked and sounded like war as lines of police with grenade launchers fired tear-gas almost point-blank at students who raised their heads above the ramparts. Concussion grenades were also lobbed among students who sang the 'Internationale' as they waited for the charge. A shouted order and the massed blue lines rushed forward to the top of the barricade. A few men who reached the summit were felled by flying paving stones. Twice the blue line struggled forward and twice it was forced to retreat. The third time, after an attack with concussion grenades, the police succeeded. Cries rose in the darkness.

The retreating students set overturned cars afire to impede the attackers' progress and moved, still shouting defiance, to the next strong point. A young man who tried to evade the charge by hiding in a doorway was beaten to the ground with rifle butts before being dragged to an ambulance.

In a dramatic middle-of-the-night meeting, top French Cabinet Ministers responsible for internal order discussed emergency measures to deal with the increasingly alarming demonstrations. The meeting, which broke up at five o'clock this morning, was attended by the Defence Minister, Pierre Messmer, acting Premier Louis Joxe, Interior Minister Christian Fouchet, and Information Minister Georges Gorse.

At 4 a.m. a Government communiqué offered to discuss constructive suggestions from the students. There was no immediate reaction from the students.

For France, host country to the Washington and Hanoi peace delegates, the riot – the most bitter in a week of student fighting – brought acute embarrassment. There is some fear that splinter groups may turn their attention to anti-Vietnam, anti-American protests.

One senior Government official, who declined to be named, said he believed the fighting could be partly blamed on 'forces hostile to the return of peace in the city while North Vietnamese and American negotiators are talking in Paris.

Evening Standard
Saturday, May 11, 1968

THE STUDENTS ROCK DE GAULLE
Shake-up in the Cabinet on the way

It is now plain that the whole future of the de Gaullist régime and, inevitably, of General de Gaulle himself, after the massive show of student power, is under discussion in Paris.

It is a debate which rages just as much in Government circles as it does in the Opposition. The crucial question which is bound to emerge is the inner story of what exactly happened last Friday night – or rather in the early morning of Saturday – when rioting in the Latin Quarter assumed insurrectionary proportions.

The General had gone to bed, and M. Joxe, who was deputising as Prime Minister in the absence in the Middle East of M. Pompidou, did not wake him until 5 a.m.

At that point the Cabinet was split between 'hawks' and 'doves'. Among the 'doves' was M. Joxe himself, M. Debré the Finance Minister, and oddly enough M. Fouchet, Minister of the Interior. The tough ones were the Minister of Education, M. Peyrefitte, and Minister of Information M. Gorse.

What was General de Gaulle's own position? On this there is considerable speculation but it is considered that he was a 'hawk' and went to bed that night giving tough instructions to the Government. If this is the case, and there seems to be overwhelming evidence that it was so, then it was M. Pompidou returning to Paris on Saturday evening who in an hour or so persuaded de Gaulle to change his mind.

This analysis of the situation, if borne out, would of course weaken the General's authority within his own Government.

On the other hand, many others, including members of the Opposition, believe that the General will ride this crisis as easily as he has ridden others.

The curious fact is that all previous instances of twenty-four-hour general strikes and massive demonstrations, which have marked the stormy ten-year history of the de Gaullist Republic, have always shown the General's astonishing political recuperative powers. It may be so this time; but this time the element of doubt goes deeper.

Earlier today it was announced that the General will address the nation later this month. He will clearly deal with the dramatic events in the city over the past ten days.

It is fully expected in Paris that drastic Cabinet changes will be made on his return from his State visit to Romania.

The General arrived in Bucharest this morning.

The changes are likely to involve the men who deputised for M. Pompidou, namely, M. Joxe, M. Peyrefitte and M. Gorse.

This afternoon the Government announced that M. Pompidou, the Prime Minister, will address the National Assembly later today on the student question.

Meanwhile, following yesterday's demonstrations, students who spent the night camped out in the Sorbonne voted to ask the Government for an hour of television time to state their case. Some militants claimed they would sabotage national TV studios unless they were given the time. And student orators warned that they would continue to sabotage university activities and they were determined to force the resignations of M. Fouchet, the Interior Minister, the Paris police chief Maurice Grimond and Sorbonne Rector M. Roche.

Today the doyens of all universities in France have issued an ultimatum to the Minister of Finance, M. Debré.

It is that necessary funds should be unblocked to build new faculties throughout France to reduce the problem of overcrowding by next October . . . otherwise they threaten to resign when the universities reopen after the summer recess.

Most observers agree that the events of the past 10 days have left the Gaullist régime badly shaken and probably irretrievably besmirched. The Government faces a vote of confidence towards the end of the week and it is thought that though it will win it the margin will be the narrowest it has ever had. The majority is likely to be as small as four.

The Opposition political parties have, of course, jumped on the student bandwagon but the student response to Opposition political leaders is as negative, if not as hostile, as it has been to the Gaullists.

All political parties underestimated the student movement, and none more so than the Communists who began by denouncing it.

The clearest expression of opposition attempts to capitalise on the student movement to topple the Gaullist régime was yesterday's General Strike. The three trade union federations are politically motivated and their leadership is in the hands of the Opposition, this being especially the case with the strongest one, which is Communist-led. The unions, however, have neither the funds nor the cohesion to play an important role in the anti-Gaullist movement. This is shown by the relative failure of yesterday's General Strike.

The inquest is now on in Paris as to what went wrong to produce so dangerous a situation out of the incidents which in themselves might have passed almost unnoticed. The answer is that the university authorities, headed by M. Roche, and the Government blundered badly at every turn.

The great lesson for the Government is to learn how to use its authority lightly and not to react to situations in an overdramatic fashion.

The only minister who emerges from this near-tragedy with an enhanced reputation is the Prime Minister, M. Pompidou, who immediately on his return to Paris on Saturday evening took matters effectively in hand.

Another lesson is that the Government, and probably all Western governments, will have to learn more of the new student movements with their Castro-ist, Mao-ist, Trotsky-ist, anarchist overtones . . . and their international affiliations.

Clearly, while making full allowance for police brutality and provocation, many of the student rioters were no angels. Some of them were disturbingly well-versed in street fighting and improvising weapons.

Meanwhile, neither the University, nor the Gaullist régime, will ever be quite the same after this astonishing and frightening week.

Evening Standard
Tuesday, May 14, 1968

THE WEEK THAT SHRANK DE GAULLE

In the weeks preceding the present students' turmoil, General de Gaulle, in the full knowledge that his remark would be repeated, took a certain malicious pleasure in telling occasional callers that he might have to stand for a third term as President of the Republic.

The next Presidential elections are in 1972 and, by that time, the General would be eighty-two. No one quite knew at that time whether his speculation on this point was to be taken seriously. Probably he was only teasing his many ambitious would-be successors.

Now, after the events of the past week, it would be difficult for him to make such a remark without evoking laughter rather than dismay.

This is a measure of the change that has come over the French political scene as a result of the students' revolt. Until a little less than two weeks ago the setting could not have been more serene for the tenth anniversary of the General's return to power. The ship of state was sailing along perfectly, wafted by an extra breeze of triumph owing to the selection of Paris as the site of the Vietnam peace talks.

Then, suddenly, it struck the reefs of student rebellion. The captain's orders were at best confusing, at worst wrong-headed. The crew itself was divided as to how they should be carried out – or even if they should be carried out at all. And the ship almost went aground. It was saved when the second-in-command in the person of the Prime Minister, M. Pompidou, returned from Afghanistan and, with a ringing 'I have decided,' took the right action – late, but not too late.

As a result, something of immense importance has happened, the consequences of which will become more and more apparent with the months and years to come. What has happened is that the direct power of the General, enshrined in the mystique of solitary decisions, solitarily arrived at, has become limited. This is not the first time that M. Pompidou has stood up to the General, but it is the first time that the disavowal of policies ordered by him has come in so striking, almost public, a fashion.

It happened once before, in 1962, when the General – furious that General Salan, who led the Algerian revolt against de Gaulle, was not sentenced to death – insisted that an earlier death sentence passed on another general, Jouhaud, should be carried out. At that time Pompidou threatened to resign – and saved Jouhaud's life.

Now, with recent events, not only has power in the French Government been kept still more in favour of M. Pompidou, but something like a real balance of power between Prime Minister and President has emerged.

It will no longer be possible, for example, in the Prime Minister's absence from Paris, for him to be replaced by almost anybody – in this case by the Minister of Justice M. Joxe, an amiable but weak man. A genuine Deputy Prime Minister will have to be appointed – probably the Finance Minister M. Debré.

To conclude: recent events cannot mean the end of de Gaulle, or even Gaullism. What it amounts to really is that a monarchy is imperceptibly giving way to a regency. The students' insurrection has revealed a manifold hypocrisy in French society.

Parents, for example, the great majority of whom are the new rich, who would never have blinked an eyelid at police brutality if it had been turned on miners, for example, react differently when the batons fall on the skulls of their sons.

Professors who have successfully blocked any move to reform French universities over the years now find themselves suddenly at one with the students. French university professors guard their privileges and their chairs as jealously as feudal chieftains guard their fiefs. Nor do they over-strain themselves in their work. Over half the professors at Lille University, for example, live in Paris and commute to Lille only to deliver their lectures and return home the same day.

It is now in danger of being forgotten, but it should be recalled, that the initial measures taken against students were by the university authorities themselves. This is no reproach, because the trouble started at the satellite University of Nanterre, where the students' rabble-rouser, Daniel Cohn-Bendit, is in his third year as a student of sociology and the situation was getting completely out of hand. There were daily riots and life at the University was totally disrupted. It was in the face of this situation that the university authorities decided to close Nanterre. This led directly to the problems of Paris when Cohn-Bendit brought his followers into the courtyard of the Paris University. They were armed and those who were not armed quickly started to improvise arms by breaking up furniture.

It was in that situation, and faced with the certainty of a clash between Cohn-Bendit's mob and the students belonging to the extreme Right organisation, Occident, that the rector of the Sorbonne decided to call in the police.

It now demands a considerable amount of courage on the part of a professor not to be starry-eyed about the student movement.

Fortunately there are some exceptions, like for example Raymond Aron and Professor Savard of Lille University.

Professor Savard, after pointing out that university education in France is free, reminds the students that even the poorest among them should consider himself as privileged as against the mass of wage-earners whose taxes pay for their education.

Professor Aron insists that the only real solution to the student problem in Paris is to end the system of unrestricted entry to the universities. He points out that successive governments have for political reasons refused to restrict entry while at the same time refusing to allocate the necessary funds to deal with a student population explosion.

These however are for the time being voices in the wilderness. The cult of the young is now the most fashionable political doctrine in Paris, and personally I find it somewhat sickening.

Evening Standard
Friday, May 17, 1968

FRANCE RIVEN BY LE 'SIT-IN'

The great French sit-in strike wave, following that of the sit-in strike of the students, continues to spread almost hourly. It now involves nearly two hundred thousand workers and has spread from the Renault works on the Paris outskirts to Bordeaux, Bayonne, Orleans, Lyons, Nantes, Le Havre and Rouen. Virtually the whole of the industrial regions of Normandy are now in the grip of strikes. In all cases the strike initiatives came from young workers, fired by the example of the students.

Their reaction seems to be that if the students can win concessions by violence, so can the working class. In all cases too, the action was spontaneous, without reference to union headquarters, and in all cases union leaders sanctioned the strikes after they had broken out.

Meanwhile a split has developed between the two major French trade union federations – the Communist-led CGT and the CFDT – regarding the attitude to be adopted towards the student movement.

The CGT and the Communist Party are flatly opposed to any link between the strike movement and the ultra-Left leaders of the student movement.

Today the CGT warned students who proposed to march in sympathy with the strikers to the Renault works at Boulogne-Billancourt near Paris that it would not tolerate any external intrusion into their affairs.

At the same time the French Communist Party has launched a violent attack on the student leaders, especially Daniel Cohn-Bendit, and warns the working class movement against being led into 'adventurism'.

The students are meeting in the Left Bank Quarter today to decide whether they should go ahead with their proposed march.

There are stirrings of possible strike movements in the railways, in public transport in Paris, in the newspaper industry, and even in French television.

The Elysée denied for the second time today that General de Gaulle would cut short his State visit to Bukarest to return to Paris.

What strikes most observers in Paris today is that the Governement seems to be acting in a void which comes from long years of over-confidence and detachment from currents of opinion and of grievances and is unable to plan any coherent action.

In this connection the Premier, M. Pompidou, whose concessions to students were applauded at the time, is being criticised on the Right for having made them in the face of rioting.

The Government has mobilised 10,000 reservists of the National Gendarmerie and at the same time security forces are being moved into Paris from as far away as Toulouse.

This morning M. Pompidou met the Minister of the Interior, M. Fouchet, the Minister of Defence, M. Messmer, and the heads of the Sûreté, the Prefecture of Police and the National Gendarmerie. The presence of M. Messmer underlines continuing reports that the Government is preparing to bring troops into the city.

The morale of the major security force, the Compagnies Républicains de Sécurité, is known to have been shaken by the events of the past week and the seeming disavowal by M. Pompidou, in a broadcast last Saturday, of its methods in its clashes with students in the Latin Quarter.

A spokesman for the trade unions representing the CRS said they have had difficulty in preventing their men from going on strike.

The major centre of industrial trouble remains the Renault nationalised car factories. This is particularly disturbing because the Renault workers are highly unionised and disciplined and the works have long enjoyed an excellent record of labour relations. So much so that Renault workers were the first in France to get four weeks' paid holiday a year. Now the red flag flies over its major assembly plant at Flins, some thirty miles west of Paris.

There are 9,000 workers occupying the plant and they have decided at a mass meeting on a strike of unlimited duration. Another 3,000 workers are holding the Renault plant at Le Mans and another 5,000 the one at Cleon, near Rouen, where the director of the plant is being kept prisoner in his office.

One encouraging sign for the Government is a perceptible swing in public opinion against the students. The newspaper *France-Soir*, which a week ago published a public opinion poll indicating overwhelming public support for the students, today prints a second poll showing that 31 per cent are for the students and 44 per cent against.

On the student front, the students themselves and their families are faced with the agonising problem of what will happen to this year's exams. If they are postponed or cancelled owing to student boycott, then it will mean a loss of a year's study, which will hit particularly hard the sons and daughters of lower middle-class and working-class families.

As the situation worsens, the Conservative elements in this largely property-owning nation are beginning to clamour for firm Government action.

The Government itself, which faces a confidence motion early next week, is likely to survive, but the events of today and of the weekend may influence the outcome. Should the Government be defeated by a confidence motion, it would have to resign and order new elections.

Evening Standard
Friday, May 17, 1968

FRANCE HALTS AS TRAINS STOP
De Gaulle hurries home — the strikes avalanche

The French strike movement was today increasingly assuming the avalanche character of a nationwide general stoppage of unlimited duration.

President de Gaulle will return to Paris tonight from his State visit to Rumania, twenty-four hours ahead of schedule, and will probably broadcast to the nation tomorrow night.

The nationwide rail strike is now almost total and stations across the country are full with stranded travellers whose trains have come to an abrupt halt.

The strike movement has now been joined by miners in the North and the Pas-de-Calais, and postal workers also came out this morning.

Many housewives in Paris are beginning to hoard basic necessities.

President de Gaulle decided to return to Paris after a long telephone conversation with M. Pompidou, the Prime Minister, late last night.

The General will arrive tonight at an Orly Airport completely paralysed by the strike, with hundreds of airport workers occupying several buildings.

Not a train was moving in and out of Paris by mid-day, although trains from the Gare de l'Est, serving Eastern France and Switzerland, had been normal for long runs, and suburban service was forty per cent this morning. The same story of complete stoppage came from Toulouse, Marseilles, Le Havre, Rouen, Limoges, Rennes, Bordeaux, Lille, Valence and Avignon. Many long-distance trains stopped during the night, some being halted by strikers before reaching their final destinations.

At Valence, in the south, workers occupied a rail depot and stopped all the trains, including the Geneva-Barcelona trans-European express. In nearby Avignon the station was also occupied by railwaymen who stopped trains and made passengers disembark.

The Government hastily put a fleet of army lorries into action between the capital and the main suburbs.

In Paris, underground trains were running but bus traffic was reduced after strikers occupied two terminal garages.

Hardly an hour went by without word of a new factory being occupied by striking workers. The number now holding their factories and plants is in the hundreds of thousands.

The big nationalised Renault automobile works, with 60,000 workers, was completely shut down and its six plants occupied.

Traffic at Orly Airport continued in disruption with many Air France flights cancelled. Control-tower operators on strike were joined by other workers who blocked entrances with trucks, as well as by hostesses and check-in clerks.

Employees at the national radio and television networks voted to go on strike, but did not set a date or fix other details.

Mail sorters stopped work in all Paris centres and distribution was expected to be affected throughout the country.

M. Pompidou had an urgent meeting this morning with Ministers of the Interior, Defence and Transport, along with top police officials.

The Government now faces little choice but to reach an across-the-board wage agreement with the trade unions involving a sizeable pay rise in the nationalised industries.

This will have serious economic repercussions and weaken still further the competitive capabilities of French industry in the Common Market and especially in the tariff-less set-up which should come into effect in June.

The student movement, it is now apparent, is collapsing and the French Communist Party and its trade union federation, the CGT, is for reasons of its own trying to contain the strike movement.

The student revolt is folding up because the overwhelming majority of students are by now refusing to follow the extremist leaders. The result is a steady decrease in the number of demonstrators and a thinning out of the ranks of those occupying the Paris University and the Odeon Theatre.

First indications of the student collapse became clear yesterday evening when their leaders indicated there would be no organised march to the striking workers at the Renault factory just outside Paris.

The students and parents — especially parents — are tiring of the seeming farce of the protest of the 'cultural revolution' launched by the Left wing, and both are becoming more and more concerned with the tough questions of the coming exams.

The calculation of the Premier, M. Pompidou, that the movement would run out of steam, is proving correct and now only some unforeseen action could revive its flagging energies.

On the strike front the motives for the evident Communist desire to check wildcat strikes will be long discussed. To some it will appear as an indication that Moscow does not wish to embarrass de Gaulle. To others a much more likely explanation suggests itself. It is that the French Communist Party is inherently suspicious of any movement which it does not itself directly inspire and control. It has become strikingly plain during the past twenty-four hours that the Communists, through their trade union agency, have checked, and are still checking, many strike movements.

The sit-in strikers now involve more than two hundred thousand workers. Managers have been forcibly kept on the premises and many workers themselves are being held against their will. One manager suffering from a serious kidney complaint was kept confined for half-an-hour before strikers allowed an ambulance to take him away.

The usual order is that no one is allowed out who is not either ill or over sixty. It is a situation which will lose its appeal to many strikers — to say nothing of their wives — as the weekend slips away.

Evening Standard
Saturday, May 18, 1968

FRENCH BANKS SHUT UP SHOP
One in three Frenchmen is now on strike

PARIS, Monday. French banks today suspended all their services, including exchange dealings, as employees joined the nationwide strike, banking sources reported. There will be no foreign exchange quotations today.

Paris today presents a scene of appalling chaos, disintegration, and almost of an approaching siege. The streets reek of uncollected garbage as though matching the stench of a decaying régime.

It took four hours of queueing to cash a cheque at one of the few banks which was still open; every street and boulevard is a snake pit of traffic jams; there is a rush to hoard essential foodstuffs; money is running out in a lot of households; and in two or three days time, if this goes on, the Government may have to put rationed Government stocks of food on the market.

Meanwhile, thousands of tons of food are rotting in rail sidings, and cattle are baying their heads off in abandoned trains.

One of the most appalling features at the moment is the lack of any sign that the Government exists. It is almost as though it has abdicated.

There are signs that newspapers may cease publication at any moment. Those which appeared today despite vigorous statements that they would not be censored 'by anyone' bore the imprint of censorship by their own printers.

Meanwhile, rioting has again broken out in the Sorbonne University — the start of all the trouble. Violent fighting broke out between students of the extreme Right and of the Left with the Right-wing students succeeding in expelling the Left-wing ones who were in possession of the Institute of Political Science.

Some reports said that between five and six thousand workers, about a third of the total labour force, were on strike. About two hundred and fifty factories have been seized and more are being taken over every hour.

Banks reported long queues, sometimes of more than three hundred people, from as early as 7.30 a.m. in front of Paris branches. Customers, they said, were withdrawing large amounts in anticipation of a possible long-term closure of the banks if cashiers went on strike. One British bank reported that some foreigners were asking for such large sums that a limit, which the bank declined to disclose, had to be imposed. The American First National City Bank on the Champs Elysées was forced to close its doors temporarily because of a shortage of cash. The Royal

Bank of Canada also closed after running out of money despite a 200-dollar limit on cheques.

Faced with such an upheaval, Frenchmen turn to their traditional haven in times of trouble — gold. Demand for the metal was heavy and the price forced up to a near-record price.

On the Paris Bourse there was some attempt to carry out business in the morning on half-staff. But there was limited business and dealers were mainly concerned with squaring up their clients' positions. But this afternoon it proved impossible to carry on, and the Bourse closed down.

Three out of four petrol stations in the Paris area are running out of supplies as motorists stock up in fear of a shortage. Workers are on strike in some of the oil refineries and a strike of petrol pump attendants is threatened.

Telegraph communications are precarious. Although essential links are still working, there is a danger that if anything goes wrong there would be no repairs. This would mean, for example, that the North Vietnamese peace talks delegation would be unable to contact Hanoi.

News was still being broadcast on the ORTF — the State-controlled radio and television network — but journalists have said they are not prepared to accept Government or police interference. All other staff on the radio service have stopped work, said a spokesman this afternoon, and apart from news there is nothing but music on the radio.

It is probable that television employees will also vote for a strike later today, and if this takes place viewers will only get a thirty-minute news programme and a feature film tonight.

Meanwhile, news of fresh strikes was reaching the capital every five minutes.

Miners in the North of France joined the wave of unrest and the country's two largest ports, Marseilles and Le Havre, closed when dock and shipworkers downed tools.

The airports of Orly and Le Bourget were paralysed. International airlines were trying to arrange coaches. Train services were also completely frozen.

Army lorries have been brought into the capital to take some of the load from taxi drivers, but it is understood that the taxi drivers themselves may take the decision to strike by tomorrow.

Most shops and offices opened as usual, but women, learning of possible shortages, queued outside food shops. Supermarkets' shelves were swept clean of sugar and canned goods by housewives who swarmed through them 'like locusts'.

Electricty plants had been occupied by workers but the power had not yet been cut. Workers have said they will provide supplies as long as there is no repression of the strike movement.

Workers opened the barricades at the huge Renault motor plant in the Paris suburbs of Boulogne-Billancourt this morning for M. Georges Seguy, leader of France's largest union, the Left-wing backed General Confederation of Labour (CGT).

M. Seguy appealed for calm. He told workers inside the factory that they should be careful. 'Any slogan calling for insurrection would change the character of your strike,' he said.

His restraining hand reflects the desire of the Communist Party to keep the situation from boiling over. It was for this reason, and because of the anxiety of Communists not to be overtaken by radical splinter groups, that the unions and students virtually parted company.

The car industry was completely idle after workers at Peugeot and Citroën plants joined their Renault counterparts in declaring 'unlimited strikes with occupation of the premises'.

Evening Standard
Monday, May 20, 1968

DE GAULLE COMES UP WITH A PLAN

General de Gaulle is planning a referendum next June on a detailed proposition that will ensure profit-sharing and co-proprietorship of French industry in the near future. On paper it looks like nothing less than the transformation of French capitalist society as we know it. Both ideas have long been cherished by de Gaulle. In fact, three months ago the first steps were taken to ensure profit-sharing in French industry.

Co-proprietorship has also been an old Gaullist idea, but now both an extension of profit-sharing and the introduction of co-proprietorship are to be, according to the General, swiftly executed and far-reaching.

These proposed reforms will be the main theme of his broadcast to the nation next Friday. Both ideas are abhorrent to the French Communist Party. In fact, the Communist Trade Union Federation has today denounced co-proprietorship as 'an empty formula'.

On these proposed reforms now hangs the life of the popular Government which faces a crucial vote of confidence tomorrow. If it falls there will be General Elections which will render the referendum pointless. But the battle cry of the Gaullists, whether it's a General Election or a referendum, will remain: 'Profit-sharing and co-proprietorship.'

The visit to Russia in 1966. De Gaulle inspecting a guard of honour in Moscow.

Soviet Premier Alexei Kosygin with de Gaulle.

The French Cabinet just after the General Election in 1967 listening to de Gaulle during a Press Conference. (First row left, from back to front) Maurice Couve de Murville, Maurice Schumann, Edmond Michelet, André Malraux. (Second row from back to front) Alain Peyrefitte, Christian Fouchet, Roger Frey, Edgar Faure, Prime Minister Georges Pompidou and among the last row, Louis Joxe and Michel Debré (partly hidden).

Pompidou, de Gaulle and Maurice Couve de Murville during the Common Market Summit of 1967 where Ministers failed to agree on Britain's entry into the European Community.

24 May 1968 – Boulevard Saint-Michel – police charge demonstrators.

24 May 1968 – Boulevard Saint-Michel – removing injured demonstrators.

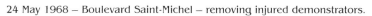

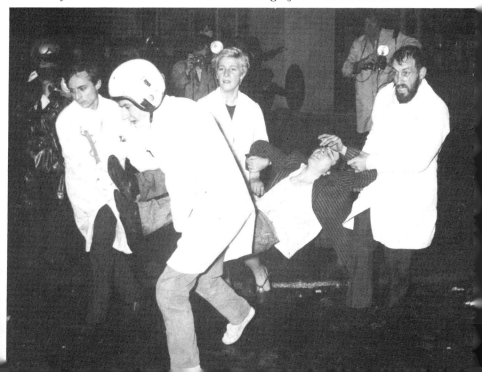

13 May 1968 — A huge demonstration involving students, teachers, and workers between the Place de la République and the Place Denfert-Rochereau.

Another street clash between demonstrators and police during the May 1968 riots.

Georges Pompidou with de Gaulle just before he was dismissed as Prime Minister in July 1968.

De Gaulle in Brittany early in 1968 where he announced the Referendum on regionalization that was to lead to his resignation.

The General is buried in the village churchyard at Colombey-les-deux-Eglises on 12 November 1970.

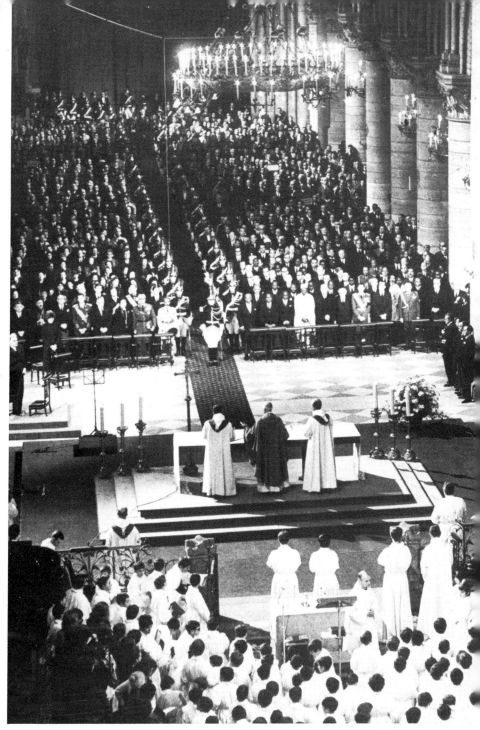

Meanwhile in Paris a memorial mass was held at Notre Dame cathedral with over one hundred Heads of State in attendance.

If the Government survives, its composition will be radically changed within a week. The posts which will change hands will be those of the Ministries of Justice, Social Affairs, Education, Youth and Information.

From this it becomes clear after days of suspense what the form and content of General de Gaulle's counter-attack on his Left-wing assailants will be. The fact that this news has been made public over the heads of the Deputies will not endear the régime or the Government to them.

The betting, which was five to three this morning, on the Government surviving, has now shortened to even odds. This is because clearly Centre-party Deputies on whose support the Government depends were prepared to compromise if they could exact a price. The price was to be a clipping of presidential powers. In fact it renders a prophecy on the outcome of the Left-wing motion of confidence in the Government more hazardous than ever.

Meanwhile among observers – even those not ill disposed towards General de Gaulle – the feeling is growing that only General Elections can provide a satisfactory issue to the struggle.

Evening Standard
Tuesday, May 21, 1968

FRENCH CABINET FACE THE AXE

The French Cabinet met for a record four hours today and its outcome will be a vast Cabinet reshuffle. Many of the present Ministers will lose their posts. All Cabinet Ministers handed in their resignations to Prime Minister Georges Pompidou this morning.

Information Minister Georges Gorse said after the meeting at the Elysée Palace that the Cabinet would meet again on Monday.

'Since the General is due to express himself to the people tomorrow night, you will understand that I cannot answer any questions,' he told a large crowd of waiting reporters and cameramen.

All that emerged from the Cabinet Meeting was a brief communiqué stating that General de Gaulle had asked each of his Ministers to give their views on the situation and that the Foreign Minister, Monsieur Couve de Murville, had reported on the international situation and especially on the President's State visit to Romania last week.

There are now prospects that negotiations between the unions and the Government to end the crippling General Strike will begin this weekend.

A major difficulty is that the Communist-led trade union federation is making pre-conditions for the opening of talks. One of the conditions is that the laws introduced earlier this year reducing the scale of social insurance health payments should be aggregated. This poses a major difficulty for M. Pompidou, who claims that this is a matter for Parliament and not one that can be negotiated in direct talks between the Government and the unions.

Apart from what General de Gaulle may say in his broadcast to the nation tomorrow evening, the other mystery concerns the real intentions of the French Communist Party and its trade union industrial arm.

Observers believe that the Communists do not want the negotiations with the present Government to succeed and that their real aim at this juncture is to overthrow the Government and the régime.

Many Ministers made frantic appeals to General de Gaulle to broadcast to the nation tonight instead of tomorrow night. The appeal fell on deaf ears.

More than ever, everything now depends on what de Gaulle says. He is behaving almost as though he is waiting for General de Gaulle to save President de Gaulle in the nick of time.

What with the students and the sinister re-appearance in the streets of Paris of gangs of extreme-Right youths looking for trouble, there is every danger that a spark may ignite dangerous street-fighting.

In the provinces there are signs of a beginning of a return to work as workers negotiating directly with managements have in some cases decided to return to work.

Even should negotiations open with the unions this weekend, a general return to work cannot be expected before the middle of next week.

Evening Standard
Thursday, May 23, 1968

PARIS — THE POWDER KEG!
Talks, but strikes go on

Paris is today a powder-keg requiring only a spark to set off an explosion. And this might come tonight as a demonstration by an expected two hundred thousand people reaches its climax just as General de Gaulle is about to make his tensely-awaited speech to the nation.

The Prime Minister, M. Pompidou, announced today that he had invited trade union leaders and members of the employers' federation to meet with him tomorrow afternoon to open negotiations for a settlement of the crippling General Strike.

The invitation was immediately accepted by the employers and by union leaders, including the head of the Communist union federation, M. Georges Seguy. M. Seguy, however, deplored that negotiations had not opened earlier and in any case the opening of negotiations would not signal a return to work. At the same time M. Seguy rejected a plea by the Paris Prefect of Police, M. Grimaud, to cancel tonight's demonstration because of the 'explosive' situation.

The Prime Minister today said he was convinced that Chinese Communist agents in France were active among the students and the younger factory workers. He thought the Government, in dealing with street rioters, was meeting highly trained professionals who knew what they were about.

Strikers and students will be marching from seven different points in the city.

The Communist trade union demonstration will be from the Bastille into the heart of the West End within half a mile of the Elysée Palace.

A warning came from the Ministry of the Interior, where the Minister, M. Fouchet, said it was known that extremist elements would join the demonstrations today and some of these would be armed. They might use these arms to provoke clashes between demonstrators and the security forces.

M. Fouchet was referring to anarchist and neo-Fascist elements belonging to the organisation Occident who have been prominent *agents-provocateurs* in the rioting last night and the night before in the Latin Quarter.

General de Gaulle recorded his, for many observers, long-overdue speech to the nation this morning. The recording lasted only seven minutes which indicates that the speech will be a remarkably, even astonishingly, brief one.

This suggests that de Gaulle will give the nation a familiar 'me or chaos' choice in inviting it to vote on June 16 in a referendum on his proposals for social and economic reforms.

The brevity of the speech suggests also that he may take executive powers under Article 16 of the Constitution pending the outcome of the referendum.

In his broadcast General de Gaulle will outline a plan for vast social changes, including profit-sharing and co-proprietorship. It will be the most important speech the General will have made since his famous war-time appeal from London urging Frenchmen to join him and carry on the War. But many commentators fear that General de Gaulle's broadcast, through being so long delayed, will be something of an anti-climax no matter what its contents.

Should grave incidents occur during the demonstrations it is conceivable that the unions will order a cut in electricity which would effectively prevent the General's broadcast being heard.

The Government, which is being severely criticised for banning student agitator Daniel Cohn-Bendit from re-entry into France and thereby rekindling student riots in the Latin Quarter, revealed today its basic reason for this decision. Ministry of Interior officials said they took this action because they considered there was a serious danger of Cohn-Bendit being assassinated by members of an extreme Right-wing students' organisation. In that case, these officials pointed out, the blame for the assassination would have been laid at the Government's feet.

Meanwhile, it is clear that the Communist trade union federation, the CGT, is having trouble with its own Left-wing. M. Andre Barjonet, one of the CGT leaders and a member of the French Communist Party, has resigned from the CGT because he considers that it is not taking full advantage of the situation to overthrow the Gaullist régime.

It became known in Paris today that the Government has already established secret contacts with the CGT. It is conceivable in those circumstances that these initial contacts may evolve into direct negotiations with the Communist Party itself.

There are two powers confronting each other, one real, the other fictitious, in France today. The real power is with the Communist Party and the trade union arm. The other, the fictitious one, is with President de Gaulle and the Government of M. Pompidou. It is by the gracious permission of the real power that General de Gaulle will be able to broadcast to the nation at all tonight.

The Communist decision to demonstrate today is seen by many as a measure designed to maintain morale on the industrial front where it is thought many workers are showing an impatience to return to work. Peasants staged nation-wide demonstrations, too, throughout France today. They say the Common Market's farm policy is forcing them out of business.

There are no newspapers in Paris today and shortages are developing everywhere. Cigarettes are running out.

Rats now maraud the streets openly; prices of foodstuffs are rocketing; and with 8,000,000 strikers the country is now almost totally paralysed except for road transport and gas, electricity and water, which the unions have agreed to maintain.

The economic outlook for France when the strikes are over is grim indeed. Economic experts predict that unemployment will grow from four hundred thousand, at which it stood before the General Strike, to close on a million.

Evening Standard
Friday, May 24, 1968

AFTER A NIGHT OF ASTONISHING FEROCITY . . .
De Gaulle's exit sign

The disintegration of France continues and is now on a nationwide scale.

Last night's riots spread right across Paris and were not restricted to the Latin Quarter. And the rioting in provincial cities like Lyons and Nantes was of astonishing ferocity.

The big question now is not what the result of the June referendum will be, but whether it will be held at all. In short, de Gaulle may be forced to quit power before the date set for the referendum.

Last night saw the first death in the Paris clashes. The victim: a demonstrator who was knifed.

This morning saw the first signs of the exodus. It was reported that there were huge traffic jams on the Swiss border as wealthy Frenchmen and their families were trying to escape from France.

General de Gaulle's agonisingly awaited speech to the nation last night was the anti-climax of all time. Why he waited a week before making it is now clear. The reason was that he wanted to make a tough speech and was restrained by members of his Government, especially by M. Pompidou, the Prime Minister.

The result was that the terms of the speech were haggled over between de Gaulle and Pompidou for the entire week and this anodyne product was the result. This would explain de Gaulle's evident lack of conviction or force in making it.

The social reform proposals which will be submitted to the nation in the referendum will be discussed by the Cabinet on Monday.

It is, of course, clear – and the General underlined it in saying he would quit if he did not win the referendum – that this, the fifth referendum since de Gaulle came to power, is more starkly a plebiscite than any previous one.

It is now felt among members of the Government that General de Gaulle has made three near fatal mistakes. The first was his decision to go ahead with his State visit to Romania. The second was not to have returned earlier. And the third was not to have gone on the air immediately on his return.

The negotiations that open today between Prime Minister Pompidou and the trade unions will be delicate but from the Government's point of view they must be brief. Time is running out and only by granting most, if not all, of the trade union demands can an early return to work be secured.

The unions want a higher minimum wage, shorter hours and more union freedom in the factories. The French Federation of Industries will be represented at the talks. Its representatives view with dismay the union claims. There is not a friendly voice in the French Press today regarding General de Gaulle's television broadcast to the nation last night.

The Left damns the speech and the Centre and Right newspapers claim that if the General is going to introduce worker participation in the running of industries then he should also broaden the base of his Government.

General de Gaulle's plans for profit-sharing and worker participation will be formulated in the form of a law which will be submitted to the June 16 referendum. But, in the light of recent events, even if the referendum is held, it is unlikely that the General will get anything like the big YES that he asked for.

In the present situation more and more observers believe that the only solution lies in new elections. In preparation for these, workers will return to work and the country's energies would be diverted to the electoral struggle.

It is an astonishing stiuation. Ten years almost to the day after General de Gaulle's return to power he finds himself in exactly the same situation, facing strikers and the trade unions, as the last government of the Fourth Republic found itself facing in the military revolt in Algeria. At that time the Government was helpless, commanding no loyalty anywhere. It was a struggle between the then Prime Minister, M. Pflimlin, and an all-powerful de Gaulle.

Today de Gaulle is in the position of the unfortunate M. Pflimlin and the all-powerful leader of the French Communist Party, M. Waldeck Rochet, is in the position of the de Gaulle of ten years ago.

Evening Standard
Saturday, May 25, 1968

THE GENERAL DECIDES TO QUIT

It can be reliably stated that whatever the outcome of the forthcoming referendum in France, General de Gaulle has decided to quit as President of the Republic before the end of this year.

He had come to this decision before his television broadcast to the nation last Friday. It is this fact which explains his lack-lustre performance and his almost resigned and uncompetitive manner.

The referendum on the Government's proposals for co-partnership between capital and labour in industry is likely to be held in three weeks' time. A Cabinet Meeting was held today to formulate these proposals.

Whatever settlement intervenes in the meantime between the Government and the trade unions the referendum, it is generally thought, will take place in circumstances highly unfavourable to the Government.

I understand that the referendum will be followed in three or four months' time by a General Election. The referendum itself may not even be held. If, for example, the opposition parties and especially the Left opposition, which have all dubbed the referendum a plebiscite, decide to boycott it, then the whole project could go up in smoke.

Holding a referendum depends on the co-operation of the mayors of cities and villages throughout France. If a sizeable proportion of these mayors – and many of them are opposed to the régime – refuse to co-operate then a dramatic situation will arise and the Government may be forced to drop the whole idea and hold general elections instead.

M. Pompidou, Prime Minister, who saw Centre Party leaders yesterday, was told by them firmly that they regarded the referendum idea as irrelevant and time-wasting. A pace-setter for the idea that the referendum should be boycotted is the former Prime Minister, M. Pierre Mendès-France.

I understand that the Finance Minister, M. Michel Debré, whose whole financial policy has come crashing around his ears, is also on the point of resigning.

This evening the Latin Quarter will be at flash-point again when a students' demonstration is scheduled.

Evening Standard
Monday, May 27, 1968

WANTED — TEN NEW MEN AT THE TOP IN FRANCE

M. François Mitterrand, leader of the Left-wing Socialist Federation and candidate of all the Left-wing parties, including the Communists, at the last Presidential elections, called today for the formation of a provisional government in France to take the place of the present régime.

M. Mitterrand began his statement at a Press conference with the words: 'Since May 3, 1968, the State has ceased to exist in France'. He urged all Republicans to say No to President de Gaulle's referendum and proposed that the provisional transition government should be composed of ten men, chosen without reference to parties or party claims. Its main task would be to organise elections for a new President of the Republic in July, after which the present Parliament would be dissolved and new parliamentary elections held in October.

M. Mitterrand said that, if necessary, he would assume the responsibility for forming such a government, but it could well be someone else — and he mentioned the name of M. Mendès-France. In any case, M. Mitterrand added, he himself would be a candidate for the presidency.

M. Mitterrand's proposals were clearly aimed at checking the growing power of the Communist Party in relation to other Left-wing parties. This is the meaning of his suggestion that the ten-man provisional government should be constituted without references to party claims or party strength. As such, it will infuriate the Communists who are more and more insistent that they should play the predominant role in any Left-wing post-de Gaulle government.

The mention of M. Mendès-France as a possible head will further arouse their suspicions that a plot is afoot to cheat them of power.

M. Mitterrand will meet Communist leaders this evening. The Communists, for the past two days, have been getting more and more angry at the delay by the Federation in answering their repeated requests for a joint programme 'of policy and of action'. They are anxious to secure an agreement as quickly as possible that will bind their non-Communist allies more firmly to them.

There is now, it is clear, a growing fear among Socialist leaders, like M. Guy Mollet and the Mayor of Marseilles, M. Gaston Deferre, that the Communists are planning to take over both the key posts and the leadership of any Left-wing government emerging after new elections in France. It is this growing fear which M. Mitterrand's statement today clearly reflected. In fact, the atmosphere in Paris is one of fear all around. The Communists fear being outflanked both in the factories and in the universities by the new revolutionary Left. The Socialists fear the Communists and the centre parties are, of course, terrified of them. The Government itself now almost fears its own shadow and is especially fearful of morale in police and security forces.

All the parties fear the revolutionary youth movement which they cannot control and which is more and more emerging as a new political force of incalculable consequence. France still remains in a darkened tunnel without even a glimmer of light in sight.

Evening Standard
Tuesday, May 28, 1968

DE GAULLE 'OUT IN TWENTY-FOUR HOURS'
He goes alone into the country

It is now generally assumed among members of the French Government that General de Gaulle will announce his resignation as President tomorrow.

The General left Paris suddenly this morning, cancelling a scheduled Cabinet meeting at the last moment, for his country home of Colombey-les-deux-Eglises, 160 miles east of Paris.

There is only one qualification regarding the meaning of de Gaulle's decision to return to Colombey, and that is that it may be intended to scare the nation into realising the consequences if he quit power. Unfortunately, in the present circumstances the effect is more likely to be that of relief rather than fright.

Cabinet member Roger Frey said: 'General de Gaulle's decision to go back to Colombey indicates that he is about to make a grave decision.'

Meanwhile, all the nine members of the Constitutional Council were alerted today to be ready to meet urgently – at any moment. One of the tasks of the Constitutional Council is to accept the resignation of the President of the Republic.

General de Gaulle, in fact, decided to resign yesterday. He was persuaded to take this decision by the Prime Minister.

Pressure is now building in all sections of French opinion and Parliament itself for an early General Election. It is generally assumed that the proposed referendum will not be held and that a General Election should be held in its stead.

As a result it is expected that Giscard d'Estaing, who leads an independent group within the Government majority, may announce today that he will withdraw his support from the Government. In that case the Government must fall.

The final blow to de Gaulle, it is believed in Paris, was the decision of the Constitutional Council that the terms of the proposed referendum were unconstitutional. This robbed the General of his favourite and only remaining weapon – a virtual plebiscite – leaving him with no choice but to retire.

It was learned today that M. Mitterrand, leader of the Left-wing federation, and Pierre Mendès-France will meet to discuss the situation that might be created by General de Gaulle's resignation.

The Communists, by far the strongest element on the Left, are viewing with increasing suspicion the manoeuvres of Mitterrand and Mendès-France which they regard as an attempt to cheat them of power in the post-de Gaulle government.

This is the meaning of a powerful demonstration by the Communist-led Trade Union Federation taking place in Paris this afternoon. It is a show of Communist strength which the non-Communist trade union federations have refused to join.

In all the chaos and the congestion and virtual abdication of the Government there emerges the Herculean figure of Premier Pompidou. He is not only Prime Minister but virtually the only voice of government and legal authority left in the country. Many political observers believe that the General is now completely alone except for a few old stalwarts.

Even among Gaullist Deputies there is mounting criticism of him and increasing talk that he should resign. All the constitutional weapons which he himself forged to protect his régime in just such a crisis are now so many pieces of paper.

Even the weapon of a referendum is useless. The referendum cannot be held while the country is in the grip of a General Strike which shows no signs of ending, and which will require the printing of the ballot papers outside France.

It is now clear beyond any doubt that the strikes have assumed an exclusively political character aimed at overthrowing the régime. In no circumstances will even the most generous offers be accepted by the unions or the strikers.

It is significant in this connection that miners in the north of France in a secret ballot voted overwhelmingly to continue the strike. The negotiations themselves, far from continuing, are petering out.

The situation today can be summed up in a few words: *It is a revolutionary situation almost of a text-book kind.*

Evening Standard
Wednesday, May 29, 1968

DE GAULLE'S DECISION
All the signs say he's staying

General de Gaulle will address the nation today . . . after presiding over a Cabinet meeting . . . but before a declaration that the Prime Minister is to make.

The General's speech will probably be televised tonight despite the strike which has blacked-out French television.

All the indications are that the General has decided to remain in power and to fight it out.

It is also thought that Prime Minister Pompidou will remain in office if and until the Government is defeated on a motion of censure.

General de Gaulle's principal asset, which he intends to exploit to the utmost, is that the strikes have now assumed a strictly political and insurrectionary character, having nothing to do with wage grievances; and that therefore he, as the legally elected President of the Republic, must defend the State against this revolutionary challenge.

Clearly only a General Election can clarify the situation in a legal manner. This he is prepared to concede and, provided there is a return to work, he is expected to announce general elections for June 23. Meanwhile with M. Pompidou still as Prime Minister the long-awaited drastic Cabinet changes will be announced.

The Government's chances of survival, however, are now negligible in view of a declaration by the Leader of the group of independent Deputies, M. Giscard D'Estaing, today that while he wished General de Gaulle to remain as President he considered it essential that the Government should resign. He suggested an interim government composed of members of all parties except the Communists and the Socialists.

If the General decides to get tough he may invoke Article 16 of the Constitution granting him emergency powers when the normal functioning of the State becomes impossible. Then the obvious power at his disposal is that of the Army.

He is generally believed to have used yesterday's journeyings by helicopter before finally arriving at his country home at Colombey to have discussed the situation with senior army officers in Eastern France and with General Massu, the famous figure from the Algerian war, who now commands the French Army in West Germany.

It became known today that units of the Foreign Legion have completed a four-day march from the South of France and are now in Melun, some thirty miles north-east of Paris.

An important article in the Paris newspaper *Le Monde* today on the state of feeling in the French Army says that its professional soldiers, numbering 160,000 officers and men, are determined to obey orders issuing from a legal government.

It makes the point that so far the Minister of Defence has resisted all attempts to use the Army in a way which might involve direct confrontation with strikers.

Tonight a great pro-de Gaulle demonstration, the first of its kind since the crisis broke, will be held in the Place de la Concorde.

The Central Committee of the French Communist Party which now wields immense power and physically controls most of the levers of power has been meeting continuously since this morning. On its decisions, almost as much as those of General de Gaulle, much of the future of France depends.

Evening Standard
Thursday, May 30, 1968

FRANCE NEARS NEW EXPLOSION
Two die — and now the Left has its martyrs

A resurgence of violence which might have the most serious repercussions, including a postponement of the general elections scheduled in two weeks' time, has broken out in France.

Two have died during the past twenty-four hours — a student drowned while fleeing from police outside the Renault works at Flins yesterday, and a twenty-four-year-old worker killed today at the Peugeot works at Sochaux, near Dijon, during a clash between strikers and police.

Surgeons at the hospital where he died declared that he had been killed by a bullet. Three other people were wounded in the course of the day's clashes, including one whose condition is described as 'grave'.

The student's death produced a renewed outburst of rioting in the Latin Quarter last night which lasted until dawn. About four thousand demonstrators built barricades and clashed with police. The result — twenty-six policemen and an unknown number of rioters injured.

The demonstrators were well-armed and dropped Molotov cocktails onto the police from roof-tops.

This evening the students' trade union has called a demonstration on the Left Bank and further serious clashes are feared.

In many cases throughout France there have been clashes between workers wishing to return to work and strike pickets.

The extreme Left in France now finds itself in the possession of two martyrs with possibly more to come in the course of the evening and during the night. It is a situation which could reproduce the dangerous deadlock of last week.

Trouble at the Peugeot works erupted after police were called in to disperse 500 hard-core strikers who were preventing a return-to-work.

The strikers set up barricades and flung missiles at the police who replied with tear gas. In the fighting a police riot truck was overwhelmed and several rifles seized and broken.

Later, police were still guarding the factory gates. A Peugeot spokesman said that a few workers were on duty and some assembly lines were running normally.

*   *   *

At Lyons several people were hurt in an incident involving strikers and plant technicians at the Berliet truck factory. And in Paris, several thousand Citroën workers marched on the Labour Ministry, demanding the right to work, after they had been turned back by strike pickets at their plant.

*   *   *

Tonight's demonstration planned by Paris students is aimed against the Government. Trade union members and all Parisians have been urged to show extra solidarity.

'We are not looking for a fight', Jacques Sauvegeot, chief of National Students' Union (UNEF), told a news conference, 'but if it is forced on us, we accept'.

Newsmen and students were wiping their eyes and sniffling from the lingering effects of tear-gas used in the violent clashes a few hours earlier between police and students.

The authorities today opened an investigation into the Seine drowning of the student – he was among several who ran away from a protest rally pursued by police – which sparked off last night's clashes.

The Latin Quarter echoed to the scream of police sirens, exploding bombs and student shouts, and the district choked under a pall of tear-gas.

A police car was set on fire and stones, cars, railings and election boards were piled into barricades. Police, armed with batons and wearing helmets, charged the demonstrators, hurling tear-gas grenades.

Soon after midnight a police charge pushed demonstrators down the Rue St. Jacques to the Sorbonne University, still occupied by the students. Abandoning their barricades, the students retreated, hurling Molotov cocktails and chanting anti-police slogans. The police then completely surrounded the University and lobbed tear-gas grenades at the windows and onto the roof of the college. Entrenched students replied by lobbing back home-made petrol bombs.

Five students were seriously injured and fifteen less badly hurt, mostly by exploding concussion and tear-gas grenades or splintering windows.

The bells of the Sorbonne chapel could be heard tolling amid the crash of the grenades.

In the main court helmeted students stood with clubs protecting a makeshift hospital where doctors were treating the injured.

The police lifted the siege after three hours and withdrew to remain on the alert in the neighbourhood.

The area around the University presented a dawn scene of desolation. Shop windows were smashed in. Glass was strewn over the sidewalks. Cobblestones from half-a-dozen streets held up traffic. Burned-out cars lay strewn at all angles.

Premier Georges Pompidou later spent forty minutes at the Elysée Palace with President de Gaulle. They obviously discussed the new flare-up.

*   *   *

TOULOUSE — A Gaullist party local headquarters was slightly damaged by a Molotov cocktail hurled into the building. No one was hurt.

Evening Standard
Tuesday, June 11, 1968

DE GAULLE BANS ALL 'DEMOS'

The French Government today banned all street demonstrations and declared illegal a number of ultra-Left organisations, including the Movement of the 22nd of March led by the German student agitator

Daniel Cohn-Bendit. This movement came into being in the satellite University of Nanterre, in Paris, and it touched off student uprisings in the Latin Quarter.

Among the organisations the Government has now declared illegal is a wide range of movements which can be variously described as Trotsky-ist, Mao-ist and Castro-ist. They are the Marxist-Leninist Union of Communist Youth, the Federation of Revolutionary Students, the Liaison Committee of Revolutionary Students, the Communist Revolutionary Youth, the Group of the Revolt, and the Workers' Voice, a Maoist labour group. The ban, according to the Government, covers the ultra-left revolutionary student fringe which has been responsible for rioting in Paris over the last five weeks, and which is trained in street fighting.

By declaring these organisations illegal the Government is now free to arrest their leaders. If, for example, Cohn-Bendit returns to France then he will be liable to automatic arrest. The Information Minister, M. Yves Guena, said violation of the order on the groups could mean prison sentences of six months to two years, according to the law.

The ban on street demonstrations is for the period of the election campaign which started last Monday and will continue for another three weeks.

M. Guena said the ban on demonstrations covers two student demonstrations planned for this afternoon in Paris. One of these was due at the building of the partially strike-bound French radio and television services. If meetings are held in defiance of the ban, they will be dispersed. Election meetings in closed places are not affected. M. Guena said anyone defying the ban on demonstrations will be prosecuted. This includes not only organisations but anyone taking part.

The Government also ordered that foreigners caught taking part in demonstrations will be expelled immediately.

The Cabinet decisions were taken in a Paris littered with riot débris.

Meanwhile a third victim has died in hospital as a result of the rioting at the Peugeot car factory at Sochaux, Southern Alsace, yesterday. He was a forty-nine-year-old worker who fell and broke his skull as he was running away from police.

A twenty-four-year-old union militant was shot dead in the clash. A riot policeman is in a critical condition after being struck across the throat with a piece of barbed wire.

Last night's rioting has left a trail of desolation right across Paris from the Gare du Nord, on the Right Bank, to Montparnasse, on the Left Bank.

This morning fire brigades were still out coping with fires started during the night while police with bulldozers were clearing away carefully constructed barricades and the carcasses of cars overturned and set on fire.

The rioting followed a day of tension in the course of which a seventeen-year-old high school boy was drowned while fleeing from the police.

To describe last night's events as student rioting would be a gross misrepresentation. As the rioters swelled outside my flat window, I could see that most were not students at all, but hoodlum types out for trouble and working in small organised bands.

The situation now is that *agents provocateurs* are clearly at work in a deliberate attempt to provoke deaths and, with deaths, more demonstrations. The renewal of rioting is bringing the Paris population to a point of pent-up rage and exasperation.

Certainly the police, heavily criticised in the early days of the rioting, would now have overwhelmingly popular approval for any measures they took to maintain order.

Last night was a nightmare one with ambulances and fire brigades shrieking through the streets until dawn.

It is difficult to bring an estimate of the number of rioters involved, but reliable sources consider that they numbered no more than three to four thousand. What they lacked in number, they made up in professionalism. They moved about as though they were skilled in the techniques of street fighting.

They were armed with missiles and Molotov cocktails and with the necessary equipment to cut down trees for barricade purposes and to open the tanks of parked cars to get at the petrol for their Molotov cocktails.

Clearly, however, there is some kind of political leadership behind the rioters and the objective is to create sufficient disorder to prevent General Elections being held. This was clearly stated by many of the demonstrators themselves whose favourite chant was 'Elections are treason'.

Paris hospital authorities said 194 injured were treated during the fighting. They included a French newsman seriously injured. Paris police put their injured at seventy-two. They announced that in Paris alone more than fifteen hundred demonstrators were arrested and taken away for questioning. Police also reported seventy-five private cars were wrecked or severely damaged in addition to ten police vehicles destroyed. Five police stations were damaged – mainly smashed windows.

Apart from about three hundred fire calls other destruction included twenty-five trees chopped down, seven lamp standards destroyed, seven police call-boxes destroyed, dozens of traffic lights out of action, and dozens of election hoardings smashed or burned.

Local authorities said more than one hundred and fifty were injured in rioting at St Nazaire last night. They included 106 mobile gendarmes.

One gendarme had his right hand blown off by a grenade explosion.
    Police said that eighty-three demonstrators were arrested at St
Nazaire, of whom fifteen were held under arrest.

Evening Standard
Wednesday, June 12, 1968

WHITHER THE REVOLUTION?

Many British observers must have been surprised, to put it mildly, that
after the near-revolution of last May, it was the Gaullists who emerged
strong from the first round of the elections last Sunday – and the Left
which lost ground.

Yet, in fact, this pattern conforms to a French political tradition which
has become more and more marked in recent years. Briefly, the tradition
is that, in times of calm and prosperity, the country allows itself the
luxury of voting Left; and, in times of trouble, it votes Right.

In the election of March of last year this protest vote gave
Communists and Socialists the illusion that they were on the very edge of
achieving power. They did not realise that many of those who voted for
them did so only because they were certain that they would remain in
opposition – and would not have dreamt of doing so if they thought they
had any serious chance of coming to power.

Again, in this context, it should be noted that, with the steady
modernisation of French industry, the political base of the French Left –
and especially the Communists – has, despite appearances, been
gradually shrinking. Thus, in the past ten years, the total Left vote has
steadily dropped from 44·50 per cent to 41·20 per cent.

For the French Left last Sunday's vote represented the end of a great
illusion – the illusion that there was a Left-wing majority in France. The
consequences of this realisation are likely to be far-reaching as
moderate Socialists draw the lesson that their real future lies not in
alliance with the Communists, but in alliance with the Centre.

For the Communists themselves there is, for the first time, a sense of
enfeeblement as they find themselves outflanked on the Left by a party –
the Party of Socialist Unity – which has doubled its vote, and which has a
revolutionary appeal for the young, which the orthodox Communists no
longer have.

It is interesting in this connection to recall a survey made recently by the French Left-wing journal, *France Observateur*. This showed that only three out of ten French Communist voters really wished to see the Communist Party in power. That there were mass desertions of Communist voters to the Gaullists last Sunday is undoubted; especially in the light of results from working class constituencies. The basic reason was probably that, having secured wage increases with the aid of the Communists, a large proportion of the French working class, and especially their wives, wished to safeguard these gains by voting Gaullist.

There is, however, a further paradox involved – in the sense that the Gaullists, and more especially General de Gaulle himself, cannot be considered as orthodox Conservatives. On the contrary, the big battle which will loom up after the elections will centre on the drastic social reforms which de Gaulle is determined to introduce, and which are already scaring the wits out of traditional French Conservatives.

The General is determined to go ahead with a referendum next autumn based on his plans for worker participation in industry. In these plans he clashes directly not only with French employers but with many members of his Government, including the Prime Minister, M. Pompidou.

Once again, we may see the remarkable paradox of the General using Right-wing forces to achieve Left-wing aims – as he did in the case of Algeria. Those in the Government and in French industry who oppose any suggestion of worker participation hope to head the General off with a watered-down and innocuous version of his ideas.

De Gaulle, however, is determined that his version of a new French revolution should be profound and far-reaching. The last aim, he told a friend of his recently, that he has set himself for the remainder of his life is to end what he calls 'the alienation' of the French working class from the nation.

Evening Standard
Friday, June 28, 1968

HOW THE LEGENDS BECAME TRUTHS, AND THE SCANDALS WERE HUSHED UP

There are those – and I count myself among them – for whom the events of last May and June in Paris evoked at the time, and now in retrospect, feelings of disgust, shame and rage. Now one of the most talented of French political analysts, Raymond Aron, justifies these feelings in a work entitled *The Illusory Revolution* which is a brilliant social, political and psychological analysis of these events.

Aron, France's leading political commentator, begins by making a remarkable disclosure. It is that during the course of the crisis he could not have his views published in France because the French Press was being censored – by the printers' trade unions. The only way he could get around this censorship was to publish in *Le Figaro* without comment de Tocqueville's views of the revolution of 1848. It was the most vicious of all forms of censorship because it was unacknowledged – and therefore unknown to the general reader.

I reported this three times at the time, and on each occasion it was formally denied. Thus the so-called 'defenders of liberty' began by attacking the most fundamental liberty of all. And they did this without protest from proprietors, editors and journalists, all of whom at the time were clamouring against Government control of television. Aron puts his finger on the main reason why the events of May could only evoke revulsion in civilised men.

'It is,' he writes, 'the disproportion of the grievances against the Gaullist régime which I dislike, between the University demands, which I consider legitimate, and this sudden decomposition of French life.' As this decomposition set in and irrationality flourished, it became almost a Parisian cult. All sorts of legends were found credible, such as that of nine million strikers and of hundreds of students killed in the Latin Quarter. In fact, there were none. Then there were the unpublicised scandals such as, for example, the monstrous one of teachers organising fourteen and fifteen-year-old schoolchildren into street fighting gangs.

Finally, there was the almost deafening scamper of rats leaving the sinking ship. The French have experience of the sudden disappearance of régimes, and many is the Prefect, civil servant and an endless variety of others who sought to come to terms with those whom they thought would be their new masters.

But Aron's main point is that the so-called revolution was itself profoundly reactionary in character. 'A society as modernised as France,' he writes, 'cannot, in fact, be governed by libertarian revolutionaries. Inevitably they would have put before France the choice of a dictatorship of the Communist Party, or a dictatorship of the Right.'

In fact, what happened was what has always happened in France after such so-called revolutions – the return to power on a more massive scale of the so-called Party of Order. And there was this fundamental difference between the May events and nineteenth-century French revolutions – it is easier to overthrow a king than a democratically-elected President.

'Why such events are possible in France,' writes Aron, 'is not only historic fragility of the French state, but the absence in France of a really strong trade union movement which leaves a mass of unorganised workers at the mercy of minorities in times of crisis'.

Evening Standard
Friday, August 23, 1968

AFTER MAY, OCTOBER

Without any reflection on the masculinity of the two men concerned, I am now tempted to describe the dismissal of the former Prime Minister M. Georges Pompidou by General de Gaulle as being the result of a lovers' quarrel.

I do not think it goes any deeper than that, and I confidently look forward to M. Pompidou's return to office in the not very distant future. I can now reveal that M. Couve de Murville, the former Foreign Minister and present Prime Minister, twice refused the post in the hope that M. Pompidou would be reinstated. When he realised, however, that if he refused it the job would go to the Minister of the Armed Forces, M. Messmer, he decided with M. Pompidou's full approval to accept it.

M. Pompidou's return to office is considered inevitable if for no other reason than that the Gaullist majority in Parliament is so huge. This makes the task of holding the party together so much more difficult and only a skilled parliamentarian with an overwhelmingly large backing inside the parliamentary party can succeed in doing that and averting major splits.

The time is now moving on towards October with bleak prophecies of a repetition of the May riots ringing in everyone's ears. In the universities some trouble confined to the universities themselves is expected. The real trouble in the universities will, in all likelihood, blow up between rival student factions, between students and professors, between professors themselves and obviously among those who decided to go along with the 'revolution' and those who remained aloof.

Nevertheless the fundamental university problem remains – which is too many students for inadequate facilities and for too few jobs. The French university system is unique in the world in so far as no selection is practised and the education is free. It means among other things that a student who passes the equivalent of, say, his 'A' level has the automatic right to go to a university of his choice. The result in the past was, and a major contributing factor to the May troubles is, that professors are forced to fail sixty per cent of first year students and that sixty per cent facing failure prefer to anticipate it by rioting.

The basic reform needed in the French university system still remains that of selection of student entries before and not after entry.

Evening Standard
Friday, August 30, 1968

THE GREAT FRENCH UPHEAVAL
But it won't do Britain much good

Still mildly dazed at being back in Paris, I survey the scene as though it had been hit by an earthquake. A few points in the landscape are familiar, but for the rest all is new or in process of change.

Change is all around one, opening up new vistas in every field. These involve the destinies of political leaders; the universities, now engaged in dismantling the Napoleonic system of higher education; regional reforms, which bring to an end the rigid centralisation which was once the heritage of the French Revolution; and, finally, changes in French foreign policy, which could cause Britain not less but considerably more disquiet.

All this has happened not over months but in the course of the last few weeks. The most obvious political change is that the Gaullist Party in Parliament now englobes virtually the whole of French political life.

As a result of last June's election, the Gaullists now have a huge majority, but, as a result, they are no longer anything like a monolithic party. Paradoxically enough, this has given a verve and validity to Parliamentary debate which has not existed since de Gaulle came to power.

There are now only three men who can be considered as candidates for the succession to de Gaulle – and they all come from Gaullist ranks. They are the former Premier, M. Pompidou, the present one, M. Couve de Murville and the Education Minister, M. Edgar Fauré.

As for the other one-time contenders, like M. Giscard d'Estaing, or any of the leaders of the orthodox Left, like M. Mitterrand, one feels they are only hanging around because no one is prepared to pay for their funeral expenses.

Then there is the drama which has overtaken the French Communist Party, the only mass working-class party in France, without which a Left-wing electoral victory is impossible.

Czechoslovakia split its leadership and demoralised its troops. For the first time in its fifty years' history the Party is threatened with disintegration, opening up the prospect, also for the first time in the half-century, of a working-class party in France emerging which will be independent of Moscow's control.

Finally, there is the French attempt to begin a courtship with Washington, and especially with the man they believe will be the next incumbent at the White House: Richard Nixon. This is now being conducted in a manner at once opportunistic and sagacious. The opportunism lies in the fact that France, far from being able to mount a new assault on the dollar, is now largely dependent on the international monetary system it has denounced in the past for survival. The sagacity consists in telling the Americans that their own pre-occupations, both domestic and super-power ones – as regards reaching agreement with Moscow – require the existence of a strong European power with an independent atomic force which, while seeking to steer a middle course, remains, in fact, a firm ally to the West.

The American deterrent, it is argued, is no longer credible, because it will not be applied against Moscow itself, immediately, in the event of a Soviet attack on West Germany.

This role of a privileged Western ally cannot be fulfilled by Western Germany without frightening the Russians: nor by Britain, whose atomic armoury, it is claimed, is tied to the US.

As a counterpart, for recognition of France's special role in Europe, it is hoped that Washington will bring pressure on the other Common Market countries to drop their support for Britain's efforts to enter the Market.

The veto against British entry will remain just as long as Paris considers it has not disengaged its atomic armoury from US control.

Evening Standard
Friday, October 25, 1968

5
The
Final Years

FOUR MORE YEARS IN OFFICE FOR THE GENERAL

General de Gaulle today announced to France and the world that he intends to remain in power until the very end of his term of office as President of the Republic — until December 1972.

The General made this announcement after a Cabinet meeting this morning through the official spokesman, the Minister of Information, M. Joel le Theule. The announcement was a blistering retort to speculation which had gathered avalanche force throughout the past few days that he might retire well before the completion of his seven-year term as President and, indeed, possibly some time this year. These speculations were touched off by a remarkable declaration in Rome last week by his former Prime Minister, M. Georges Pompidou.

Speaking to a group of French journalists, M. Pompidou announced that he would be a candidate for the Presidency of the Republic when that post became vacant. It was immediately assumed that M. Pompidou was speaking with the authorisation of the General. He was in Rome on a semi-official mission for General de Gaulle and he had had a long interview with the General before leaving Paris.

It seemed inconceivable that anyone of M. Pompidou's political finesse and intimate knowledge of the General should casually announce his candidature for the presidency without direct encouragement from the Elysée's present occupant.

However, it soon became known that M. Pompidou had spoken without the General's authority and that his remark had detonated an explosion of fury at the Elysée Palace.

Today's statement said: 'In performing the national task which is mine, I was re-elected President of the Republic for seven years by the French people on December 19, 1965. I have the intention and the duty to fulfil my mandate until it expires.'

M. Pompidou's statement was particularly damaging to the present Prime Minister, M. Couve de Murville, who immediately, in the light of the speculation it touched off, found his own authority both in the Government and in the country seriously undermined.

Ever since the furore created by M. Pompidou's confession that he had presidential ambitions, the former Prime Minister has been bending over double to try and prove that his remark was entirely innocuous and totally speculative. This, however, simply won't wash.

It is not merely the fact that M. Pompidou is the first Gaullist to speculate out loud on the possibility that the General may not be immortal, but he must have realised that in the present political context in France it would be instantly assumed that the post of President of the Republic was about to fall vacant.

The question now that is agitating political circles in Paris is: Why did M. Pompidou say it? Was it perhaps a deliberate nudge to the General to leave the scene in circumstances which still left his 'historic image' relatively undamaged? Whatever prompted M. Pompidou to make his remark there is no doubt as to the tonic effect it had on the morale of the Gaullist Party.

The bulk of the party is now convinced that the best hope of its survival is an early retirement by General de Gaulle, with M. Pompidou as a candidate for the succession.

It was not only assumed by the party as a whole that M. Pompidou had de Gaulle's blessing and encouragement in putting himself forward as his successor but that a tentative date had been fixed between the two men for the General's retirement. This, it was assumed, would follow the holding of a referendum later this year on General de Gaulle's plans for greater regional autonomy.

Now General de Gaulle's firm announcement that his 'duty and intention' to remain in power until December 1972 brings the relationship between the two men to breaking point. This relationship underwent severe strains during the troubles of May and June last year. At that time, M. Pompidou went fairly near to advising the General to quit.

In any case, when the General left Paris mysteriously at the height of the crisis, allegedly for his country home but in fact to visit the French armed forces in Germany, M. Pompidou was kept in ignorance of the

General's movements and was convinced that he was about to quit.

General de Gaulle's categoric statement will disappoint many, dismay others – but will at least dispel illusions both in France and abroad.

Evening Standard
Wednesday, January 22, 1969

FRANCE PROTESTS OVER OUR 'LEAKS'

Mr Christopher Soames, Ambassador to Paris, was today handed a tough Note of Protest by the permanent head of the French Foreign Office, M. Hervé Alphand, concerning the Anglo-French dispute as to what General de Gaulle did or did not say to Mr Soames over lunch on February 4 and the subsequent leakage of this talk by the British Government to France's five Common Market partners.

The Note accused Britain of spreading a 'distorted' version of the conversation and one which at no time had received the approval, contrary to British claims, of either the French Foreign Office or the Elysée Palace.

Mr Soames, who had returned from seeing Mr Stewart and Mr Wilson yesterday, asked this morning to be received by the French Foreign Minister, M. Michel Debré. Instead he was told to see M. Alphand, who handed him the Note, the contents of which were immediately conveyed to the British Government.

In a sense M. Debré's action in refusing to see the Ambassador may be taken in conjunction with other indications as an attempt by the French to 'downgrade' the dispute. Had M. Debré himself delivered the protest Note, it would have had a far more serious implication than one delivered by the Secretary General of the French Foreign Office.

Other indications that the French are trying to lessen the consequences of the Anglo-French dispute came this morning with a broadcast by the French Prime Minister, Monsieur Couve de Murville, in which he said, 'What seems to be now useful and even essential is to examine everything that has led to the present storm.'

But he added, 'One must beware of polemics.'

A colossal misunderstanding seems to be at the root of the British claim that the summary of Mr Soames's conversation with General de Gaulle on February 4, which was released by the British Government on Friday, was approved by both sides.

As the British Embassy itself makes clear, Mr Soames's version of the talks submitted for approval to the Elysée on February 6 was criticised on several points by General de Gaulle's right-hand man, Monsieur Tricot. M. Tricot, however, suggested the whole matter might be cleared up when Mr Soames saw M. Debré later in the week.

According to British sources, M. Debré approved of Mr Soames's summary as a whole, but they did not discuss what seemed to both of them the contentious point of a so-called 'inner council' composed of Britain, France, Germany and Italy which would provide the political leadership for a broadened European community replacing the Common Market and including Britain.

This 'inner council' has since been referred to by the Foreign Secretary, Mr Stewart, as a *directoire* which, to French ears anyway, is a plain distortion of the meaning conveyed in Mr Soames's summary.

The truth of the matter is that both M. Debré and Mr Soames were passionately eager to have the General's suggestions accepted by London and did not, in fact, give the necessary concentration to the finer points of Mr Soames's summary.

In M. Debré's case, he is a passionate Anglophile who was overjoyed at the prospect of an Anglo-French reconciliation.

In Mr Soames's case he saw General de Gaulle's proposals as the promised 'breakthrough' in Anglo-French relations on which he had set his heart.

He urged from the start that de Gaulle's suggestions should be taken up and explored and he protested vehemently to London at the revelation by Mr Wilson to Herr Kiesinger in Bonn of the contents of these talks without at least trying to get prior French approval.

Mr Soames's situation is now a considerable personal tragedy overshadowed by the immense tragedy of this setback to Anglo-French reconciliation in the foreseeable future. It is no exaggeration to describe Mr Soames as being in despair and furious with the turn events have taken.

The reason is that the French now regard Mr Soames as something of an ally and a man they can do business with. Furthermore, as far as Mr Soames is concerned, he considers that the European ferment which produced General de Gaulle's proposals will continue, will lead to a renewal of these proposals, and, in that case, he will be in a better position than anyone to see them through to fruition.

This is, of course, a highly optimistic view for in the present situation the climate of distrust not only between Britain and France, but within all of Western Europe, is such that no early end to the crisis is at the moment even foreseeable.

His situation and that of M. Debré are so similar in their respective disappointments that when the two met at the French Foreign Office on Saturday evening they did not even have the heart to engage in recriminations. They almost, in the words of one confidant, wept on each other's shoulders in despair.

Mr Soames's future is now open to every kind of speculation. He could resign, but that is rendered almost unthinkable by the fact that, if he did so, he would hand the French a great diplomatic victory. He could be declared *persona non grata* by the French, but that is in the highest degree unlikely.

Evening Standard
Monday, February 24, 1969

ALAS, POOR SOAMES, HIS FUTURE LOOKS VERY BLEAK . . .

It is interesting to poke about in the still radio-active fall-out of the Soames affair (poor Soames incidentally – as the innocent victim he does not deserve to have his name pinned to an act of considerable diplomatic villainy).

Let us, however, begin with the Ambassador himself. His position has been rendered so seemingly hopeless that the resignation he offered last Sunday to Mr Stewart will most probably be renewed in three or four months' time.

This is, of course, all the more tragic because he was on the verge of making precisely the diplomatic breakthrough that he had set for himself when he first came to Paris six months ago.

His mission, about which he made no secret, was to forget about the Common Market as such and to open a wide dialogue with de Gaulle as to the possibility of Anglo-French cooperation in the creation of an independent Europe.

The view in British Embassy circles now is that when the dust settles on the present row de Gaulle will discreetly renew his offer of discussions which can be taken up without overmuch scruple about drowning the Common Market baby in its bath, strangling old Auntie NATO and, horror of horrors, negotiating with the French 'behind the backs' of our friends and allies.

In that case, and so runs the argument, Mr Christopher Soames will come into his own again as a negotiator whom the French can trust.

I am sceptical about this prospect. First of all M. Bernard Tricot, de Gaulle's Secretary-General, now holds the view that no fruitful negotiations are possible with the Wilson Government. Secondly General de Gaulle himself expressed privately the opinion only three days ago that while he considers the British Ambassador to have been the innocent victim of his own Government's Machiavellianism he nevertheless believes that his credibility as an ambassador has been largely destroyed.

De Gaulle has thereby reverted to his original view that only a Conservative Government would bring Britain into Europe and he may well envisage the day when he's talking to Mr Soames as Foreign Secretary of a Conservative Government rather than Mr Soames as Mr Wilson's envoy in Paris.

The Soames view of his role as Ambassador in Paris infuriated the Foreign Office which already disliked the idea of a political choice of Ambassador to Paris and which was in any case dedicated to ways of outsmarting the French. In Paris, however, his views created instant interest especially in the Elysée Palace and with strongly pro-British French Foreign Minister, M. Michel Debré.

As far as de Gaulle is concerned he had long ago realised that Anglo-French rivalry in Europe was getting neither country anywhere and he had openly spoken of a larger association including Britain and its EFTA partners which would create a looser grouping than the existing Common Market.

Soames asked for his interview with de Gaulle on December 14. The interview was originally scheduled for early January but had to be postponed chiefly owning to the Ambassador's one-month long illness. It is an intriguing possibiity that, had the interview taken place in early January instead of in a climate conducive to mischief-making possibilities as a result of the Western European meeting and the impending visit of Mr Nixon, it would have got off to some kind of start.

I have taken a canvass of opinion among most of the ambassadors in Paris of the so-called 'Friendly Five' — Holland, Belgium, Italy, Luxembourg and West Germany. These it would appear from the Foreign Secretary's statement would have been most horrified at an Anglo-French get-together behind their backs.

Whatever their feelings might have been as a result of possibly garbled reports of Mr Soames's conversation with General de Gaulle at the time, their feelings now are of keen disappointment that the negotiations did not begin. Even among the most pro-British Five there has long been a feeling that the crisis inside the Common Market could only be resolved by bilateral Anglo-French talks. As one ambassador of the 'Friendly Five' put it to me: 'We would have understood the need for secrecy at the beginning but of course we would have wished to be kept informed once serious negotiations began.'

He went on to say that the current Anglo-French dispute removes even the remotest of possibilities for British entry into the Common Market. He continued: 'This is a situation which we now have to recognise. As a result, instead of paralysing the Common Market in anticipation of a possible British entry in the future we may now be driven to conclude that we must face facts and make the Common Market as now it exists become once again a functioning organism.'

Evening Standard
Friday, February 28, 1969

FRANCE: 'BACK TO DISORDER' FEARS GROWING

Is France heading for a repeat performance of the events of last May–June?

This is a question the French nation is asking itself today following last night's breakdown in wage negotiations between the Government and the trade unions. The collapse of the talks was immediately followed by a trade union announcement of a twenty-four-hour General Strike scheduled for next Tuesday.

The Government refuses to yield to union demands for a six per cent wage increase which would compensate workers for the rise in the cost of living since the fifteen per cent wage increase last May. The Government contests both the unions' statistics in the matter of price rises and the sheer feasibility of a wage increase on that scale at this time.

Meanwhile it is now authoritatively known that General de Gaulle has resolutely set his face against devaluation.

Wage increases followed by slashing devaluation is the course favoured by some sections of French industry. It is a course, however, which the General is not prepared to follow and a Government spokesman has let private industry know that if they increase wages in anticipation of devaluation then they would be gravely mistaken.

General de Gaulle takes the view that devaluation would be disastrous, repeating what he considers to have been the historic mistake of the Popular Front Government of 1936, which accompanied large wage increases with devaluation. This, then, according to him, became the pattern of conduct for post-war governments with disastrous inflationary consequences. He is determined to see that what he calls 'the psychoses of inflation' should not return to France.

In those circumstances, wage increases would be economic lunacy. French industry is barely competitive as it is and new wage increases would rule large segments of French industry out of the world market.

Is the Government bluffing or are the unions? This is the test as it will be provided by the next few days and weeks.

An encouraging sign from the Government's point of view is that the call for a twenty-four-hour General Strike is made in due legal form giving five days' notice of strike action. This was never the case during the May–June events.

The General Strike will hit the nation just as General de Gaulle addresses it on television to launch his referendum campaign for regional reform.

In this speech he will no doubt stress the heavy representation and it will be given to the trade unions on the newly formed regional councils and in the Senate.

He will also stress the union reforms carried out by the Government earlier this year which for the first time give the unions legal rights at the shop floor level never before granted them in France.

Evening Standard
Friday, March 7, 1969

FRANCE PUTS HER MONEY ON DE GAULLE

Gold prices took a spectacular tumble and French industrial shares rose sharply on the Paris Bourse today.

It was a remarkable display of confidence that the French Government could handle current labour difficulties as symbolised by today's twenty-four-hour General Strike without recourse to devaluation.

Gold prices dropped sharply in today's trading when the Bourse re-opened normally despite the General Strike.

Part of the explanation for this sudden burst of confidence in the franc is to be found in the ragged nature of today's strike, in which the strike call launched by France's three major trade union formations was observed with only partial success. While the strike succeeded in crippling the greater part of industrial activity throughout the country it was nowhere followed with anything like the same unanimity as the strikes of last May and June.

The response varied from ninety per cent in the mines, docks and public transport to only fifty per cent in such key sectors as, for example, the railways.

The call by the teachers' union for a General Strike was a flop, with only a feeble response in the Paris area where most schools functioned normally.

As usual it is difficult to estimate how many are actually on strike and how many have been forced to stay at home by power cuts and transport difficulties.

In Paris itself gas and electricity are still available in most parts of the city. The large stores are open but there are no buses and few underground trains.

Suburban trains are, however, maintaining a reduced service.

Internal air traffic is normal and most main line trains are running. At various high schools in Paris there have been clashes between students among those wishing to attend classes and those seeking a shutdown.

Today's strike will be climaxed by a demonstration from the Place de la République to the Bastille later today.

Revolutionary student elements are expecting to join in the demonstration, although trade union leaders have made it clear that their presence would be unwelcome.

The greater part of the strike wave will end later today and the electricity situation will be normal by the time General de Gaulle broadcasts to the nation this evening.

There are no evening newspapers today and there will be no morning papers tomorrow.

It is difficult to say whom the strike scares most – the Government or the French trade union leaders.

Called five days ago following the breakdown of Government–union negotiations on wage adjustments to compensate for price increases since last year's fifteen per cent wage rise, today's strike raises the spectre of a repetition of the chaos of May and June, 1968. This fear haunts France like a family ghost and is responsible for the current tribulations of the franc.

The French trade union movement, divided into three different federations and impoverished by last year's strike, fears almost as much as the Government that the twenty-four-hour strike will somehow slip into the control of ultra-Left-wing groups which last year captured temporarily the leadership of the revolt sparked by the students.

Coupled with uncertain and divided trade union leadership, France's political Left fears that it may be walking into precisely the same trap which resulted in a major defeat at the polls last year.

The strike takes place against a background of financial panic which reached its peak towards the end of last week and is now tailing off, as the full extent of France's financial reserves and the General's determination not to devalue the franc is beginning to sink in on the financial opinion at home and abroad.

Nevertheless the fate of the franc remains linked to the outcome of today's strike, for if there is not a general return to work tomorrow and strikes continue in some key industries then a new wave of financial panic can be expected in the course of the week.

Evening Standard
Tuesday, March 11, 1969

POMPIDOU AND DE GAULLE — ACT OF ABSOLUTION

The former French Prime Minister M. Georges Pompidou and Mme Pompidou will dine alone with General and Mme de Gaulle at the Elysée Palace tonight. The invitation to the Pompidous became known yesterday and created a considerable stir for both political and personal reasons.

Now that M. Pompidou's name has been publicly mentioned as a possible witness in the current Markovic affair the invitation to dine with the de Gaulles can be interpreted as an act of absolution by the President for his former Prime Minister, clearing him in the public mind of any suspicion of involvement no matter how tenuous in the scandal.

Politically it can be taken as an act of forgiveness by the General for M. Pompidou's remark two months ago in Rome, which caused considerable fury in the Elysée Palace, in which he declared himself a candidate for the Presidency of the Republic.

As for the Markovic affair proper, it entered an important stage today when the film star Alain Delon was questioned once again by the examining magistrate, M. René Pétard, regarding the murder of his friend and bodyguard, the Yugoslav Stefan Markovic, nearly six months ago.

Delon has already endured two periods of intensive questioning, the last being for thirty-six hours during which time he was held at police headquarters. Today's questioning of the actor, which began this morning, threatens to last three full days.

M. Pétard has a list of 110 questions to put to Delon, all connected with the relations between himself and the victim; the relations between

Delon and, so far the only accused in the case, the Corsican ex-gangster Marcantoni; relations between Delon and his now divorced wife Nathalie; and finally certain contradictions which have appeared in the evidence given by Delon and the evidence of other witnesses.

One of the vital questions concerns exactly as to how, when and from whom Delon learned of Markovic's death. The examining magistrate also wants to know who exactly visited Delon's villa at St Tropez where he lived between September 22 and the beginning of October last year.

The examining magistrate will also want to know if Delon was aware of the contents of a long letter written by Nathalie to Markovic which has fallen into M. Pétard's hands.

As for Nathalie Delon, she is still filming in Italy and she is expected to return to Paris next Thursday. She will be questioned on March 24 while Delon himself will be in Rome filming in his turn.

Evening Standard
Wednesday, March 12, 1969

SECRETS OF THE SIX MISSING HOURS IN THE LIFE OF GENERAL DE GAULLE

What happened on that astonishing day in May of last year when, at the height of the crisis – with all France seemingly crumbling into chaos – General de Gaulle vanished from the scene for six agonising hours? The full story of that day – May 29, 1968 – is only now beginning to emerge with a publication in Paris of Jean-Raymond Tournoux's book, *The General's Month of May*.

With the events of last May still haunting France, Tournoux's book, obviously based on massive confidences from the then Prime Minister M. Pompidou, provides a striking account of how de Gaulle coped with what he himself considered to be an impossible situation.

It might be subtitled, ''The Torment of de Gaulle''. The General, it will be recalled, on May 29 suddenly cancelled a Cabinet meeting and told M. Pompidou that he was helicoptering to his country home at Colombey for twenty-four hours of 'reflection' and 'to catch up on some sleep'.

The General Strike was then entering into its fourth week, despite an agreed wage settlement, and the Communist Trade Union Federation had called for a demonstration dangerously close to the Elysée Palace for that evening. In view of the chaos that reigned, the Government's obvious lack of authority, and the evident demoralisation of the security forces it was a situation in which anything could happen. An assault on the Elysée Palace was not only not to be ruled out, but was a distinct possibility. Willy-nilly, the Communists were being driven into the situation where only they had the means of restoring order – by seizing power.

This was the situation in which the General flew off, presumably to Colombey but in fact to the French forces in Germany, with their headquarters at Baden-Baden. When it was discovered that he had not in fact arrived at Colombey, official circles in Paris were seized by panic.

M. Pompidou himself had become almost convinced, as the result of a telephone conversation with the General that morning, that he might be intending to quit. He was particularly disturbed by the General's final words: 'I embrace you.'

A fact not mentioned in the book is that de Gaulle's temporary disappearance so unnerved Pompidou that he asked the TV network to hold itself in readiness to broadcast an appeal to the nation that evening. What was de Gaulle up to in Baden-Baden, where he conferred with the Commander-in-Chief of the French forces in Germany, General Massu?

He demanded the Army's unconditional loyalty to the legal régime and then told Massu that, in the event of a revolution in Paris, the President of the Republic would establish the Government on the West Bank of the Rhine.

A remarkable feature of the situation was that the only political leaders to receive news of what was cooking in Baden-Baden were the Communists. The French Army, through channels available to itself, let the French Communist leaders know something of General de Gaulle's intentions. By nightfall on the 29th it was clear that calm reigned in Paris and that the General could safely return in triumph.

Evening Standard
Friday, March 14, 1969

IT LOOKS BLACK FOR DE GAULLE

The latest public opinion poll carried out by the French Institute of Public Opinion which will be made public late today has de Gaulle well and truly beaten in next Sunday's referendum.

According to its poll 51 per cent will vote against de Gaulle and 49 per cent for. This gives de Gaulle the slightly better score in another public opinion poll made public yesterday which gave 53 per cent against and 47 per cent for.

The French Institute of Public Opinion has a high reputation for the accuracy of its forecasts, especially in referendums. It will take a further poll tonight and tomorrow morning – on the eve of Sunday's vote and following General de Gaulle's broadcast speech to the nation tonight.

The General will speak to the nation tonight in what will be in effect a final effort to turn the tide which threatens him with defeat in Sunday's referendum.

The public opinion polls are beginning to show a majority of noes to his constitutional reform proposals which he has made into a vote of confidence. These polls show that a little over 30 per cent of the nation is still undecided as to which way to vote. Among the electorate, too, 54 per cent are sceptical as to whether de Gaulle will carry out his threat to resign if defeated. These sceptics should be left in no doubt as to his intention to quit if he loses after his televised speech tonight. Whatever the outcome, it promises to be a narrow one.

I understand that if it is so narrow that he is only saved by the votes from France's overseas territories, which habitually vote overwhelmingly for him, then he will still resign on the grounds that, as his regional reform plans concern only Metropolitan France, he cannot be satisfied with a minority vote in France itself.

Meanwhile the wheeling and dealing among the opposition leaders has already begun as though de Gaulle's overthrow can be considered as certain. It is not an appetising sight as they set about carving up the body before the victim is actually dead. It is also one which may swing many last-minute votes to de Gaulle. For what is involved is precisely the same unprincipled political bargaining which characterised the Fourth Republic.

There is, for example, a secret agreement between Conservative politicians and M. Guy Mollet that while the Socialists will put up their own candidtate in the next Presidential elections they will swing in the second round of voting behind the Conservative leader, M. Giscard d'Estaing.

The Socialists have already firmly turned their backs on the Communists with whom they were in electoral alliance until recently. The belated excuse is, of course, the events in Prague.

This about-turn of the Socialists has dismayed the Communists who are now spending as much time attacking this plotted turn to 'third force' politics as they are de Gaulle. It has had a dispiriting effect on their 5,000,000 followers. many of whom are certain to express their disgust by abstaining next Sunday.

What is clear, too, is that 'big money' in France, which has always detested de Gaulle but has accepted him as a lesser evil, has now decided to dump him. It feels safe to do so because there is no danger of a left-winger succeeding de Gaulle in the Elysée Palace.

The unfortunate M. Mitterrand, who was a candidate of the Left at the last Presidential elections and who ran de Gaulle to a humiliating second round, has been forgotten to such an extent that none of the Left-wing parties would give him any of their campaign time on television.

The result is a line-up of opposition of a range de Gaulle has never encountered before.

The theorising about the outcome continues to be matched by theorising as to why de Gaulle exposed himself to this danger.

With an overwhelming parliamentary majority won only eight months ago, he has dismayed even his closest followers by exposing himself to the risk of a referendum.

He has become particularly vulnerable, too, because the current catch-phrase has caught on: 'A NO for de Gaulle is a YES for Pompidou.'

The answer cannot be that he was simply jealous of Pompidou as the man largely credited with last summer's election victory. He knew all along that in the short run, whatever the outcome of the referendum, he could not match Pompidou's success and would emerge from the contest diminished.

The answer can only be that he feels in duty bound to submit a constitutional protest to a referendum and that in any case he is committed to a programme of radical reform which demands a renewed mandate.

The present project for regional reform is part and parcel of a package deal, part of which has already been delivered and this concerns university reform and legalisation of trade union activity in the factories.

If he wins this referendum he will go on to his even larger reform project — that of worker participation in industry.

*   *   *

FOOTNOTE: General de Gaulle left Paris for his country home at Colombey-les-deux-Eglises this morning after recording his broadcast to the nation which will be delivered tonight.

If he is defeated on Sunday night he will not return to Paris. He will make his resignation known in a communiqué issued from his village home. The outcome of the referendum may well hang on the 700,000 votes of the French overseas territories.

Evening Standard
Friday, April 25, 1969

DE GAULLE, ONCE UPON A TIME . . .

This has been what can only be described as Political Fiction Week in Paris, with everyone speculating as to what would happen if de Gaulle were defeated in next Sunday's referendum.

Visions flit between the Elysée Palace and de Gaulle's country home at Colombey-les-deux-Eglises, where he will be with his family this weekend.

Some have him sulking at his country home and making no statement beyond a brief communiqué that he has resigned.

Others have him returning to Paris to hand over the interim powers of the presidency to M. Alain Poher, the President of the Senate, in accordance with the Constitution, until new presidential elections are held.

There are, of course, those incorrigible addicts of de-Gaulle-the-Fascist myth, who expect to wake up on Monday morning with tanks at every street corner and all the leaders of the Opposition under arrest and a state of siege declared.

There is, of course, not the slightest doubt that, if defeated, the General will go.

On the other hand, I would not dismiss entirely the possibility of his political resurrection. Technically, nothing could prevent him, having resigned, standing again as a candidate for the Presidency.

One can imagine the pleasure the General would take in giving events so mischievous a twist. He would, of course, wait a few days to allow the French — and the world Press — to bury him under mountains of flowers and brickbats. Then would come the laconic communiqué from Colombey, announcing that he was a candidate for his own succession. Consternation: it would be like Napoleon's return from Elba. M. Pompidou would, of course, have to stand aside for him.

By this time the French nation would be in a contrite mood all too conscious, if I may continue to mix my historical metaphors, of its crime in having lit the faggots under Joan of Arc.

It would be — again, forgive the fantasy — Napoleon's Hundred Days all over again, except that this time (if he won) the General would have a mandate to rule for another seven years. Goodnight, children, and pleasant dreams!

Evening Standard
Friday, April 25, 1969

213

DE GAULLE MINISTER STORMS OUT

General de Gaulle's functions as President came officially to an end at midday today when M. Alain Poher, 60, President of the French Upper House, the Senate, who was virtually unknown to the general public until a few short weeks ago, took over as interim President until new Presidential elections are held in four weeks' time.

The constitutional council met this morning to take official note of de Gaulle's resignation which he announced shortly after midnight.

M. Poher, former civil servant in the Ministry of Finance, was moving into the Elysée Palace this afternoon. There he will consult the Prime Minister, M. Couve de Murville, who presided over the Cabinet meeting this morning, and tonight he will broadcast to the nation.

It became known this morning that a member of the Cabinet, M. René Capitant, Minister of Justice, has resigned. M. Capitant, an eminent jurist who is one of the oldest and most devoted of General de Gaulle's followers, in his letter of resignation to M. Poher, explained that he was resigning because he could not bring himself to sit at Cabinet meetings presided over by M. Poher, who, as an opponent of the referendum, had played such a prominent part in bringing about General de Gaulle's defeat. His resignation is expected to be followed by that of another veteran de Gaullist, M. André Malraux, Minister of Culture.

Removers began taking General de Gaulle's personal archives from the Elysée Palace early today. In effect few of his personal papers remained at the Elysée because he had moved most of them to his country home in Colombey-les-deux-Eglises during the troubles of last May and June.

Although he is now a private citizen, his country home at Colombey, La Boisserie, continues to be heavily guarded. It is to be protected by heavy forces of police.

The General has so far received no visitors but some old followers were expected to make a pilgrimage to Colombey, 120 miles east of Paris, later today.

A Paris evening newspaper publishes today a full-page photo of the General, grey-haired and solitary, walking in the gardens of his home. It quotes as caption the last lines of the final volume of General de Gaulle's Memoirs: 'Old man, exhausted by ordeal, detached from human deeds, feeling the approach of the eternal cold, but always watching in the shadows for the gleam of hope.'

The main reaction in Paris to the not-unexpected news that General de Gaulle had lost his referendum battle over regional reform and the

Presidential succession and duly abdicated was one of 'The king is dead, long live the king'.

The feeling, with possibly a touch of wishful thinking, is that he will be succeeded by his heir apparent and former Prime Minister, M. Georges Pompidou. This feeling is, of course, strongly reinforced by the already apparent disunion that reigns in the ranks of the victors.

*   *   *

The final official returns for Metropolitan France were:

Against – 11,966,550 (52.87 per cent);
For – 10,669,550 (47.13 per cent).

*   *   *

Of the votes for the NOES, 25 per cent must immediately be deducted as belonging to the Communists. Of the rest, these are split between extreme Left Socialists, Socialists, Radicals, Liberals, Conservatives, Right-wing Conservatives, and a traditional 3 per cent of the extreme Right.

To speculate on a cohesive coalition emerging from this kind of opposition is to build on sand. It is obvious that with 47 per cent of the vote de Gaullists remain by far the strongest single party in the country. They must remain the principal political polar attraction for any new government rather than any of the segments of the opposition.

What became apparent in the early hours of this morning on the radio networks of the country was the disunity and uncertainty that reigns among the opposition parties. There was only one exception to this and that was the Communist Party, which denounced any move to form a Centre Left coalition excluding the Communists.

The Communists were backed in this by their trade union federation, the CGT. As for the Socialist leader, M. Guy Mollet, he clearly envisaged a centre-Left Government without the Communists, with a Socialist backing for M. Poher in a run-off fight at the Presidential elections with M. Pompidou.

What was significant about M. Mollet's attitude, which has been known for some time, is that he has specifically ruled out a strong president after the model created by de Gaulle and advocated the return to the president as 'mediator' after the Fourth Republic model.

M. Mollet then went on to say that while a government of the Left, including the Communists, was impossible and, after Prague, undesirable, he would nevertheless support the Communists if in the second round of voting the run-off fight was reduced to one between a Communist and M. Pompidou.

A spokesman for the so-called Centre Party envisaged a coalition ranging from M. Giscard d'Estaing on the Right to M. Gaston Deferre, the Moderate Socialist Mayor of Marseilles.

Evening Standard
Monday, April 28, 1969

THE LONG, BITTER RIFT BETWEEN THE GENERAL AND POMPIDOU

There was something almost laconic about the way General de Gaulle threw away power. It was rather like a player throwing away his racquet in disgust after a bad match at tennis. His bad match commenced with events of May–June last year when he muffed every shot and limped towards every stroke – all except the last, which was a smash hit.

This was when he left Paris at the height of the storm, the origins of which baffled and intrigued him to virtually repeat in miniature his famous flight from crumbling France to London in 1940.

Now, as then, like a good general, he was averting being imprisoned by events which he frankly confessed he could not control, to establish a base from which he could defend and finally re-establish a 'legitimacy' which he felt he represented, first against treason from London and now from Alsace-Lorraine if need be against a French relapse into revolutionary anarchy.

This was the sense of that astonishing escapade of his when, keeping his intentions secret even from his Prime Minister, he flew off to see his Army chiefs; not to ask them favours but to tell them of his intentions and secure their allegiance.

Then, realising that nothing dramatic had happened in Paris during his absence, that the revolution had, in fact, shot its bolt, he returned to the capital the next day to make his electrifying broadcast announcing that he was staying and that he had ordered a General Election.

This last was a concession wrested from him only minutes before he made his broadcast by his Prime Minister, M. Pompidou. Right up to that minute a quarrel had raged between them and had even reached an acrimonious pitch, with Pompidou insisting on a General Election which he was certain he would win and de Gaulle insisting on a referendum, which Pompidou was certain he would lose.

If de Gaulle had won that struggle, the May revolution would have claimed its victim not yesterday but ten months ago.

Ever since then de Gaulle has been off balance as though a victim of that 'shipwreck' which he called old age.

It is easy to say now that he called yesterday's referendum against the unanimous advice of all his staff and all his ministers in order to prove that he, and not Pompidou, was still the top man in France. There may be something in that; but there are other factors also.

Pompidou was scheduled for dismissal way back in March 1967. He was only saved by the fact that the Gaullists sneaked in by so narrow a majority in the elections of that year that they needed a good parliamentary boss to handle the situation and that, in any case, Couve de Murville, his chosen successor, had been defeated as a parliamentary candidate.

The rift between de Gaulle and Pompidou in fact preceded the events of last May. It was based on what might be called temperamental differences of ideology.

Pompidou is a liberal Conservative; de Gaulle sees himself as a revolutionary who, as a nationalist, accomplishes the very reforms the Left have been clamouring for for generations and never been able to achieve.

De Gaulle believes that it is his mission to end the class war of France whereas Pompidou believes that enlightened capitalism has already rendered the very idea of class war an outdated nineteenth-century concept.

De Gaulle blamed Pompidou's conservatism for the May explosion. As for himself, he claimed not entirely without justice that he had been clamouring for reforms, especially university reforms, to no avail ever since the Presidential election of 1965.

To get de Gaulle in perspective one must recall something of his background. He is a man from Lille whose family were upper middle-class Catholics. The northern French Catholics differed from the southern ones in that they were familiar with the horrors of nineteenth-century industrialisation and were instinctively drawn to the earliest Christian Socialist movement.

His grandmother was an evangelical propagandist for workers' rights; his father defended Dreyfus against the French Right. This was the atmosphere in which de Gaulle was brought up. A mixture of Catholicism, patriotism and social uplift.

His pre-war experiences in Paris and later in London developed these two latter aspects of his thinking. Peddling his military ideas in Paris based on the creation of a professional French armoured striking force he met with indifference on the Right, which was already knee-deep in capitulation, and political objections from, for example, Léon Blum, the Socialist head of the pre-war Popular Front government, who told him that though his idea seemed excellent, the Socialists would never support the creation of such an élite military force, in case it would turn against the workers.

Then came de Gaulle's hallucinating arrival in London after the collapse with virtually no one from the higher echelons of politics, army or the civil service to join him.

Two blistering hates which never left him developed as a result – against the political parties which had reduced France to its plight and against the whole French Establishment, the nation's so-called élite.

'The Left is against the nation and the Right is against the Republic,' he reflected sadly at the time.

Some time later, as the liberation of France approached, he noted that his colleagues whilst prattling of revolution were, in fact, preparing to return to the old political ways.

'I reflected then that among all these so-called revolutionaries I was the only serious one.'

His forebodings about the future proved justified.

Against his advice, the nation by referendum adopted a constitution which in effect restored the Third Republic, lodging both legislative and executive power in an all-powerful assembly. Ironically enough in view of the defence of the French Upper House by the French Left in the current referendum, at the time the entire Left clamoured for its abolition.

De Gaulle retired in dignity, referring to himself as 'the sidetracked leader'. He was replaced by someone called Félix Gouin.

What followed was what de Gaulle called 'the régime of parties'. This should be understood in its French context for it means and meant at the time quite literally that party caucuses against even the terms of the constitution could decide on the withdrawal of ministers without the Government even being defeated in the Assembly. What with that and ungovernable assemblies, governments fell with the regularity of a guillotine working overtime.

It is interesting to speculate now on what would or would not have happened if de Gaulle had remained in power. I am convinced, for example, that neither the Indo-Chinese war (which broke out under a Socialist government) nor the Algerian war would have taken place.

Of course there could be no question for him after the War but that of re-establishing French sovereignty over the lost colonies; but once re-established, as his subsequent de-colonisation policy showed, independence within or outside the French union would have been negotiated.

In colonial policy as in foreign policy he zigzagged according to circumstances; but there was never any real deviation from course. As a man he divided his life into two rigid compartments – the de Gaulle of the history books and the family man.

As a political animal he could be both repulsive and fascinating. He had a deep cynicism about men and a deep pessimism about the future, which occasionally swept him away on cataclysmic visions.

His guile was, of course, notorious but – curiously enough – few statesmen have stated their intentions so clearly and followed the course of their ideas so resolutely.

He was no enemy of our country, for which he had a profound admiration and, certainly as far as the United States is concerned, he may have rendered it a greater service by denouncing the folly of the Vietnamese war than any other so-called friends did by condoning it.

In his family life and among close friends, mostly the very large family circle, he was both a gentle father and grandfather who displayed great sweetness of character.

His private life was scarred by the tragedy of his mentally-handicapped daughter, Anne, who died in her twenties and to whom he was devoted.

He consoled Mme de Gaulle at the time of the funeral with the words: 'Now at last she is like other children.'

Memories are short and people forget. It is not fashionable now to recall the Fourth Republic and compare it with the Fifth. Having lived under both I can honestly say that both as a reporter and a resident I felt more free and secure under the Fifth than under the Fourth.

It is not that the men of the Fourth were evil or corrupt or that the Gaullist Party does not have its fair share of crooks or adventurers (it might be noted in passing that the most notorious of them long ago passed into the ranks of the opposition).

The politicians of the Fourth were by an overwhelming majority both honest and patriotic. It is simply that the uncertainties the system generated and the impotence it imposed upon them meant inevitably that the scum rose to the top.

I hope history will not repeat itself.

Evening Standard
Monday, April 28, 1969

POMPIDOU, FIRST OFF, MAKES THE RUNNING

Georges Pompidou, General de Gaulle's former Prime Minister, who was a hot favourite for the Presidency of the Republic following General de Gaulle's resignation, shot ahead still further today when he was the first to declare himself a candidate for the post. He did so before a meeting of the Gaullist majority in the French Parliament. He received the party's endorsement afterwards – but by declaring his intentions beforehand he sought to demonstrate that he was not the product of party machinations.

This was particularly important in view of the striking contrast it provides to the situation among the various factions of the Opposition. Their feverish party and inter-party consultations were going on to designate a candidate either of a united Left stretching to the Communists or a moderate Left stretching to the extreme Right.

So far the indications are that the French Socialist Party will join with various conservative parties to back the candidature of M. Alain Poher, sixty-year-old President of the Senate and, as such, interim President of the Republic.

On the other hand M. Pompidou has the support of the Gaullist party including its Left Wing which has previously been critical of him.

There seems to be no doubt too that he has the implicit support of General de Gaulle himself although whether that support will become explicit remains a matter of speculation.

It is, however, clearly in a reference to the likely victory of M. Pompidou in the coming presidential elections that General de Gaulle referred to in his last broadcast to the nation last Friday when he spoke of 'the massive army which supports me and which in any case will hold the keys to the future'.

Apart from his enormous influence in the country – as a virtually unknown Rothschild's Bank executive he was chosen by President de Gaulle as Prime Minister – M. Pompidou will enjoy two clear advantages over other candidates.

First, he will benefit from a certain 'guilt' complex the nation is suffering from for its sacking of de Gaulle and the inevitable reaction will play heavily in his favour.

Secondly, if elected, there will be no need for new Parliamentary elections, whereas if any of his opponents are chosen a dissolution of Parliament and new General Elections will have to be held.

This would make three electoral confrontations in something like three months in a country that is tired of electioneering and tired of being dragged to the polls.

M. Pompidou's main electoral theme will be that he defends the Constitution created by General de Gaulle which has given the country a period of unprecedented political stability and that his opponents seek to dismantle the structure and revert to the institutions of the Fourth Republic.

M. Pompidou really has a powerful base from which to operate in the fact that the Gaullists polled 47 per cent of the vote in Sunday's referendum. At last year's elections the Gaullists polled 46 per cent of the vote and secured a 120 Parliamentary majority.

As no candidate is likely to secure an absolute majority in the first round of voting, M. Pompidou's chances of winning in the second round must be reckoned to be bright, if not positively brilliant.

The presidential elections are likely to be held on June 1, with the run-off between those two candidates who poll the highest votes a fortnight later.

M. Pompidou can also draw comfort from the disarray on the Left and among the Centre parties.

There is a tacit agreement stretching from M. Giscard d'Estaing, a former Finance Minster of General de Gaulle, who played an important part in his defeat, to sections of the French Socialist Party to support either M. Giscard d'Estaing himself or M. Alain Poher, the President of the Senate and interim President of the Republic in the second round of voting.

This has dismayed the Communists who can muster very nearly 25 per cent of the vote and who are now bringing heavy pressure on the Socialist Party leader, M. Guy Mollet, for a common candidate of the Left in the presidential elections.

This was the situation in 1965 when M. Mitterrand was the Left's candidate and polled 44 per cent of the vote.

M. Mitterrand has said he would not stand unless the Left wing parties reached prior agreement on his candidacy.

Some pressure has also been brought to bear on M. Antoine Pinay, a former Prime Minister, who is a year older than General de Gaulle, to stand and to stay in power only until 1972 which would have been the year when General de Gaulle's term of office would normally have ended. M. Pinay has reacted with a ferocious refusal by saying he will only return to politics if the country finds itself in a 'dramatic' situation.

What is being attempted by politicians like M. Giscard d'Estaing, M. Deferre, the Socialist mayor of Marseilles, and M. Mollet is to re-create the pre-de Gaulle so-called 'third force' between Gaullism and Communism which governed France in the fifties.

This in its turn, if successful, would mean watering down the Gaullist institutions so as to effectively reduce the power of the President and increase the power of the National Assembly.

The prospects on the Opposition side, therefore, are confused and this may result in three or four candidates running against M. Pompidou in the first round.

Evening Standard
Tuesday, April 29, 1969

POMPIDOU MOVES IN AT THE ELYSÉE

M. Georges Pompidou moved into the Elysée Palace today to become General de Gaulle's successor as President of France.

Meanwhile, uncertainty continues as to the composition of his Government, which it is now expected will not be formed before Sunday. All that is known so far is that his Prime Minister will be, as expected, the former Speaker of the French Parliament, and Mayor of Bordeaux, M. Jacques Chaban-Delmas.

M. Pompidou arrived at the Elysée this morning dressed in a morning coat and accompanied by the outgoing Prime Minister, M. Couve de Murville. The new President was received by the interim President, and his rival in the presidential election campaign, M. Alain Poher. M. Pompidou was smiling and relaxed as the two exchanged a limpish handshake.

Also present in the Elysée Palace courtyard was the President of the Constitutional Council, M. Gaston Palewski, who gave the official reading of the results of the presidential election. At that moment a twenty-one-gun salute echoed across Paris in the traditional greeting to the new President.

Later in the morning in the gilded main salon of the Elysée, M. Pompidou, as all incoming Presidents traditionally are, was decorated with the ribbon of Grand Master of the Legion of Honour. The ceremony was carried out by Admiral Cabanier, titular head of the Order. This afternoon M. Pompidou was laying a wreath on the Unknown Soldier's tomb at the Arc de Triomphe, before driving in state across Paris.

Evening Standard
Friday, June 20, 1969

THIS TOUCHING FLIRTATION BETWEEN TWO OLD POLITICAL HAS-BEENS . . .
I'm talking, of course, about de Gaulle and Ben-Gurion

One of the most touching as well as one of the oddest love affairs in history must be the one between that old Israeli lionheart David Ben-Gurion and General de Gaulle.

It has now been going on for ten years and has survived such little difficulties as the General's embargo on arms to Israel as well as his famous declaration, which gave such widespread offence, dubbing the Jews as 'an élite sure of itself and domineering'.

Now Ben-Gurion is expected in Paris next week and he's coming here with the express intention of seeing de Gaulle. For this purpose, in case the meeting takes place at the General's country home at Colombey-les-deux-Eglises, a helicopter chartered by Ben-Gurion is standing by in Paris to whisk him there.

The entire project is meeting with the sniffiest of sniffy disapproval both from the Israeli Government and the Israeli Embassy in Paris. The latter in fact feels so strongly about the projected meeting that it has refused to act as a channel of communications between Ben-Gurion and de Gaulle. As one high Israeli official put it: 'It is true that the two old men feel very sentimental about each other, but I have the strong suspicion that Ben-Gurion is considerably more sentimental about de Gaulle than de Gaulle is about Ben-Gurion.'

He went on to add that he would suspect something sinister if the General agreed to see Ben-Gurion. 'I would suspect,' he said, 'that if the General saw him, it would be in order to clear himself before history of the charge of anti-Semitism his description of the Jews provoked at the time.'

In fact, the charge seemed absurd to me at the time and now, two years later, re-reading the remark in its context it seems to me positively grotesque. De Gaulle, I should say, clearly intended his remarks as a compliment.

One of the few people, especially abroad, to recognise this was Ben-Gurion. At the time when the storm over the General's words was at its height he wrote to de Gaulle deploring 'the unjust criticism formulated by many people who have not examined your observations with all the attention needed'.

Will de Gaulle then see Ben-Gurion? At the moment it seems highly doubtful. The noises out of Colombey seem to indicate that the General will refuse on the plea that, now that he is out of office, he must adhere, for the time being anyway, to the strict rule of not receiving political figures, either domestic or imported.

Ben-Gurion is a determined man, however, and he can counter de Gaulle's plea by pointing out that he too is now out of office and resides in the same political Valhalla as the General. It would not surprise me in the least if the two old men finally met up.

Evening Standard
Friday, October 17, 1969

DE GAULLE REMEMBERS

This week marks the eleventh anniversary of the day on which General de Gaulle became effectively President of the Republic.

The anniversary has passed unnoticed and provoked no comment. It is remarkable, however, to what degree he has remained true to himself since his retirement and falsified every prophecy of the ignorant and malicious.

Far from attempting any comeback or even seeking to interfere in any way in the affairs of state, his retirement remains total and his isolation from political life complete, so much so that the offices placed at his disposal in Paris by the French Government remain unused and even occasions which might have provided a dignified way of visiting Paris have remained unexploited.

In fact it can be stated with the utmost confidence — it would have been greeted with general derision six months ago — that the General's retirement from public life is complete and irrevocable.

He is now, despite good health, engaged in a race against what might be considered to be a more than normal life span to complete the three volumes of his memoirs, *Memoirs of Peace*, to supplement his three volumes of War Memoirs.

Those who see him, and they are almost entirely members of his family and of his personal secretarial staff, describe him as being not only in robust health, but cheerful and even enthusiastic in outlook.

The typing involved in writing his memoirs is entrusted to his daughter Mme de Boissieu, the wife of a general. In this way, seemingly small but highly important, the de Gaulle family forms an indestructible and tightly-knit unit.

As for Mme de Gaulle, those who have seen her recently remark on the contentment she finds in her husband's retirement and M. Malraux has gone so far as saying that she looks twenty years younger.

In a curious way, de Gaulle in retirement has found that consensus of national respect for his name and character which always escaped him during his turbulent life.

By accepting defeat as he did by resigning instantly and without a word of recrimination, by holding himself aloof from political life ever since, he has not only served Democracy well, but enhanced the prestige of the office now held by his successor.

Evening Standard
Friday, January 9, 1970

DE GAULLE: HE KNEW ALL THE TIME . . .

It is altogether fascinating that the first manifestation of public life General de Gaulle has given since his retirement has been provoked by Nasser's death.

Many close associates of de Gaulle's have died at home and abroad in the past eighteen months without once the text of a message of condolence being made public.

This time, however, in a manner which is almost a usurpation of the head of state's role, de Gaulle has empowered the Egyptian Ambassador in Paris to make public the text of his message.

De Gaulle's epitaph on Nasser could very well have been Nasser's epitaph on de Gaulle if he had outlived him.

'Exceptional courage . . . imcomparable services to his country . . . never ceased to fight for his country's honour, independence and greatness . . . thus we both profoundly understood and respected each other.'

Actually de Gaulle owes Nasser a considerable debt for once providing him with an occasion for exercising his well known and almost mystical prescience.

The story is told in the best-selling Paris book by the French journalist Philippe Alexandre, *The de Gaulle-Pompidou Duel*. It concerns de Gaulle's statement to a Cabinet meeting in May 1967, just before the outbreak of the Six-Day War.

De Gaulle is quoted – and there is overwhelming evidence that the quotation is exact – as breaking off the Cabinet meeting with the words: 'I now have to meet the Israeli Foreign Minister but I want you to know what I'm going to tell him.

'I will tell him: "You are heading for war and if there is a war you will win it and win it quickly. However, your victory will have the gravest possible consequences. Firstly, it will mean a Russian implantation in the Middle East; secondly, moderate régimes in the Arab world will give way to extremist ones; thirdly, Western and especially European supplies of petrol will be threatened; finally, the Palestine problem, which at the moment is no more than a refugee problem, will become a great national problem."'

Evening Standard
Friday, October 2, 1970

225

DE GAULLE DIES AT SEVENTY-NINE
'France is a widow' says Pompidou

General Charles de Gaulle died last night of a heart attack – seated in an armchair, playing a game of patience and waiting for the television news.

The seventy-nine-year-old general, who quit as President of France in April last year, was at his country home, La Boisserie, in Colombey-les-deux-Eglises, 100 miles from Paris.

It was 7.30 p.m. His wife Yvonne was with him. Suddenly he slumped in his chair . . . his face became contorted with pain.

Mme de Gaulle summoned the doctor and the village priest.

This evening the General 'lay in state' in the drawing-room, dressed in the uniform of a two-star Brigadier-General, wearing one decoration – the Order of Liberation – and covered in the Tricolour.

The news of his death, just thirteen days before his eightieth birthday, came as a complete surprise to Paris this morning. It was just after five o'clock that Colombey's mayor passed the news to the French Government.

De Gaulle's successor, President Pompidou, called an emergency meeting of the Cabinet and then appeared on television calling on Frenchmen to be worthy of the lessons given by the General. 'De Gaulle is dead,' he declared in a shaky voice, his face strained with emotion. 'France is a widow.'

Then followed another announcement about the funeral which will be on Thursday, private and at Colombey. De Gaulle had already decreed this in a 'last wishes' letter.

The letter, beginning with the words 'General de Gaulle' and dated January 16, 1952, read:

*   *   *

'I wish that my funeral be held at Colombey-les-deux-Eglises. If I die elsewhere, my body should be transported to my home, without the slightest public ceremony.

'My tomb will be there where my daughter Anne already lies, and where, one day, my wife will lie. Inscription: Charles de Gaulle (1890–   ). Nothing else.

'The ceremony will be set forth by my son, my daughter, my son-in-law, my daughter-in-law, aided by my secretariat, in such a way that it should be extremely simple. I do not wish a national funeral. No President, no Ministers, no parliamentary committees, no representatives of government organs.

'Only the French military service may take part officially, as such; but their participation should be of very modest proportions, without bands, fanfare or bugles.

'No speech will be pronounced either at the church or elsewhere. No funeral orations in Parliament. No seats will be reserved at the ceremony, except for my family, for my companions of the Order of Liberation, for the municipal council of Colombey.

'The men and women of France and other countries of the world may, if they wish, do my memory the honour of accompanying my body to its last resting place. But it is in silence that I wish it should be conducted.

'I declare that I refuse in advance any distinction, promotion, honour citation, decoration, whether it be French or foreign. If any such should be awarded me, it would be in violation of my last wishes.'

Village priest Claude Jaugey said today he hurried to a second-floor room and arrived to find the General stretched out on the floor.

He was dressed in a dark suit. 'De Gaulle was not dead,' he said, 'but seemed to be unconscious. He was suffering terribly.

'I gave him the last rites.' Mme de Gaulle, he added, reacted to her husband's death 'with perfect dignity, even nobility'.

Father Jaugey said that about nine o'clock some security guards asked him what was going on.

'They asked if anything was abnormal. I said "No",' the priest added with some hesitation. 'I lied.'

'I listened to the radio to see if there had been any leaks of the news, There was nothing, and I was pleased,' he said.

The church in the village of Colombey, which is in the Champagne region, is tiny, and will restrict the size of any planned ceremonies.

There are only 140 inhabitants – and yesterday started for them and the General like many they have passed together.

In the afternoon de Gaulle strolled under the tall trees in his garden. Then he went to his study in the tower that he added to his home and started work on his memoirs.

The first volume of *Memoirs of Hope* relating the history of his return of power in 1958 appeared a month ago.

He was half-way through the second volume. When he left his study yesterday afternoon he quietly sat down to play patience and wait for the television news.

Then came the heart attack.

Now his memoirs – the crucial third volume was to detail the events of May 2, 1968, and his subsequent defeat and resignation – will remain an unwritten secret.

Thursday in France will be a day of national mourning. Government offices, banks, businesses and schools will be closed.

President Pompidou and the rest of the Government will remain in Paris and attend a religious ceremony at Notre Dame as the Colombey funeral takes place.

There will be one corner of France where the name of de Gaulle will be fondly remembered . . . the home for backward boys and girls at Milton-la-Chappelle, near Paris, which is named after de Gaulle's daughter Anne, who died in 1948, aged twenty.

The Anne de Gaulle Foundation, as it is known, has been receiving the proceeds from the sale of the General's memoirs.

Evening Standard
Tuesday, November 10, 1970

DE GAULLE'S FUNERAL

In a moving, almost starkly simple, memorial Mass for General de Gaulle at Notre Dame Cathedral a congregation which included more than a hundred heads of state prayed for the former French President.

The ceremony, conducted by the Archbishop of Paris, Cardinal Marty, opened with an organ and choir rendering of Bach's 'St Matthew's Passion'. It ended on an almost unprecedented note for such an occasion with priests offering Communion to those who wished to take it. Steady processions of dignitaries moved through the congregation towards the nearest priest to take Communion. The simplicity of the ceremony with no eulogy of himself was in strict conformity to de Gaulle's wish.

In the subdued light shed by the stained glass windows the only splashes of colour were provided by the mourning covers of violet and occasionally striking attire of African heads of state.

Black faces almost seemed to predominate among the first ranks of the congregation, striking tribute to de Gaulle's popularity in Black Africa and especially among the former French colonies to which he gave independence.

Two striking figures in the front row were the seemingly ageless Haile Selassie, Emperor of Ethiopa, and Archbishop Makarios of Cyprus.

President Nixon was there, flanked by two uniformed White House aides, a few feet from the Russian delegation headed by President Podgorny, and between them there was the hunched figure of Israel's Ben-Gurion.

Queen Juliana of the Netherlands was there also, standing next to Lord Avon, and so was King Baudouin of the Belgians.

The Epistle was from St Paul's two letters to Timothy. Some members of de Gaulle's family, including several grandchildren, were among the congregation.

President Pompidou, who was accompanied by members of the Government as well as leading Opposition figures, sat apart from the congregation in a special place reserved for him.

More than ten thousand police in Paris were mobilised for special security surveillance in view of the influx of foreign leaders. The result was that the Ile de la Cité, on which Notre Dame stands, bristled with police and police rooftop watchers.

Even Communist China was represented at the funeral by its Ambassador in Paris and the French are impressed by Mao's gesture in calling at the French Embassy in Peking yesterday.

There was a last-minute change in Soviet representation with President Podgorny coming instead of Mr Kosygin which put paid to any idea of a summit meeting between President Nixon and the Russians.

At noon, Paris buses stopped for one minute – the staff's homage to General de Gaulle.

Evening Standard
Thursday, November 12, 1970

PROGRESS FOR THE PILGRIMS

Mme de Gaulle has been officially invited to take her place in the saluting stand in this year's July 14 parade. If she accepts it will be her first public appearance since her husband's death and probably her first return to Paris since he quit office.

Meanwhile in the de Gaulle village of Colombey-les-deux-Eglises a great transformation has taken place to cope with the tourist influx.

The French Foreign Office now has a special section dealing with VIPs who may wish to visit the General's grave or may receive sympathetically a suggestion that they should do so.

In Colombey itself private enterprise takes over where the Foreign Office task ends. By the beginning of next month a new hotel will be opened in the village named Hotel des Dhuys after the forest which de Gaulle's house overlooks and in which he often walked. It is confidently expected that on the 18th of this month, which is the anniversary of de Gaulle's famous London broadcast, Colombey will receive some thirty thousand people.

The village boasts only one café-restaurant, Chez Jeanine. Mme Jeanine has completely modernised her installation and her bar and attached to her establishment a small shop selling de Gaulle souvenirs. These are chiefly small busts of the General.

All these innovations in Colombey are worrying Mme de Gaulle, who is concerned about the prospects of maintaining her own privacy in a village now given over to what, without disrespect, might be described as the 'pilgrimage industry'.

Evening Standard
Friday, June 4, 1971

FOND MEMORIES OF DE GAULLE

Now that de Gaulle has been dead for a year something like a national pride in the man has emerged in the course of ceremonies marking the first anniversary of his death.

During his lifetime there was always curiosity in that, whereas his name was always revered in countries aspiring to liberty, in his own country the Left should have wasted so much of its breath in assailing him as a Fascist.

True, the dwindling regiments of the doctrinaire Left still remain embattled in the positions they dug for themselves at the time of the Dreyfus trial and partisans of Vichy and French Algeria have learnt nothing and forgotten nothing.

I think the change is best exemplified by Francois Mitterrand, leader of the French non-Communist Left, who in the early Sixties published a vicious book on de Gaulle entitled *The Permanent Conspiracy*. Now he has written a scholarly and sensitive essay on the General which almost amounts to a eulogy.

It is hard now to recall the hysteria with which de Gaulle's constitutional reforms were greeted at the time, especially the one affecting the change in the role of the President of the Republic from figurehead to effective head of Government.

Widely attacked at the time as putting France on the high road to dictatorship, the reform has now been accepted not only without a murmur but as though it had never even been contested. I always thought attribution of maniacal anti-British and anti-American obsessions to de Gaulle were of an absurd vulgarity and it is interesting now to recall that, for example, during the Cuban missile crisis, when all America's allies wavered, de Gaulle gave Washington his solid approval and support.

Whatever follies he may have committed in international relations nothing seems more absurd now than Mr Douglas Jay's notorious castigation of him as a man who had created the most mischief in the world since Hitler. In fact, in retrospect, it now seems that in his unfreezing 'cold war' attitudes, when everybody else was assuming the 'cold war' was still on, he was something of a pioneer.

A noted French writer, M. André Frossard, once described de Gaulle as 'a Napoleon in reverse'. It was an amusing theory which greatly amused de Gaulle. M. Frossard argued that just as Napoleon disembarked from an island, in his case Corsica, so did de Gaulle – in his case Britain. And just as Napoleon organised his own coup d'état so de Gaulle organised his own departure from power. In short, it was a kind of coup d'état in reverse.

The only discordant note in the anniversary of the General's death has been struck by the emergence of a disagreeable breed which could only be described as 'Gaullist prigs'. They are old-time associates of the General who have constituted themselves into a kind of myopic guardian of what they deem to be the Gaullist conscience.

Chief among them is the former Minister, Jean-Marcel Jeanneney, who resigned from the Gaullist Party just as the anniversary of the General's death was approaching. This carefully-timed piece of political play-acting was accompanied by a statement saying that, though no-one had the right to interpret de Gaulle's thoughts in any given circumstance, nevertheless he felt that M. Pompidou had gone off the strictly orthodox rails.

One of his proposals was based on the admission of Britain into the Common Market which, he claimed, would loosen the ties binding the existing six members. The fact that there were no real ties to loosen seems to have escaped him – and also the equally important fact that it was de Gaulle himself in his last months of power who opened the way for an Anglo-French agreement to re-cast the Europe of the Six.

The most tragic element in de Gaulle's last days in office was the way he was disorientated by the student riots of 1968. That so great a man should in fact have been toppled by so lunatic an event constitutes the essence of tragedy.

*   *   *

NO GHOSTING FOR DE GAULLE

For forty years of his life General de Gaulle lived under a considerable literary cloud. It was the most menacing of all clouds that can hang over a writer's head – he had been accused of plagiarism. Throughout those years de Gaulle never bothered to reply to either the charges or the insinuations which crept into the history books covering that period.

Now, as it were from the grave, he speaks by authorising in his will that his son Philippe should release the correspondence he exchanged with the late Marshal Pétain over a thirteen-year period from 1925 to 1938, on the subject of a book de Gaulle published just before the outbreak of war entitled *France and its Army*. The correspondence began when de Gaulle was a mere captain and Pétain was already the legendary hero of Verdun and a Marshal of France. The correspondence is fascinating, for not only does it clear de Gaulle of any suspicion of plagiarism, but it shows this junior officer risking his entire career by challenging Pétain on a matter of principle.

The principle involved concerned a book which Pétain wanted de Gaulle to write for him and which would appear under Pétain's name. From this point on a clash of vanities became inevitable. Pétain wanted a book published in his name because he wanted the ultimate consecration of being elected to the French Academy and he was unable to fulfil the essential qualification of producing a literary work. De Gaulle was even at that early date a serious and talented writer beginning to be proud of his literary prowess.

Therefore, Pétain, clearly worried that his own notorious inability to construct a sentence would contrast too obviously with the brilliance of de Gaulle's style, ordered that the book should be rewritten by his staff officers. At this point de Gaulle exploded. He wrote a polite but firm letter to the Marshal pointing out that the book was entirely his own work and if any changes were to be made in it he would make the changes himself rather than have them made by others.

The correspondence continued in a mounting tone of mutual

exasperation accompanied by threats that if de Gaulle published the work under his own name he would lose two years of seniority equivalent to the two years he had spent on the book on the Marshal's orders.

In March 1938 de Gaulle wrote a final letter to Pétain saying he was going ahead with the book's publication. He wrote that he would acknowledge the encouragement he received from the Marshal but that apart from that the work was entirely his own and in no sense a piece of literary ghosting.

The letter ends with the words: 'You will appear in a more generous light as a patron of a literary work than one who seeks to appropriate the work of someone else.'

There the correspondence ends, but there is an ironic footnote to it. It occurs in the memoirs of Paul Reynaud, Prime Minister at the time of the 1940 collapse. On June 5 of that year Reynaud told Pétain that he had appointed de Gaulle Under-Secretary of State for War. Reynaud writes: 'The Marshal seemed displeased and mumbled something about a quarrel over a book which they had written together.'

Evening Standard
Friday, January 26, 1972

RUSSIAN SALUTE

This is the second anniversary of General de Gaulle's death and the Russians have paid him the compliment of publishing a work by one of the most eminent historians, Professor Moltchanov, on the subject.

Professor Moltchanov, while not denying that the General was a bourgeois, albeit an intelligent one, covers him with such lavish praise that it is going to be positively embarrassing for the local comrades in what is, after all, an election year in France.

To add to their embarrassment the Russians have published a French translation of the work of which some twenty thousand copies have reached our French Communist bookshops.

To underline the revived Soviet interest in de Gaulle, the Soviet Ambassador in Paris, Monsieur Abrassimov, paid a highly publicised visit to de Gaulle's grave. One point which the professor brings out in his book, and which though true is not generally known in France, is that when de Gaulle went to Washington for President Kennedy's funeral he was warned by the FBI that an attempt might be made to assassinate him. In view of this the FBI offered an armour-plated vehicle to take the General to and from the funeral. This the General firmly refused.

Evening Standard
Friday, November 3, 1972

DE GAULLE – A RIDDLE SOLVED . . .

I slipped across to Dublin over Christmas to clear up a mystery concerning General de Gaulle which has been nagging me over the past few years (I might mention here incidentally that there are few pleasanter places for such a task than Dublin, involving as it does a great deal of weaving across St Stephens Green from hostelry to hostelry).

To return to the mystery, it concerns the banquet given in de Gaulle's honour by the then President of the Irish Republic, Mr De Valera, in his residence in Phoenix Park on June 18, 1969, at the conclusion of a holiday the General and Mme de Gaulle had taken in that country.

Only a few weeks earlier he had been defeated in a referendum and this defeat signalled his retirement and disappearance from the political scene. The defeat still rankled and as he tramped about from beauty spot to beauty spot in Galway and Killarney, Ireland began to take on something of the contours of another Elba.

The General's gloom was only relieved by the prospect of his meeting with De Valera whom he had long admired, but never met before. He looked forward to the meeting with the greatest relish, especially as he had made a pre-holiday study of Irish history and had taken advantage of the holiday to brush up on his own family's genealogical links with Ireland.

At the end of the banquet there would be toasts and he had prepared his own toast with consummate care. The mystery, which I set myself to clear up, was what exactly de Gaulle's toast was, for oddly enough its text has remained a matter for conjecture to this day. The Irish have remained mute on the subject and so have the French.

The interpreter at the banquet was the French Ambassador to Dublin – he is still Ambassador there – M. Emmanuel D'Harcourt, and his account of the proceedings is lodged with the French Foreign Office and has never been made public.

What is clear, however, is that even before the banquet the General's

Irish hosts feared a great de Gaulle gaffe along the lines of his notorious 'Vive le Quebec libre' speech.

As a result, they took special precautions to ensure that there was no newspaper coverage of the event. De Gaulle got off to an excellent start at the dinner by turning to his host and saying to him: 'Now tell me about Ireland.' This De Valera proceeded to do with great verve and gusto until the time came for toasts. De Valera raised his glass to the French Republic and to de Gaulle, whom he described as the saviour twice over of his country. Then came de Gaulle's turn, and the tension mounted.

Here, for the first time, is the text of de Gaulle's toast. He said: 'I raise my glass to the whole of Ireland' (In French it reads: 'Je lève mon verre à l'Irlande tout entière'). To his audience the meaning was clear and de Gaulle's words were a thinly-veiled reference to a united Ireland.

Immediately the Irish took the decision to suppress the text and next day M. D'Harcourt asked why the text had not been released. He was told that the tape recording of the speeches ran out just before the General's toast.

Shades of Watergate on the Liffey!

Evening Standard
Friday, January 4, 1974

THE MAN DE GAULLE LISTENED TO

It should be noted in connection with the death this week of France's greatest modern writer, André Malraux, that from the turmoil of war occupation and liberation France produced only two genuine revolutionaries: de Gaulle and Malraux himself.

It is this which gave a strange air of complicity to the companionship which bound them from the moment they first met in liberated Paris until the General's death. They were privy to each other's innermost thoughts and it was their thoughts which shaped de Gaulle's actions more effectively than any Cabinet meetings.

De Gaulle's anti-colonial stand, for example, especially in relation to Algeria, was greatly influenced by Malraux's own fierce anti-colonialism. 'Our greatest victory,' Malraux said on the day of Algerian independence, 'because it is a victory over ourselves.' And de Gaulle echoed these words.

De Gaulle's interest in the third world and Latin America were all fostered by Malraux: and no one understood better from his own experiences the deeper causes of the Communist revolution in China as lying in the humiliations inflicted on that country by foreign imperialists. This was de Gaulle's guide to action in his early recognition of the Communist régime.

Sometimes this influence bordered on the absurd, as when Malraux, then Minister of Culture, intervened in a Cabinet debate on whether the franc should be devalued with the words: 'de Gaulle does not devalue for that would be to devalue France.' There were excellent reasons why the proposed devaluation should not take place but the meeting broke up on that note, and the franc was not devalued.

Apart from this rapport with de Gaulle, Malraux's death underlines the extraordinary worldwide influence he had on his own and subsequent generations. Never openly a Communist himself (although I suspect that he was for a time a Comintern agent) his two greatest novels, *Man's Fate*, on the Chinese civil war, and *Man's Hope*, on the Spanish, rolled in wave after wave of converts to Communism.

I recall feeling the tug myself after reading *Man's Fate* in far off Melbourne. He was then the idol of the international Left and when, after the War, he emerged as a Gaullist the stupefaction on the Left quickly gave way to venom. The vilification was such that many of his Left-wing writer and painter friends vowed never to speak to him again and in fact never did so, except when they had a favour to ask from him when he was Minister of Culture.

Picasso himself never came to the huge retrospective of his work in Paris some years ago, largely, it is said, because Malraux had organised it. It is significant of the change in the climate of opinion – both regarding Malraux and de Gaulle – that the French Left has on his death once again claimed him as its own.

The Communist daily, *L'Humanité*, for example, devoted four pages of lavish praise to him and never a sour note. As to his influence on his fellow writers, this too has been enormous. As one French critic put it: 'He introduced the machine gun into the modern novel', anticipating all the so-called liberation terrorists and anarchist movements of our time: the idealists as gunmen.

No French writer of any importance, and especially Camus and Sartre, has failed to reap where Malraux sowed; and this, I should say, is particularly true of our own Graham Greene.

Efforts to debunk Malraux as a man of action should not be taken seriously. His record as an airman in the Spanish Civil War and in the French Resistance is too well documented to reveal him as anything but a man who put his actions where his mouth was.

One aspect of his personal life has always puzzled me, and that is his romance with the French novelist Louise de Vilmorin. A writer of fashionable romances, she came from an entirely different world to that which Malraux inhabited – a world of fashion, money and high society. It was as unlikely a love affair as one between, say, Graham Greene and the late Nancy Mitford.

Evening Standard
Friday, November 26, 1976

MISUNDERSTANDING DE GAULLE

It is now ten years since General de Gaulle retired after his defeat in the 1969 referendum and the event is being celebrated by a fresh flood of books on the man. When the tone is not frankly idolatrous, there is a *mea culpa* air about some of the books written by former critics – especially those on the Left. The atmosphere has changed considerably from the days when the General could be dismissed as at best a bleak reactionary, and it is now fashionable to confess one's past misjudgments on him. Thus, for example, probably no one misunderstood de Gaulle more often in his lifetime than Jean Daniel, the editor of the Left-wing *Nouvel Observateur*; now, in his latest volume of reminiscences, Daniel makes honourable if posthumous amends for past mistakes.

The seeds of doubt over de Gaulle's abilities were of course sown by French socialist refugees in London during the War, who delighted in depicting him to their horrified British counterparts as a royalist and a member of the ultra-reactionary *Action Française*. Now, forty years later, comes a book written by no less an authority than the Pretender to the French throne, the Count of Paris, which seeks to slap some flesh on that alleged skeleton in de Gaulle's cupboard. The Count, a stout-hearted if inept intriguer all his life, was never more active as such than during the War – first in Vichy, to which he offered his services, and later in Algiers.

In the turmoil that followed the assassination of Admiral Darlan by a young royalist, the Count saw the possibility that he might be entrusted with some kind of mission by de Gaulle. Nothing came of it and he remained missionless after the liberation of France. It was not until de Gaulle's return to power in 1958 that something like a solid relationship was struck up between the two men. By then de Gaulle had apparently given some thought to the role the French royal family might play in the nation's affairs and had decided to back the Count (the move failed, incidentally) for the presidency of the French Red Cross.

The Count, however, in his account of their relationship, especially during the years 1961 to 1963, would have it otherwise. According to him de Gaulle had by then decided to restore the monarchy and wished him to succeed de Gaulle as a kind of king-president in the presidential elections of 1965. 'Prepare yourself' was, according to the Count, de Gaulle's repeated advice to him during the lengthy conversations they had – usually late at night, so that their meetings might pass unnoticed. If that was the purpose of holding them at unusual hours then it failed, since it was at about that time that the French Press began openly to speculate about de Gaulle's supposed intention to restore the monarchy. It was really too good a chance to miss, especially with new elections looming, and the Left-wing press made the most of it.

As the 1965 elections approached, the Count began to detect something of the absurdity of his position. He then explained to de Gaulle that it would, obviously, be a contravention of monarchic principles for him to stand for election, and he would only consider doing so if he had de Gaulle's endorsement. He would then be, as it were, the beneficiary of the legitimacy that the nation had already conferred on de Gaulle. To the Count's consternation de Gaulle refused his request and the entire story ends on a note of farce with the Count baffled over the reasons why the General should have let him down. The answer is obvious enough, however – the Count mistook the respect and consideration of de Gaulle showed him as a descendant of 'the forty kings who had made France' for a declaration of intent to restore the monarchy.

The Count's book has created an enormous stir here but, fortunately, another book has appeared almost at the same time which corrects some of his more extravagant meanderings on the subject of de Gaulle and the monarchy. This is a book by that master of contemporary French history, Jean-Raymond Tournoux, and it sketches with meticulous documentation de Gaulle's views on the subject. Here is for example de Gaulle spelling it out to his former Secret Service chief, Colonel Passy, who had some royalist sympathies: 'The monarchy is well and truly finished in France. It has absolutely no chance.' And here he is quoted by Beuve-Mery the founder-editor of *Le Monde* from an interview in 1958: 'Naturally you think me a monarchist. I have a great respect for it. The monarchy made France but it did not know how to adapt itself. Today all this is finished. It would be ridiculous . . .' Or this from his statement to a Cabinet meeting when the speculation in the Press regarding his relationship with the Count of Paris was raised: 'I have respect for what the Count of Paris represents. As a candidate for the presidency of the Republic, however, he does not exist.'

One could fill an entire chapter with similar quotations, and Tournoux does. By the end there is nothing left of the Count's claims except the possibility, indeed the likelihood, of a major misunderstanding. It is tempting to blame the Count entirely for this but, on the other hand, the ambiguities of the General's style were notorious and he may not therefore have been entirely blameless. Respect, yes, but a political role for the Count of Paris, never – this, according to Tournoux, was de Gaulle's consistent attitude to the royal family throughout. And, as he says, he cannot find a single member of de Gaulle's entourage or any member of the de Gaulle family who will contradict him on that point. Sentiment might have made de Gaulle a royalist; reason however made him a republican. This is Michel Debré's verdict on the matter also, and it is a verdict which history will uphold.

Evening Standard
Friday, May 12, 1979